THOR

THE MIGHTY AVENGER

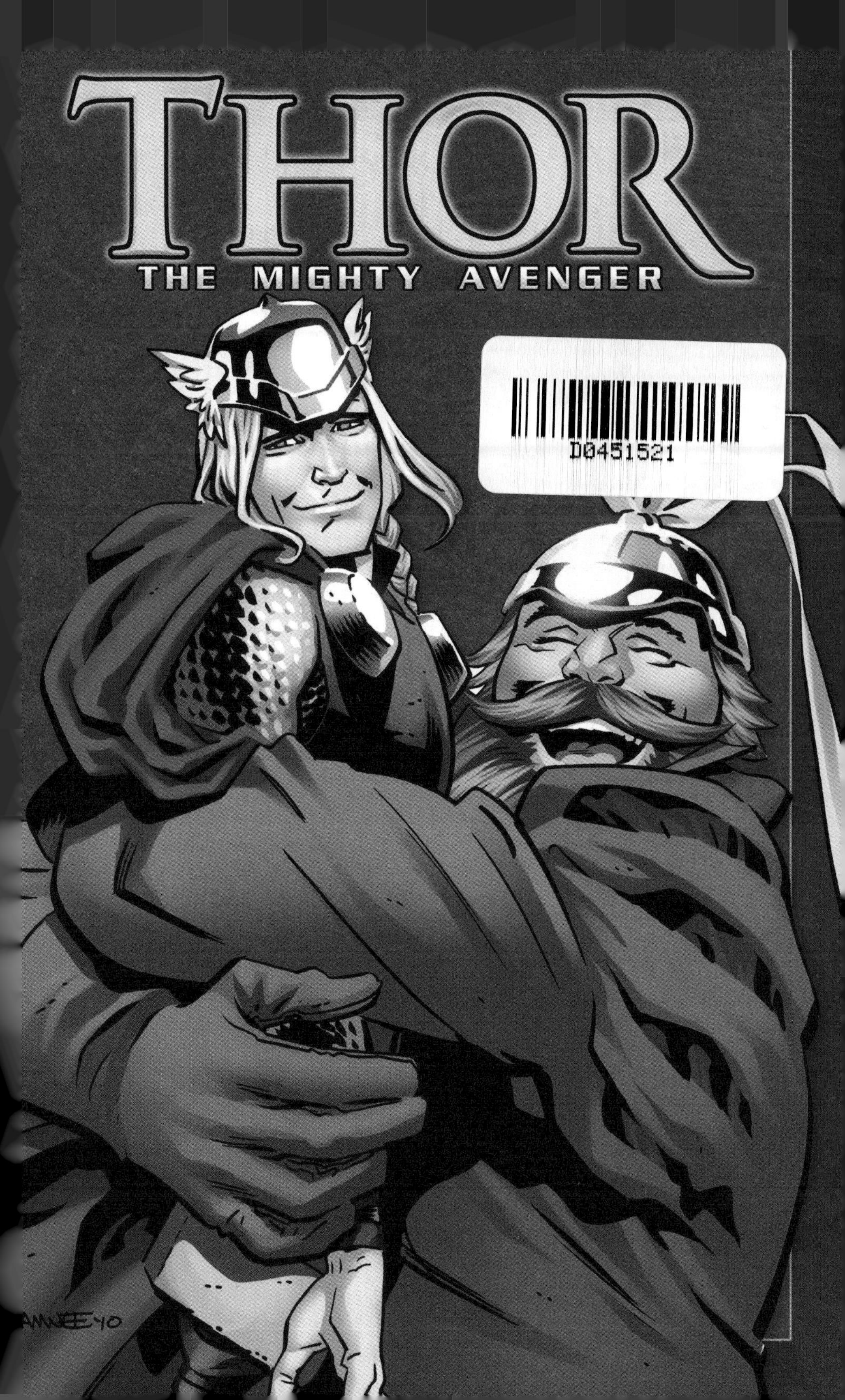

THOR
THE MIGHTY AVENGER

Writer
ROGER LANGRIDGE

Artist
CHRIS SAMNEE

Colorist **MATTHEW WILSON**

Letterer **VIRTUAL CALLIGRAPHY'S RUS WOOTON**

Cover Artist **CHRIS SAMNEE WITH MATTHEW WILSON &
CHRISTINA STRAIN**

Assistant Editor **MICHAEL HORWITZ**

Editor **NATHAN COSBY**

Collection Editor **CORY LEVINE**

Editorial Assistants **JAMES EMMETT & JOE HOCHSTEIN**

Assistant Editors **ALEX STARBUCK & NELSON RIBEIRO**

Editors, Special Projects **JENNIFER GRÜNWALD
& MARK D. BEAZLEY**

Senior Editor, Special Projects **JEFF YOUNGQUIST**

Senior Vice President of Sales **DAVID GABRIEL**

Book Design **ARLENE SO**

Editor in Chief **JOE QUESADA**

Publisher **DAN BUCKLEY**

Executive Producer **ALAN FINE**

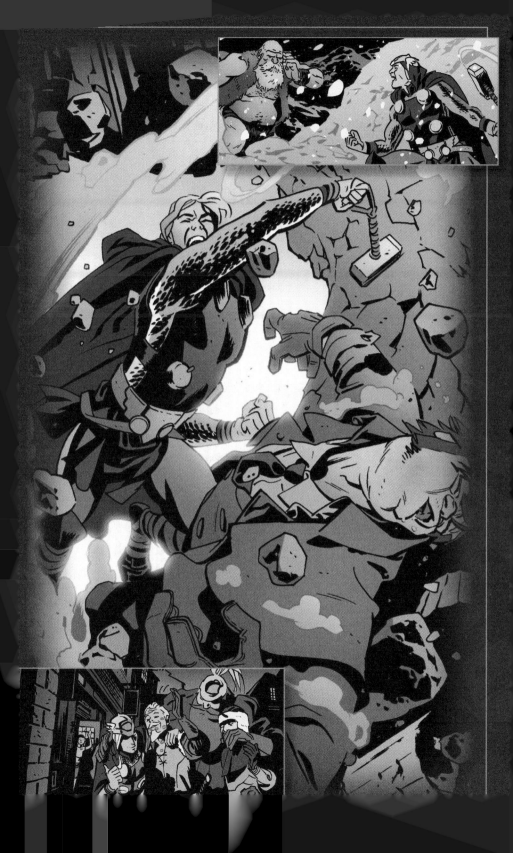

THOR THE MIGHTY AVENGER #1

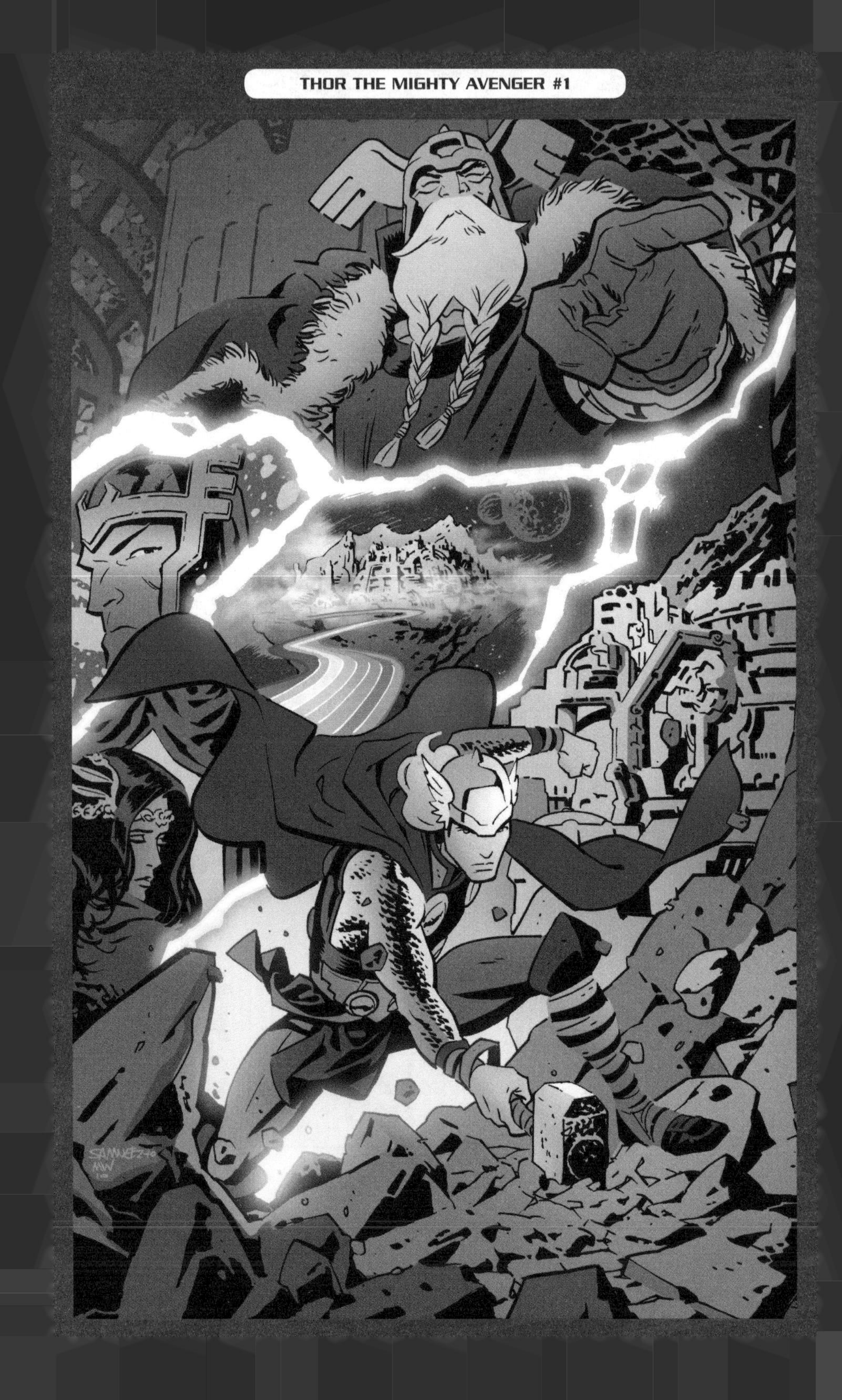

THOR THE MIGHTY AVENGER #1 VARIANT BY CHRIS SAMNEE

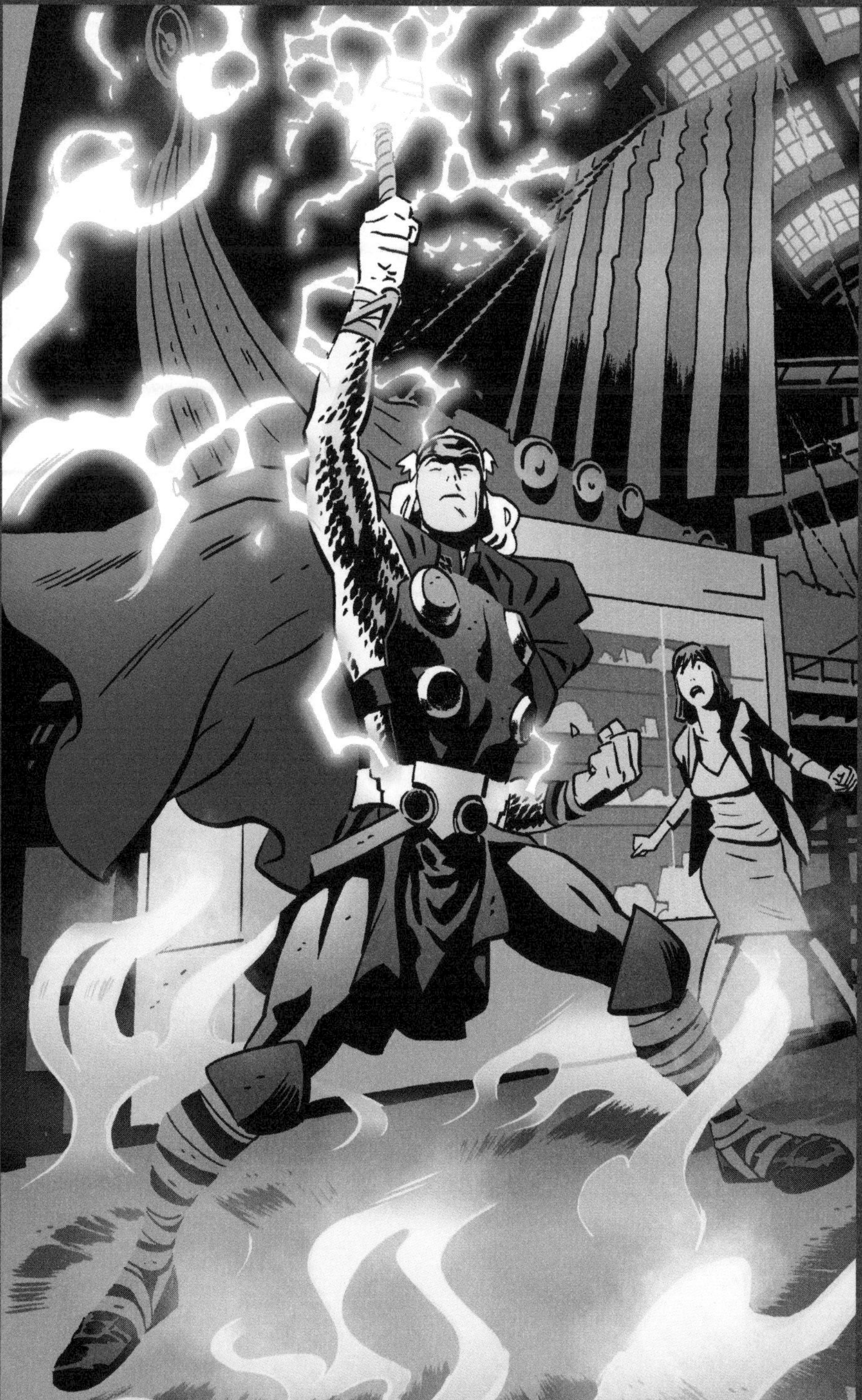

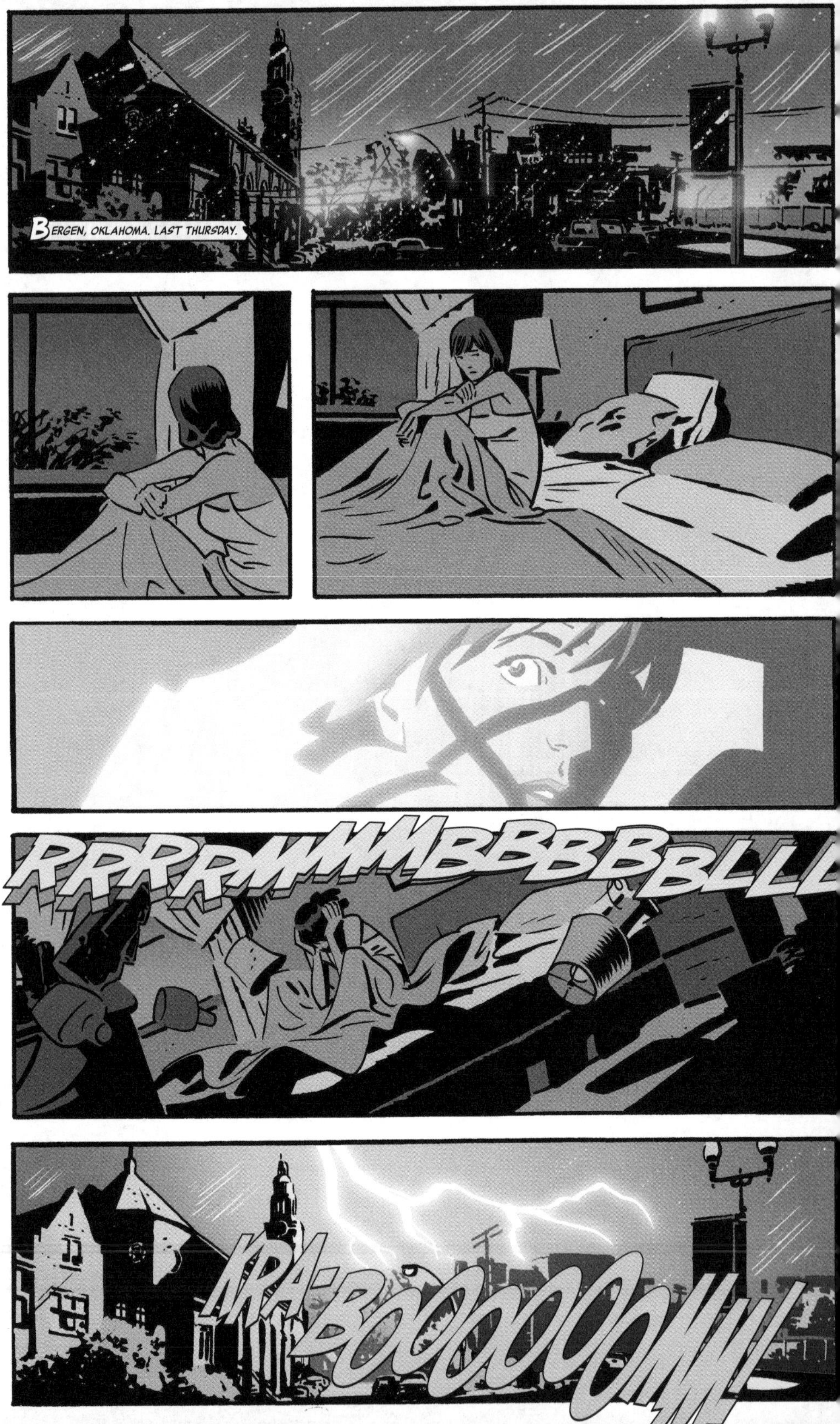
BERGEN, OKLAHOMA. LAST THURSDAY.
RRRRMMMBBBBBLLL
KRA-BOOOOOOMM!

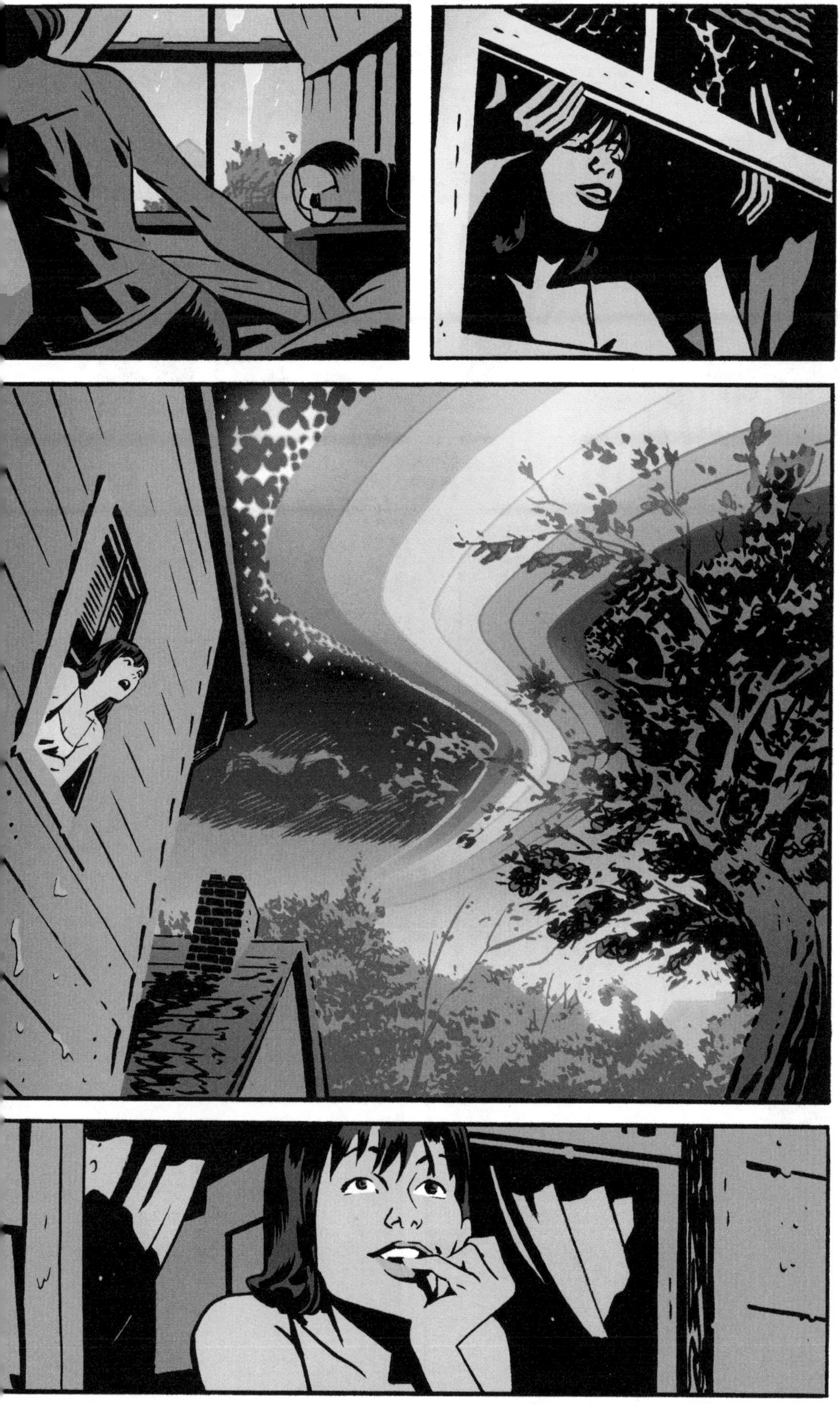

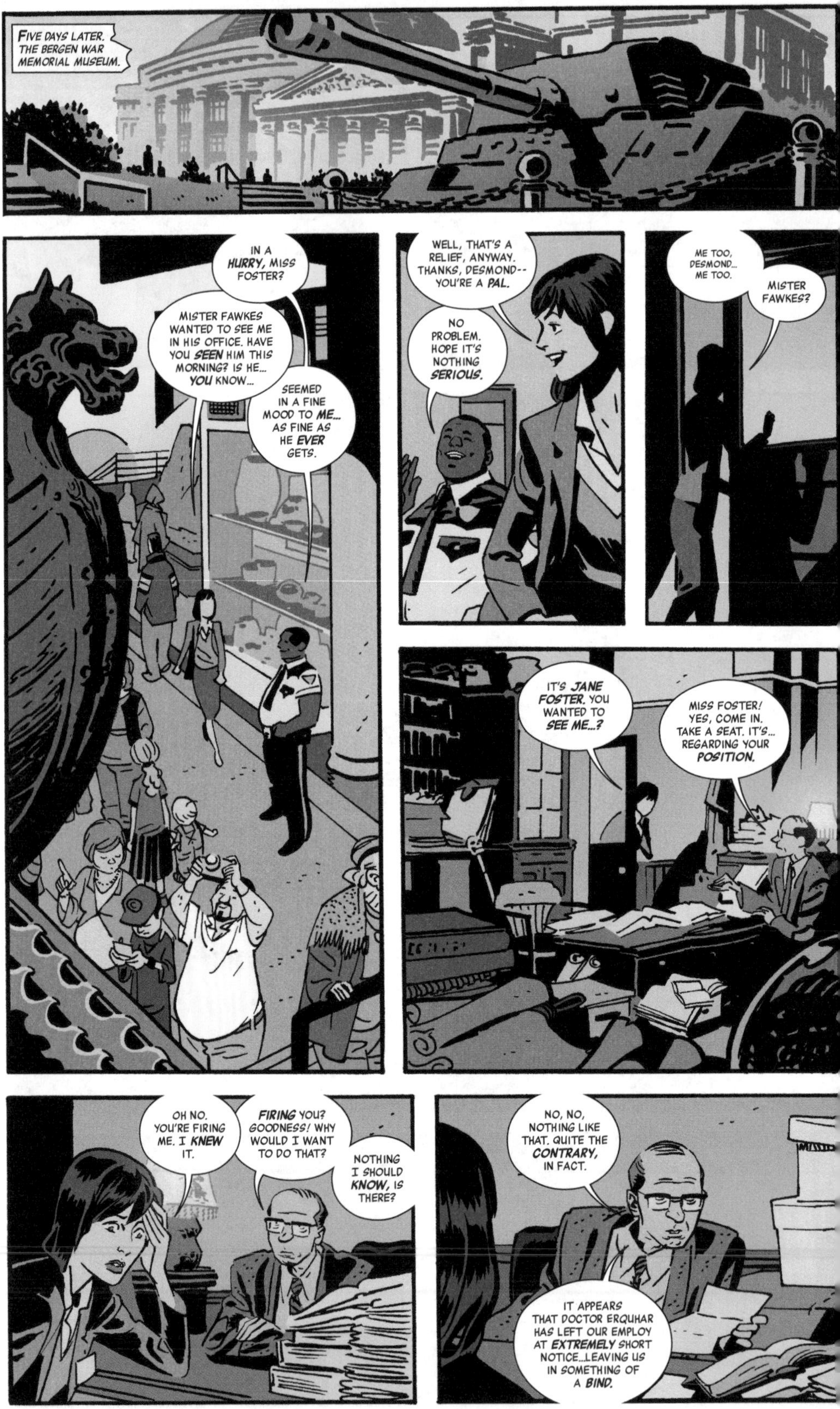
FIVE DAYS LATER. THE BERGEN WAR MEMORIAL MUSEUM.
IN A HURRY, MISS FOSTER?
MISTER FAWKES WANTED TO SEE ME IN HIS OFFICE. HAVE YOU SEEN HIM THIS MORNING? IS HE... YOU KNOW...
SEEMED IN A FINE MOOD TO ME... AS FINE AS HE EVER GETS.
WELL, THAT'S A RELIEF, ANYWAY. THANKS, DESMOND-- YOU'RE A PAL.
NO PROBLEM. HOPE IT'S NOTHING SERIOUS.
ME TOO, DESMOND... ME TOO.
MISTER FAWKES?
IT'S JANE FOSTER. YOU WANTED TO SEE ME...?
MISS FOSTER! YES, COME IN. TAKE A SEAT. IT'S... REGARDING YOUR POSITION.
OH NO. YOU'RE FIRING ME. I KNEW IT.
FIRING YOU? GOODNESS! WHY WOULD I WANT TO DO THAT?
NOTHING I SHOULD KNOW, IS THERE?
NO, NO, NOTHING LIKE THAT. QUITE THE CONTRARY, IN FACT.
IT APPEARS THAT DOCTOR ERQUHAR HAS LEFT OUR EMPLOY AT EXTREMELY SHORT NOTICE...LEAVING US IN SOMETHING OF A BIND.

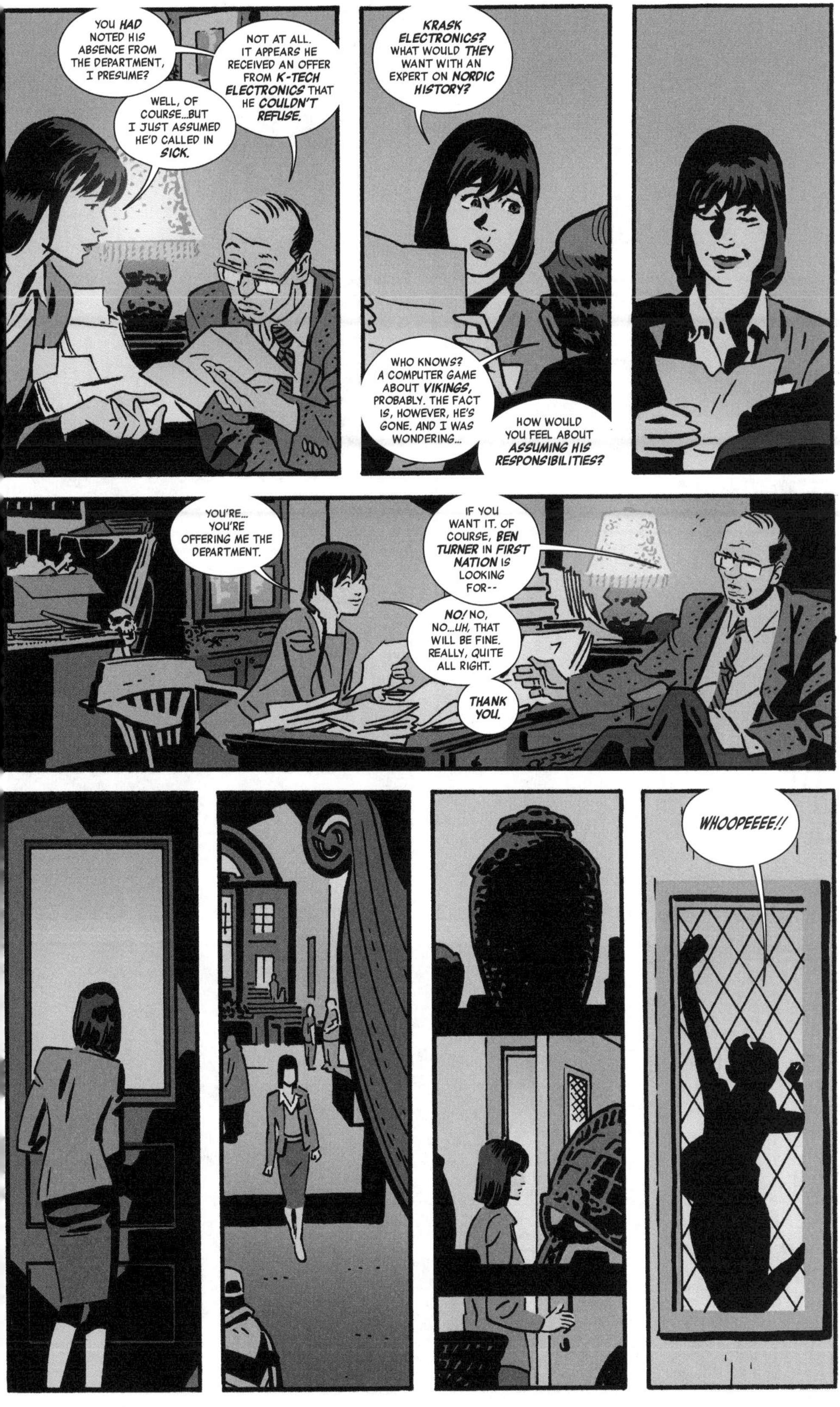

YOU HAD NOTED HIS ABSENCE FROM THE DEPARTMENT, I PRESUME?
WELL, OF COURSE...BUT I JUST ASSUMED HE'D CALLED IN SICK.
NOT AT ALL. IT APPEARS HE RECEIVED AN OFFER FROM K-TECH ELECTRONICS THAT HE COULDN'T REFUSE.
KRASK ELECTRONICS? WHAT WOULD THEY WANT WITH AN EXPERT ON NORDIC HISTORY?
WHO KNOWS? A COMPUTER GAME ABOUT VIKINGS, PROBABLY. THE FACT IS, HOWEVER, HE'S GONE. AND I WAS WONDERING...
HOW WOULD YOU FEEL ABOUT ASSUMING HIS RESPONSIBILITIES?
YOU'RE... YOU'RE OFFERING ME THE DEPARTMENT.
IF YOU WANT IT. OF COURSE, BEN TURNER IN FIRST NATION IS LOOKING FOR--
NO! NO, NO...UH, THAT WILL BE FINE. REALLY, QUITE ALL RIGHT.
THANK YOU.
WHOOPEEEE!!

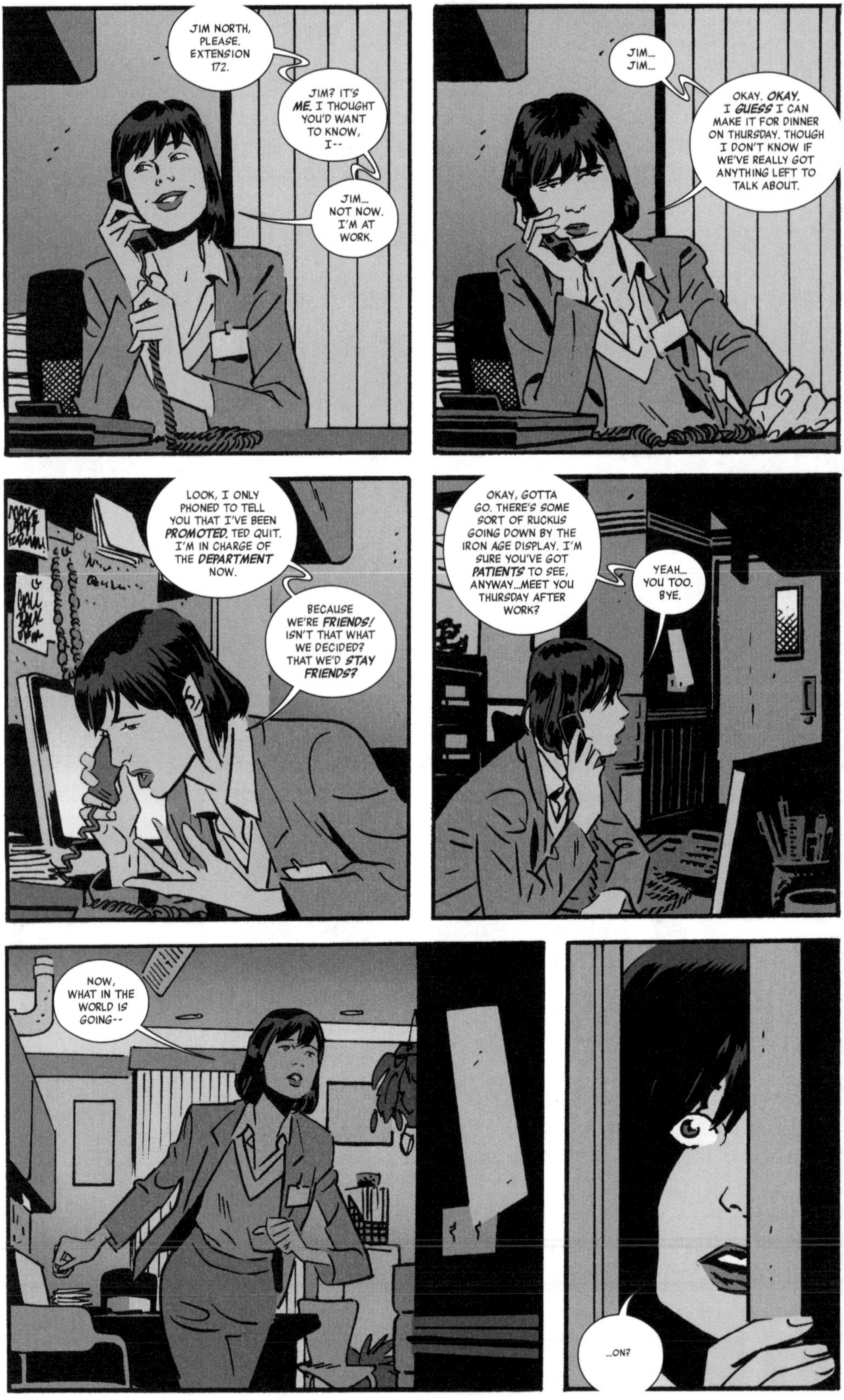
JIM NORTH, PLEASE. EXTENSION 172.
JIM? IT'S ME. I THOUGHT YOU'D WANT TO KNOW, I--
JIM... NOT NOW. I'M AT WORK.
JIM... JIM...
OKAY. OKAY. I GUESS I CAN MAKE IT FOR DINNER ON THURSDAY. THOUGH I DON'T KNOW IF WE'VE REALLY GOT ANYTHING LEFT TO TALK ABOUT.
LOOK, I ONLY PHONED TO TELL YOU THAT I'VE BEEN PROMOTED. TED QUIT. I'M IN CHARGE OF THE DEPARTMENT NOW.
BECAUSE WE'RE FRIENDS! ISN'T THAT WHAT WE DECIDED? THAT WE'D STAY FRIENDS?
OKAY, GOTTA GO. THERE'S SOME SORT OF RUCKUS GOING DOWN BY THE IRON AGE DISPLAY. I'M SURE YOU'VE GOT PATIENTS TO SEE, ANYWAY...MEET YOU THURSDAY AFTER WORK?
YEAH... YOU TOO. BYE.
NOW, WHAT IN THE WORLD IS GOING--
...ON?

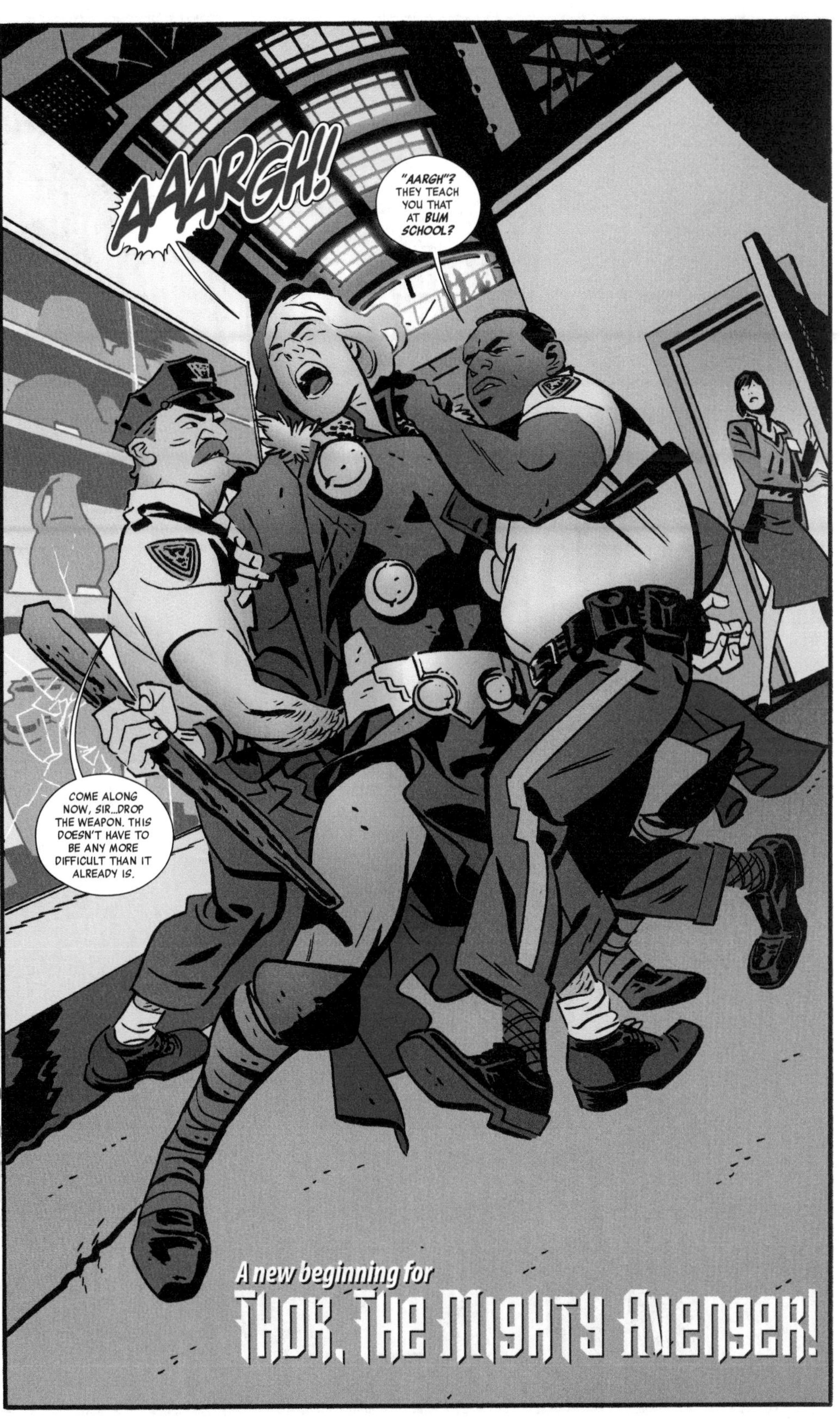
AAARGH!
"AARGH"? THEY TEACH YOU THAT AT BUM SCHOOL?
COME ALONG NOW, SIR...DROP THE WEAPON. THIS DOESN'T HAVE TO BE ANY MORE DIFFICULT THAN IT ALREADY IS.
A new beginning for
THOR, THE MIGHTY AVENGER!

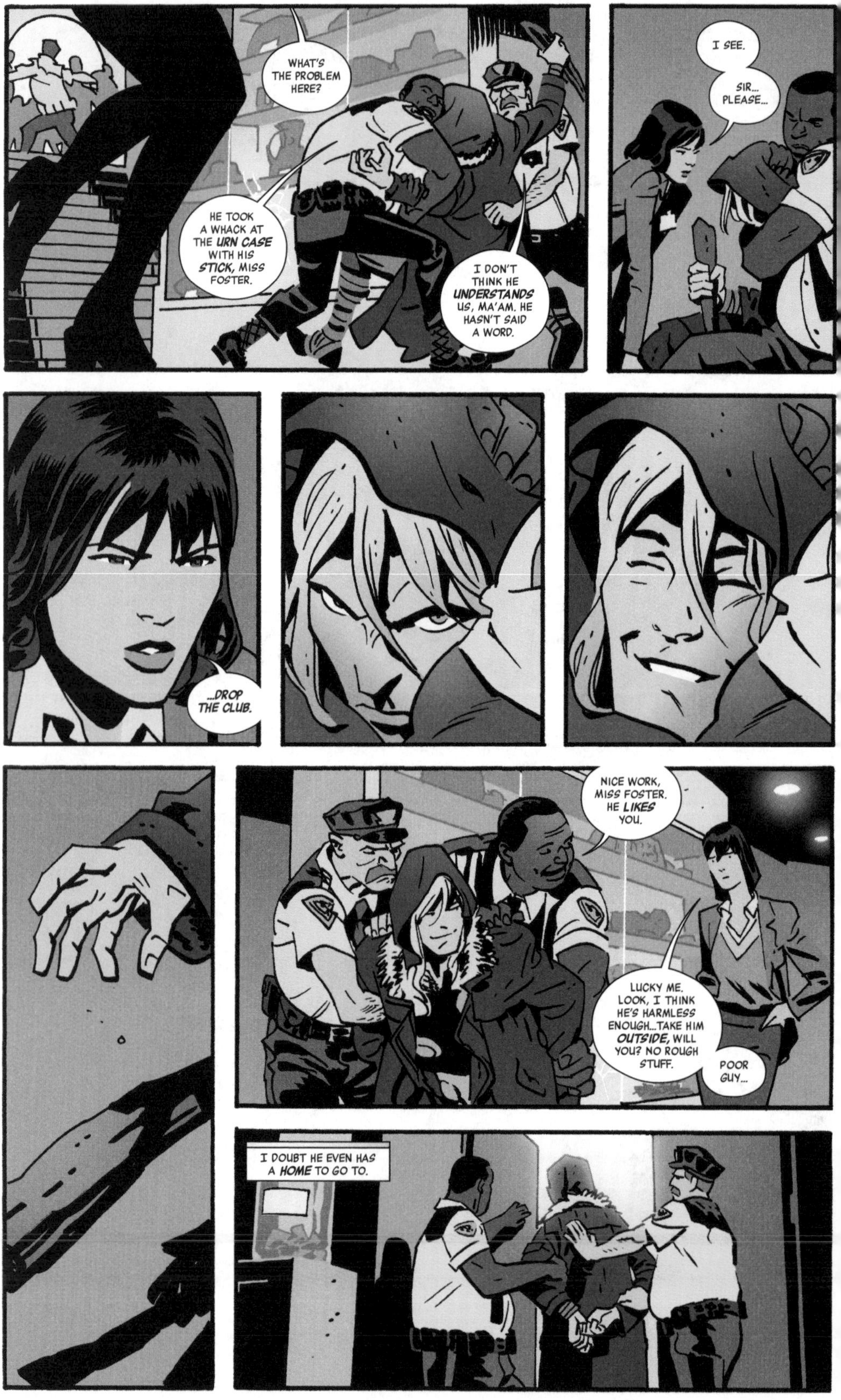

WHAT'S THE PROBLEM HERE?
HE TOOK A WHACK AT THE URN CASE WITH HIS STICK, MISS FOSTER.
I DON'T THINK HE UNDERSTANDS US, MA'AM. HE HASN'T SAID A WORD.
I SEE.
SIR... PLEASE...
...DROP THE CLUB.
NICE WORK, MISS FOSTER. HE LIKES YOU.
LUCKY ME. LOOK, I THINK HE'S HARMLESS ENOUGH...TAKE HIM OUTSIDE, WILL YOU? NO ROUGH STUFF.
POOR GUY...
I DOUBT HE EVEN HAS A HOME TO GO TO.

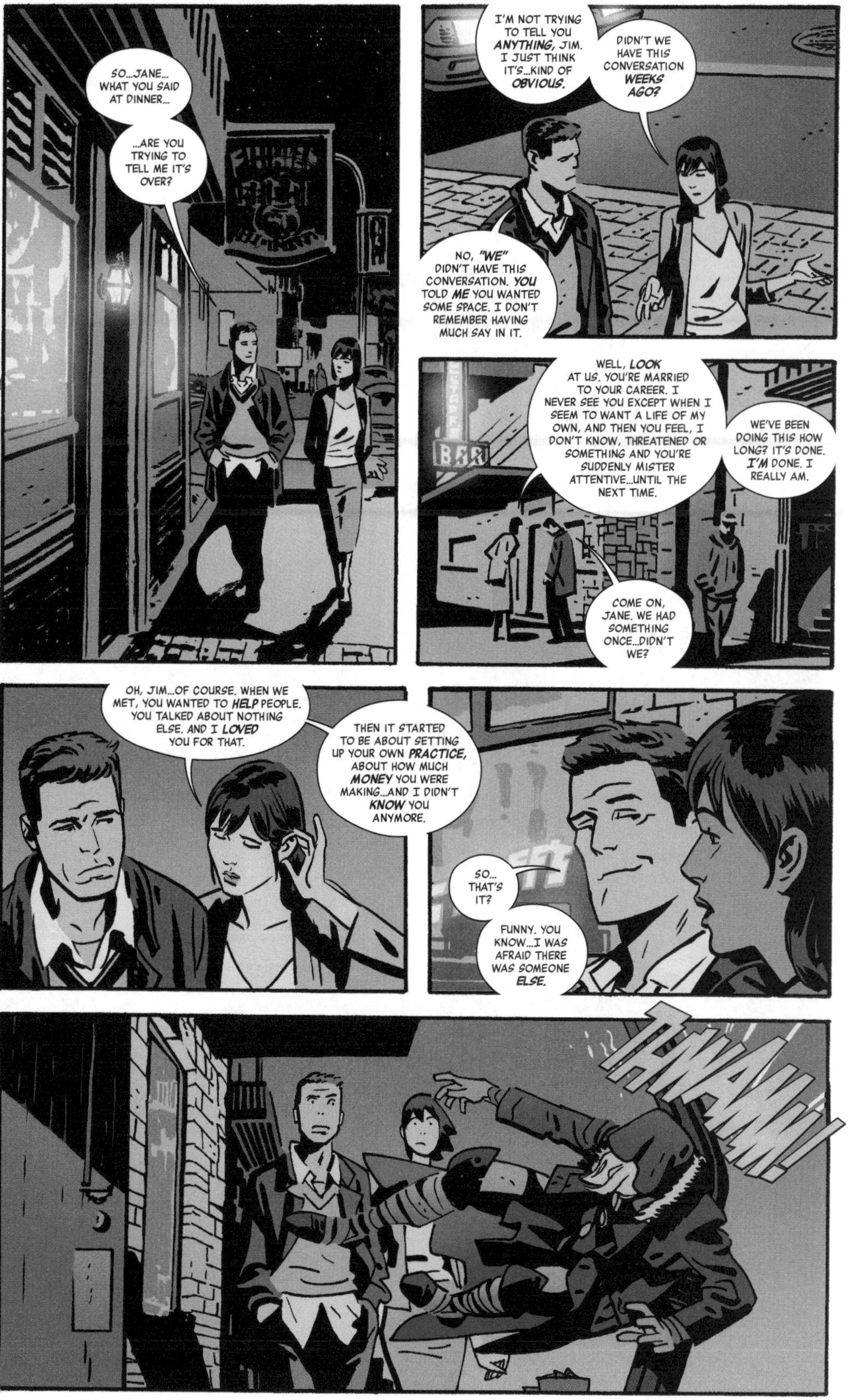
SO...JANE... WHAT YOU SAID AT DINNER...
...ARE YOU TRYING TO TELL ME IT'S OVER?
I'M NOT TRYING TO TELL YOU ANYTHING, JIM. I JUST THINK IT'S...KIND OF OBVIOUS.
DIDN'T WE HAVE THIS CONVERSATION WEEKS AGO?
NO, "WE" DIDN'T HAVE THIS CONVERSATION. YOU TOLD ME YOU WANTED SOME SPACE. I DON'T REMEMBER HAVING MUCH SAY IN IT.
WELL, LOOK AT US. YOU'RE MARRIED TO YOUR CAREER. I NEVER SEE YOU EXCEPT WHEN I SEEM TO WANT A LIFE OF MY OWN, AND THEN YOU FEEL, I DON'T KNOW, THREATENED OR SOMETHING AND YOU'RE SUDDENLY MISTER ATTENTIVE...UNTIL THE NEXT TIME.
WE'VE BEEN DOING THIS HOW LONG? IT'S DONE. I'M DONE. I REALLY AM.
COME ON, JANE. WE HAD SOMETHING ONCE...DIDN'T WE?
OH, JIM...OF COURSE. WHEN WE MET, YOU WANTED TO HELP PEOPLE. YOU TALKED ABOUT NOTHING ELSE. AND I LOVED YOU FOR THAT.
THEN IT STARTED TO BE ABOUT SETTING UP YOUR OWN PRACTICE, ABOUT HOW MUCH MONEY YOU WERE MAKING...AND I DIDN'T KNOW YOU ANYMORE.
SO... THAT'S IT?
FUNNY. YOU KNOW...I WAS AFRAID THERE WAS SOMEONE ELSE.
THWANNN!

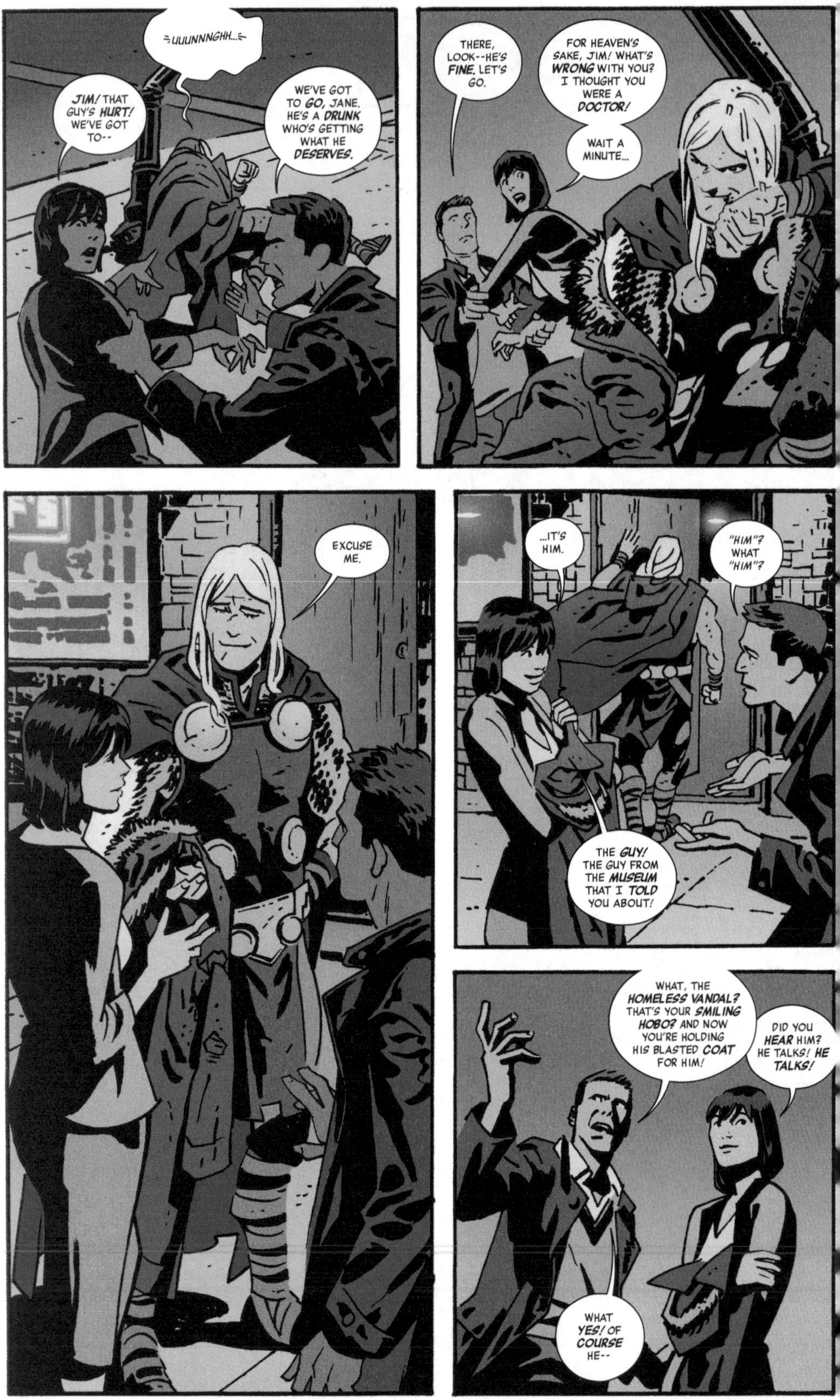

≈UUUNNNGHH...≈
JIM! THAT GUY'S HURT! WE'VE GOT TO--
WE'VE GOT TO GO, JANE. HE'S A DRUNK WHO'S GETTING WHAT HE DESERVES.
THERE, LOOK--HE'S FINE. LET'S GO.
FOR HEAVEN'S SAKE, JIM! WHAT'S WRONG WITH YOU? I THOUGHT YOU WERE A DOCTOR!
WAIT A MINUTE...
EXCUSE ME.
...IT'S HIM.
"HIM"? WHAT "HIM"?
THE GUY! THE GUY FROM THE MUSEUM THAT I TOLD YOU ABOUT!
WHAT, THE HOMELESS VANDAL? THAT'S YOUR SMILING HOBO? AND NOW YOU'RE HOLDING HIS BLASTED COAT FOR HIM!
DID YOU HEAR HIM? HE TALKS! HE TALKS!
WHAT YES! OF COURSE HE--

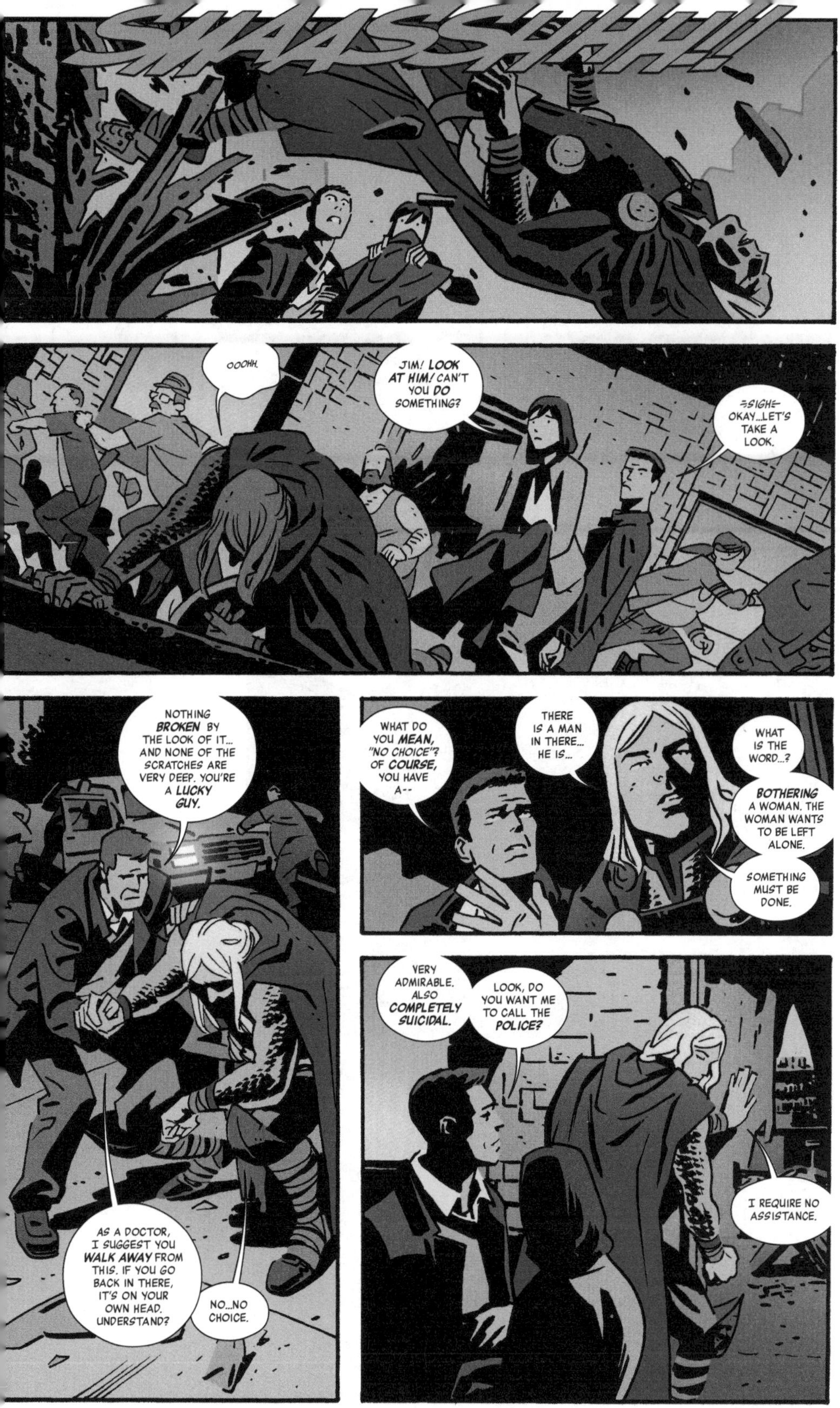
SHAASSHHH!!
OOOHH.
JIM! LOOK AT HIM! CAN'T YOU DO SOMETHING?
=SIGH= OKAY...LET'S TAKE A LOOK.
NOTHING BROKEN BY THE LOOK OF IT... AND NONE OF THE SCRATCHES ARE VERY DEEP. YOU'RE A LUCKY GUY.
AS A DOCTOR, I SUGGEST YOU WALK AWAY FROM THIS. IF YOU GO BACK IN THERE, IT'S ON YOUR OWN HEAD. UNDERSTAND?
NO...NO CHOICE.
WHAT DO YOU MEAN, "NO CHOICE"? OF COURSE, YOU HAVE A--
THERE IS A MAN IN THERE... HE IS...
WHAT IS THE WORD...?
BOTHERING A WOMAN. THE WOMAN WANTS TO BE LEFT ALONE.
SOMETHING MUST BE DONE.
VERY ADMIRABLE. ALSO COMPLETELY SUICIDAL.
LOOK, DO YOU WANT ME TO CALL THE POLICE?
I REQUIRE NO ASSISTANCE.

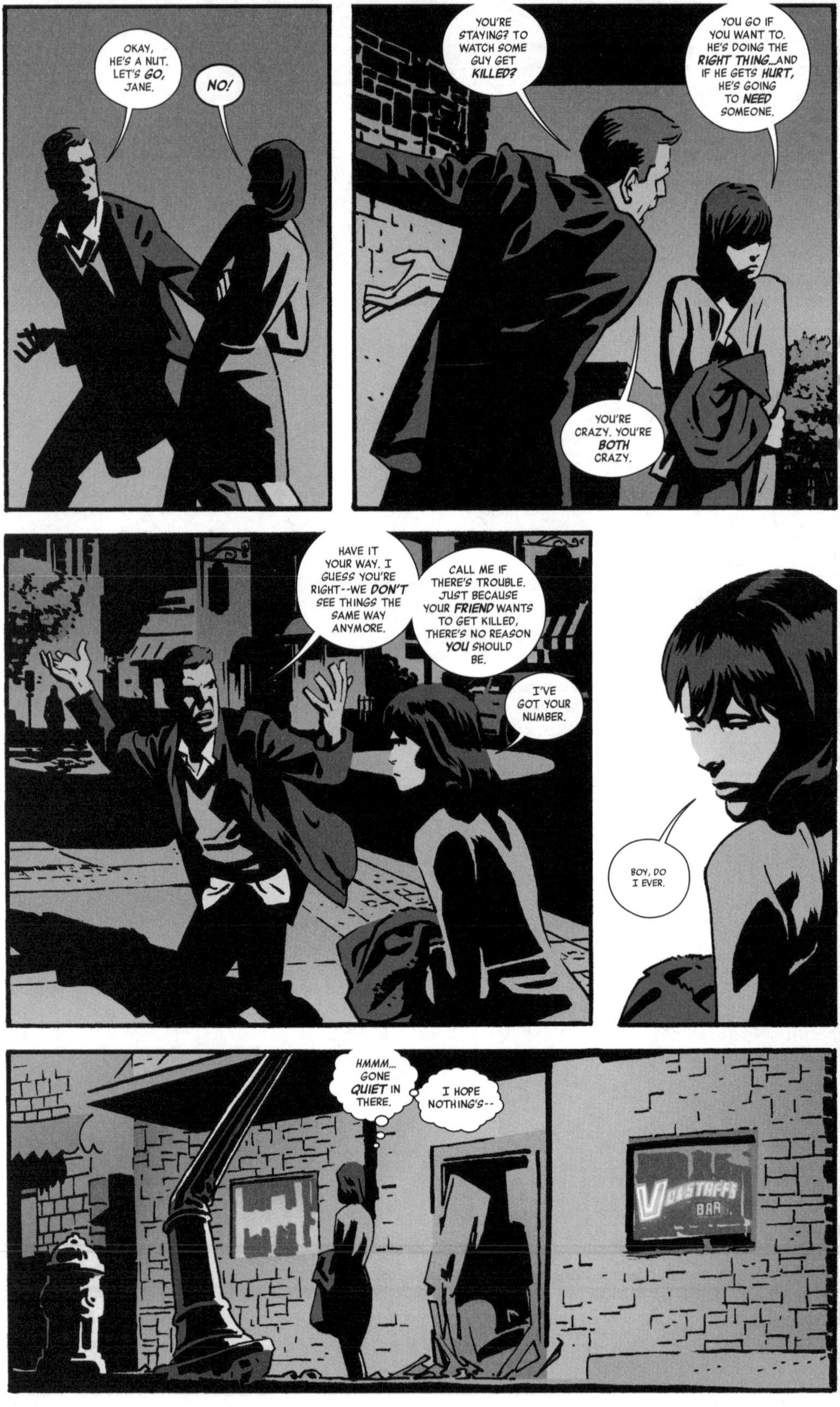
OKAY, HE'S A NUT. LET'S GO, JANE.
NO!
YOU'RE STAYING? TO WATCH SOME GUY GET KILLED?
YOU GO IF YOU WANT TO. HE'S DOING THE RIGHT THING...AND IF HE GETS HURT, HE'S GOING TO NEED SOMEONE.
YOU'RE CRAZY. YOU'RE BOTH CRAZY.
HAVE IT YOUR WAY. I GUESS YOU'RE RIGHT--WE DON'T SEE THINGS THE SAME WAY ANYMORE.
CALL ME IF THERE'S TROUBLE. JUST BECAUSE YOUR FRIEND WANTS TO GET KILLED, THERE'S NO REASON YOU SHOULD BE.
I'VE GOT YOUR NUMBER.
BOY, DO I EVER.
HMMM... GONE QUIET IN THERE.
I HOPE NOTHING'S--
BAR

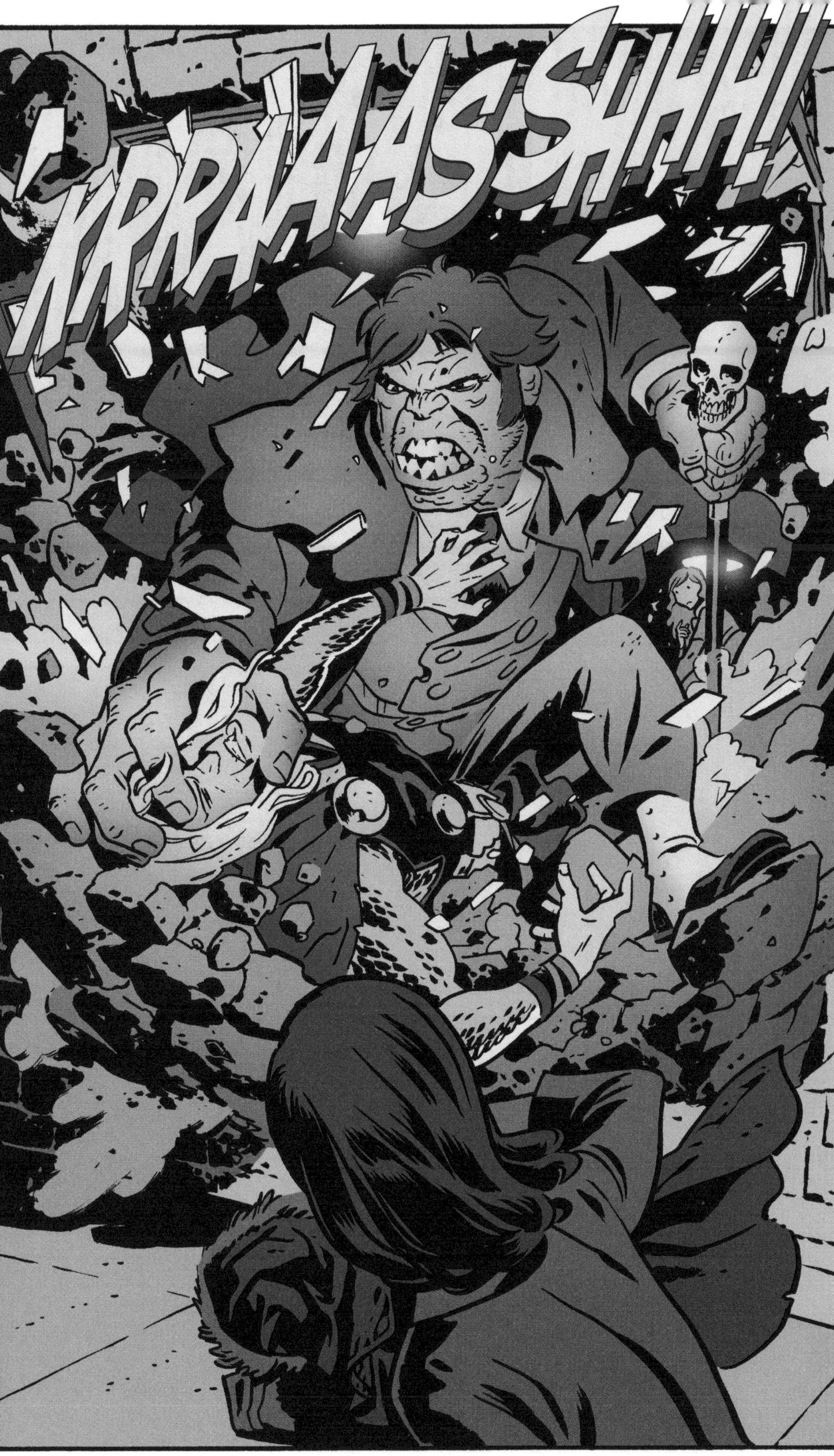
KRRAAAASSHHH!!

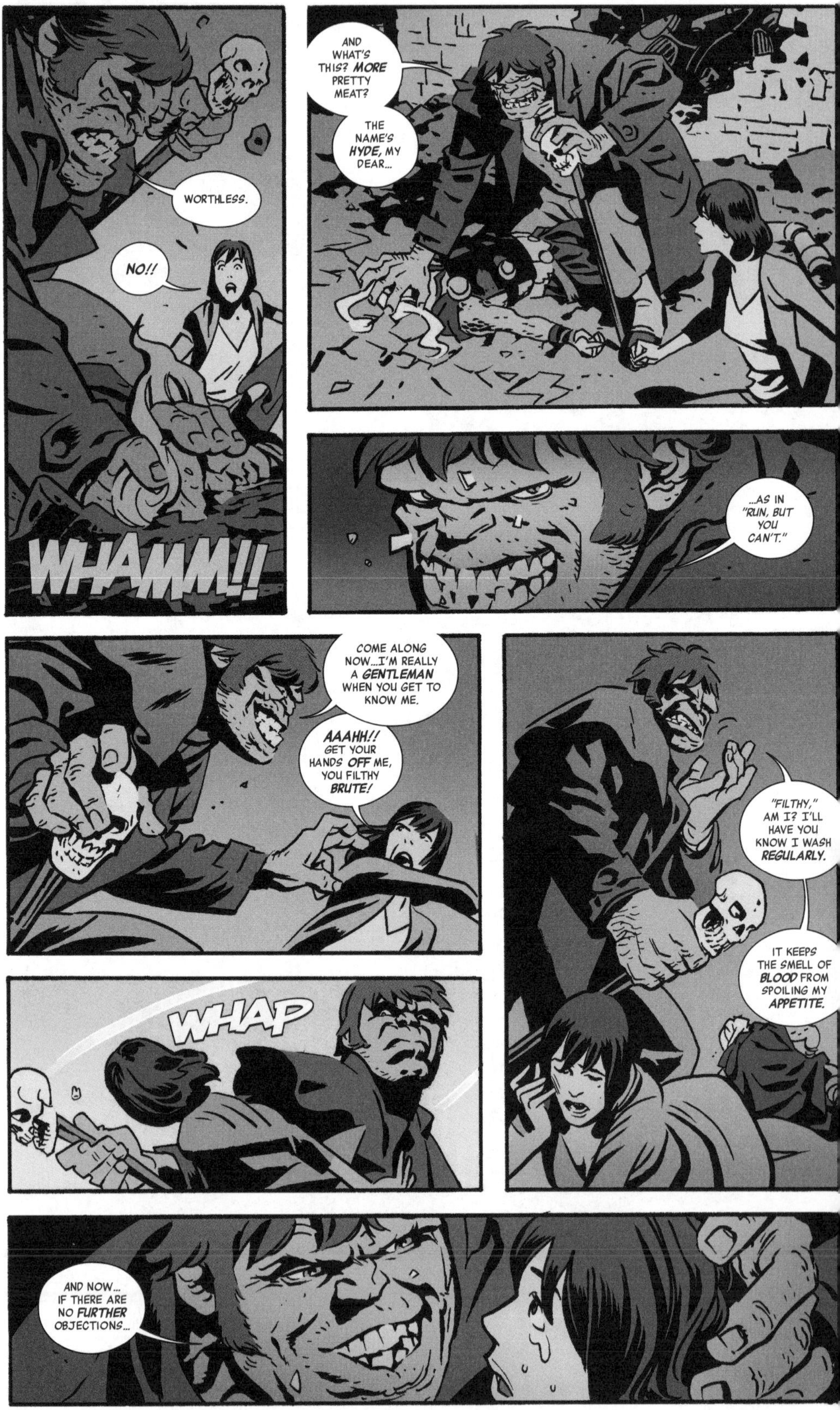
WORTHLESS.
NO!!
WHAMM!!
AND WHAT'S THIS? MORE PRETTY MEAT?
THE NAME'S HYDE, MY DEAR...
...AS IN "RUN, BUT YOU CAN'T."
COME ALONG NOW...I'M REALLY A GENTLEMAN WHEN YOU GET TO KNOW ME.
AAAHH!! GET YOUR HANDS OFF ME, YOU FILTHY BRUTE!
"FILTHY," AM I? I'LL HAVE YOU KNOW I WASH REGULARLY.
IT KEEPS THE SMELL OF BLOOD FROM SPOILING MY APPETITE.
WHAP
AND NOW... IF THERE ARE NO FURTHER OBJECTIONS...

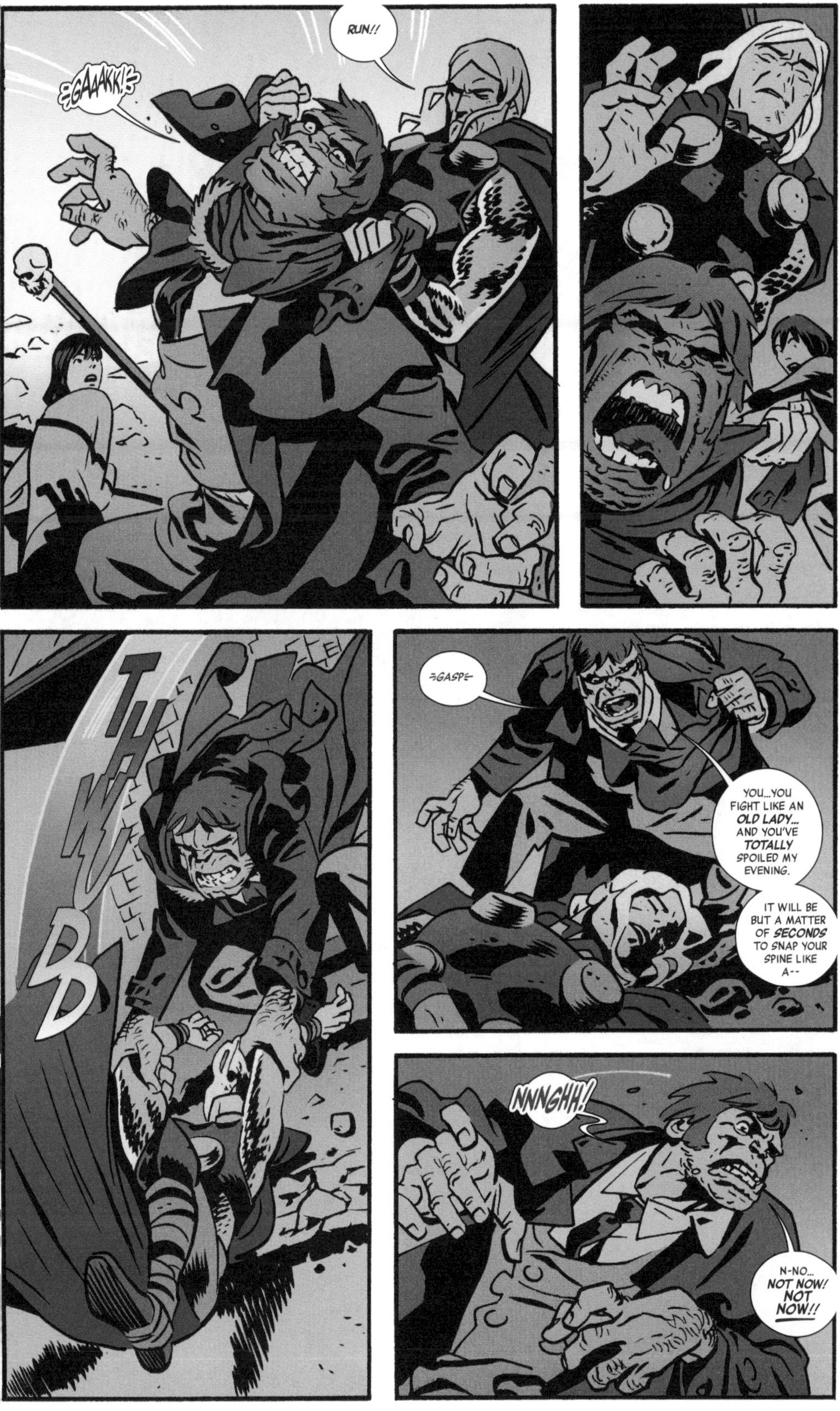
RUN!!
GAAAKK!
=GASP=
YOU...YOU FIGHT LIKE AN OLD LADY... AND YOU'VE TOTALLY SPOILED MY EVENING.
IT WILL BE BUT A MATTER OF SECONDS TO SNAP YOUR SPINE LIKE A--
THWOBB
NNNGHH!
N-NO... NOT NOW! NOT NOW!!

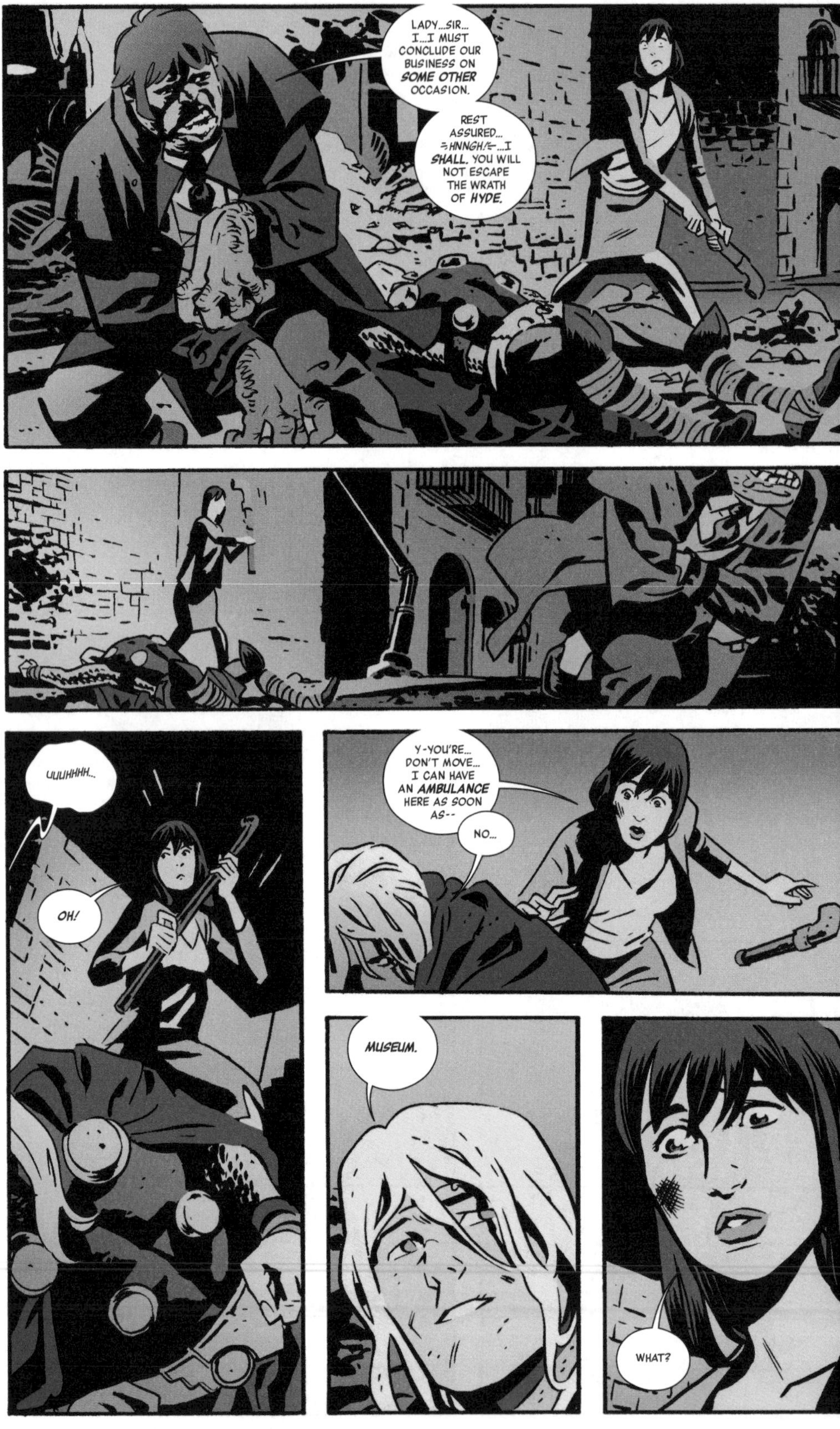
LADY...SIR... I...I MUST CONCLUDE OUR BUSINESS ON SOME OTHER OCCASION.
REST ASSURED... =HNNGH!=...I SHALL. YOU WILL NOT ESCAPE THE WRATH OF HYDE.
UUUHHHH...
OH!
Y-YOU'RE... DON'T MOVE... I CAN HAVE AN AMBULANCE HERE AS SOON AS--
NO...
MUSEUM.
WHAT?

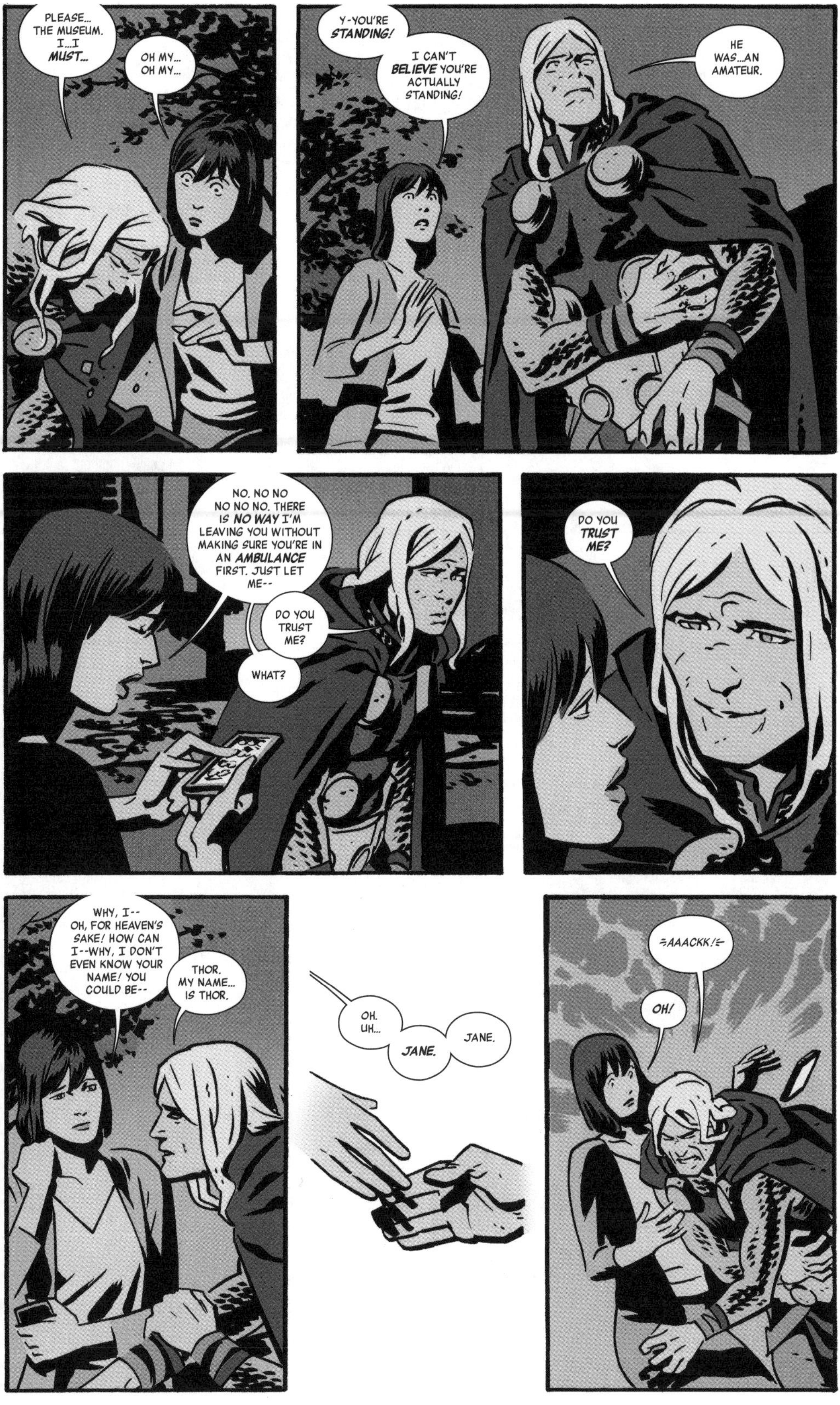
PLEASE... THE MUSEUM. I...I MUST...
OH MY... OH MY...
Y-YOU'RE STANDING!
I CAN'T BELIEVE YOU'RE ACTUALLY STANDING!
HE WAS...AN AMATEUR.
NO. NO NO NO NO NO. THERE IS NO WAY I'M LEAVING YOU WITHOUT MAKING SURE YOU'RE IN AN AMBULANCE FIRST. JUST LET ME--
DO YOU TRUST ME?
WHAT?
DO YOU TRUST ME?
WHY, I-- OH, FOR HEAVEN'S SAKE! HOW CAN I--WHY, I DON'T EVEN KNOW YOUR NAME! YOU COULD BE--
THOR. MY NAME... IS THOR.
OH. UH...
JANE.
JANE.
AAACKK!
OH!

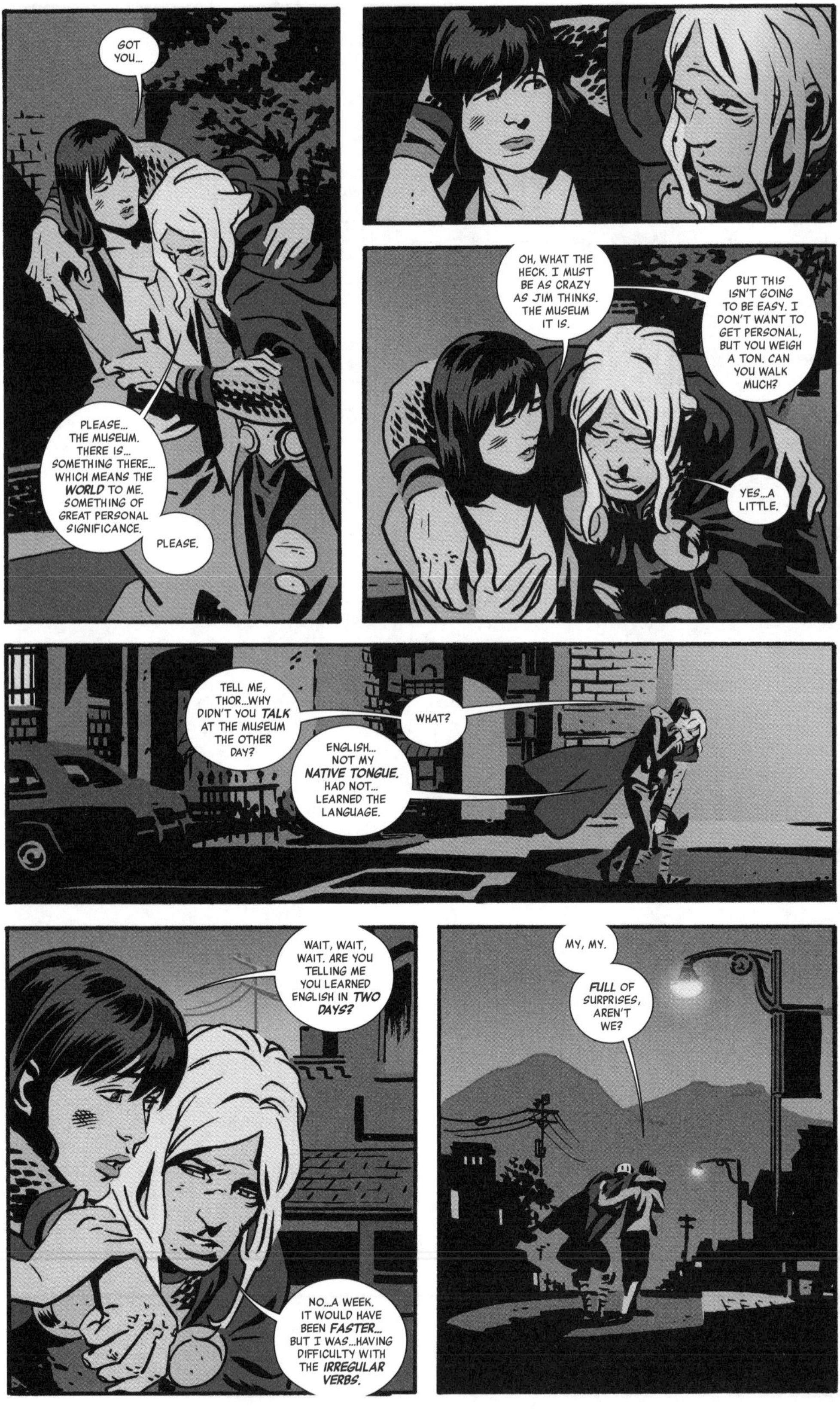
GOT YOU...
PLEASE... THE MUSEUM. THERE IS... SOMETHING THERE... WHICH MEANS THE WORLD TO ME. SOMETHING OF GREAT PERSONAL SIGNIFICANCE.
PLEASE.
OH, WHAT THE HECK. I MUST BE AS CRAZY AS JIM THINKS. THE MUSEUM IT IS.
BUT THIS ISN'T GOING TO BE EASY. I DON'T WANT TO GET PERSONAL, BUT YOU WEIGH A TON. CAN YOU WALK MUCH?
YES...A LITTLE.
TELL ME, THOR...WHY DIDN'T YOU TALK AT THE MUSEUM THE OTHER DAY?
WHAT?
ENGLISH... NOT MY NATIVE TONGUE. HAD NOT... LEARNED THE LANGUAGE.
WAIT, WAIT, WAIT. ARE YOU TELLING ME YOU LEARNED ENGLISH IN TWO DAYS?
NO...A WEEK. IT WOULD HAVE BEEN FASTER... BUT I WAS...HAVING DIFFICULTY WITH THE IRREGULAR VERBS.
MY, MY.
FULL OF SURPRISES, AREN'T WE?

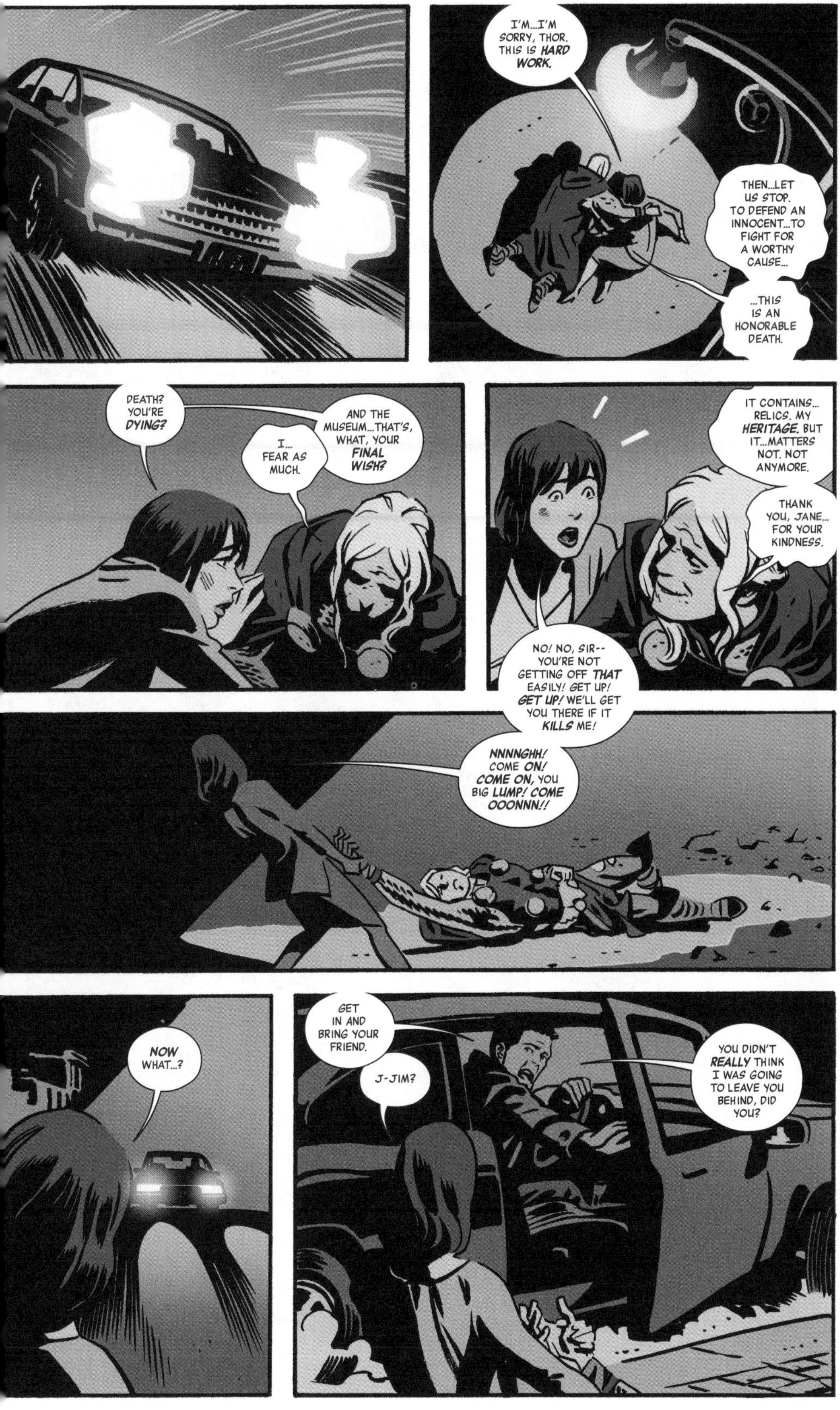
I'M...I'M SORRY, THOR. THIS IS HARD WORK.
THEN...LET US STOP. TO DEFEND AN INNOCENT...TO FIGHT FOR A WORTHY CAUSE...
...THIS IS AN HONORABLE DEATH.
DEATH? YOU'RE DYING?
I... FEAR AS MUCH.
AND THE MUSEUM...THAT'S, WHAT, YOUR FINAL WISH?
IT CONTAINS... RELICS. MY HERITAGE. BUT IT...MATTERS NOT. NOT ANYMORE.
THANK YOU, JANE... FOR YOUR KINDNESS.
NO! NO, SIR-- YOU'RE NOT GETTING OFF THAT EASILY! GET UP! GET UP! WE'LL GET YOU THERE IF IT KILLS ME!
NNNNGHH! COME ON! COME ON, YOU BIG LUMP! COME OOONNN!!
NOW WHAT...?
GET IN AND BRING YOUR FRIEND.
J-JIM?
YOU DIDN'T REALLY THINK I WAS GOING TO LEAVE YOU BEHIND, DID YOU?

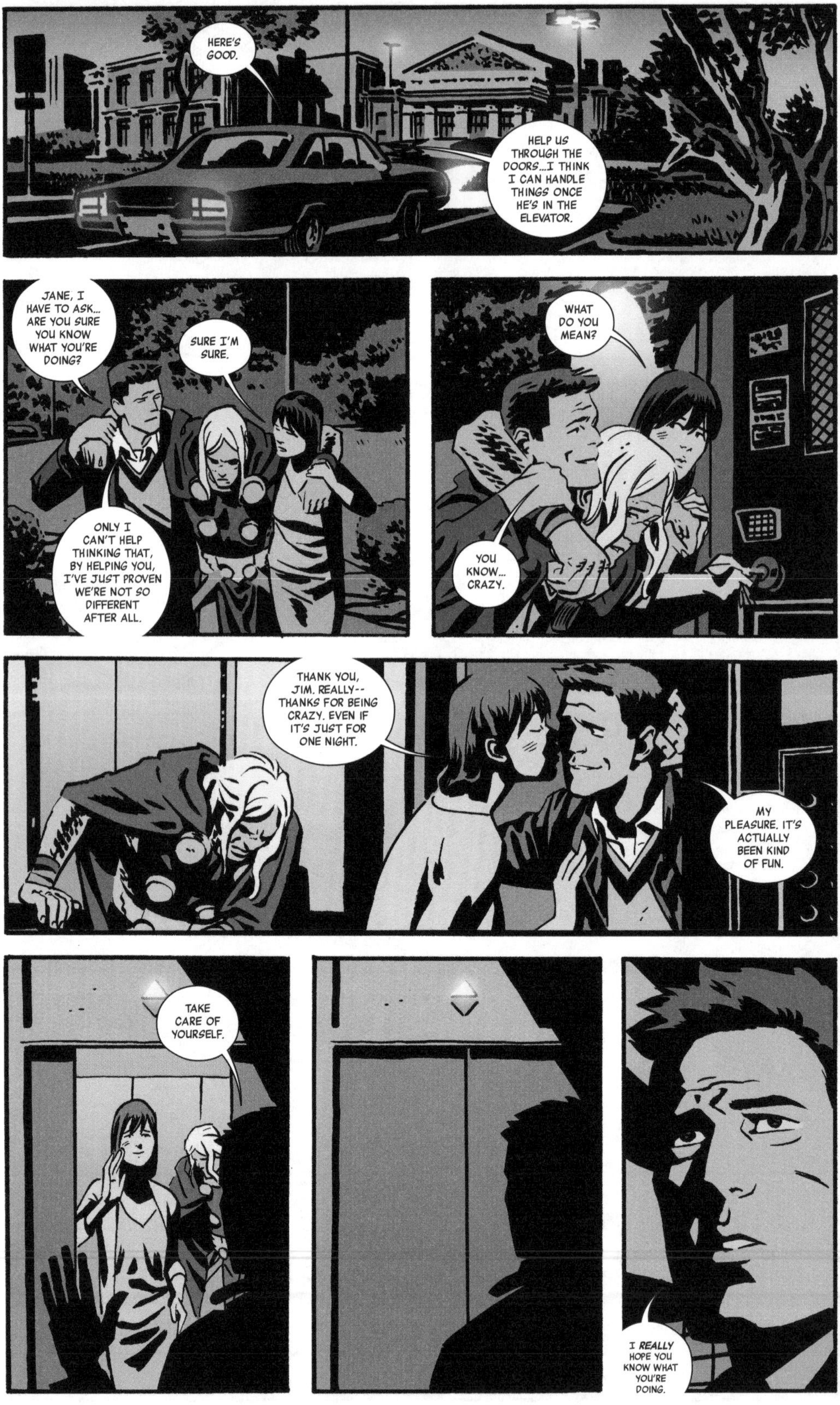
HERE'S GOOD.
HELP US THROUGH THE DOORS...I THINK I CAN HANDLE THINGS ONCE HE'S IN THE ELEVATOR.
JANE, I HAVE TO ASK... ARE YOU SURE YOU KNOW WHAT YOU'RE DOING?
SURE I'M SURE.
ONLY I CAN'T HELP THINKING THAT, BY HELPING YOU, I'VE JUST PROVEN WE'RE NOT SO DIFFERENT AFTER ALL.
WHAT DO YOU MEAN?
YOU KNOW... CRAZY.
THANK YOU, JIM. REALLY-- THANKS FOR BEING CRAZY. EVEN IF IT'S JUST FOR ONE NIGHT.
MY PLEASURE. IT'S ACTUALLY BEEN KIND OF FUN.
TAKE CARE OF YOURSELF.
I REALLY HOPE YOU KNOW WHAT YOU'RE DOING.

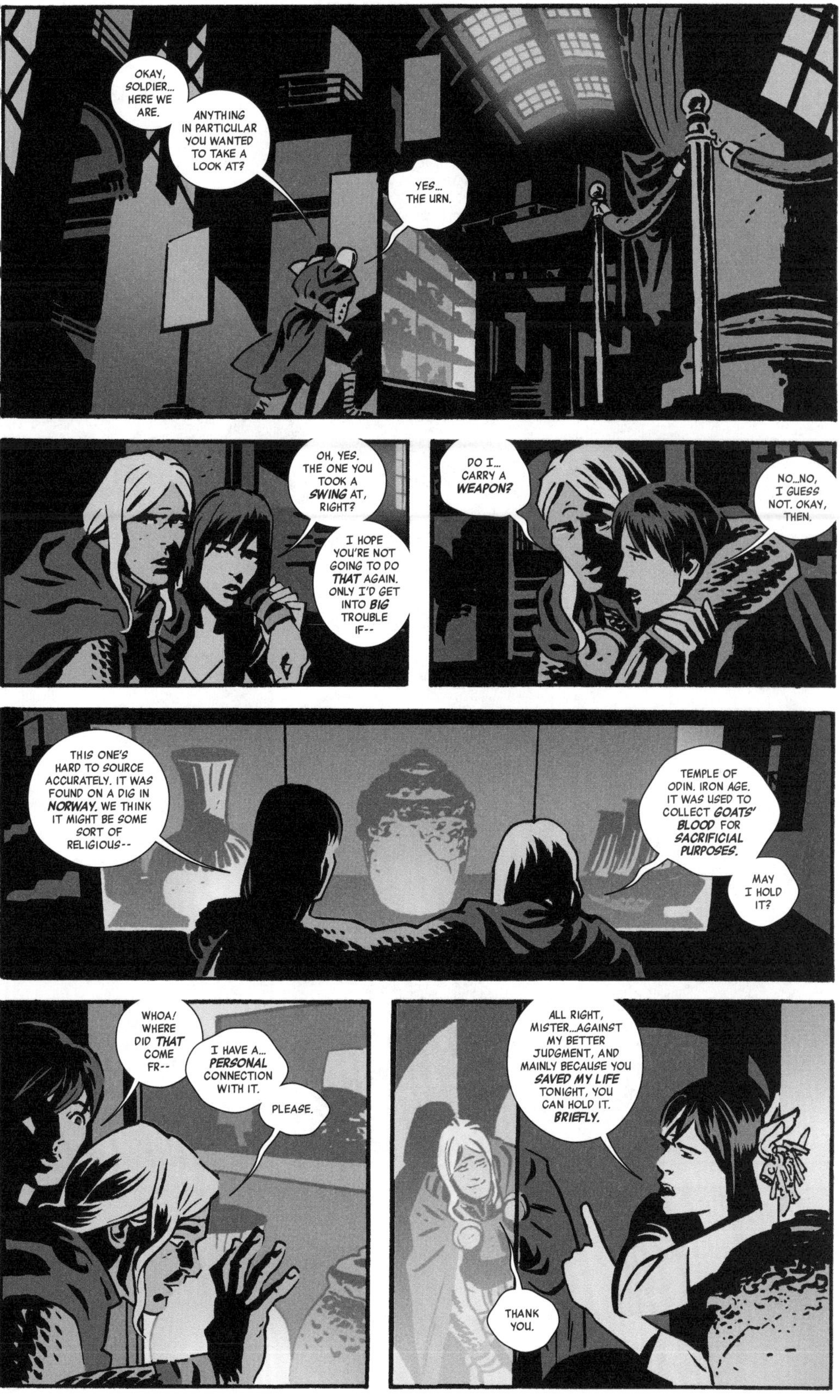
OKAY, SOLDIER... HERE WE ARE.
ANYTHING IN PARTICULAR YOU WANTED TO TAKE A LOOK AT?
YES... THE URN.
OH, YES. THE ONE YOU TOOK A SWING AT, RIGHT?
I HOPE YOU'RE NOT GOING TO DO THAT AGAIN. ONLY I'D GET INTO BIG TROUBLE IF--
DO I... CARRY A WEAPON?
NO...NO, I GUESS NOT. OKAY, THEN.
THIS ONE'S HARD TO SOURCE ACCURATELY. IT WAS FOUND ON A DIG IN NORWAY. WE THINK IT MIGHT BE SOME SORT OF RELIGIOUS--
TEMPLE OF ODIN. IRON AGE. IT WAS USED TO COLLECT GOATS' BLOOD FOR SACRIFICIAL PURPOSES.
MAY I HOLD IT?
WHOA! WHERE DID THAT COME FR--
I HAVE A... PERSONAL CONNECTION WITH IT.
PLEASE.
ALL RIGHT, MISTER...AGAINST MY BETTER JUDGMENT, AND MAINLY BECAUSE YOU SAVED MY LIFE TONIGHT, YOU CAN HOLD IT. BRIEFLY.
THANK YOU.

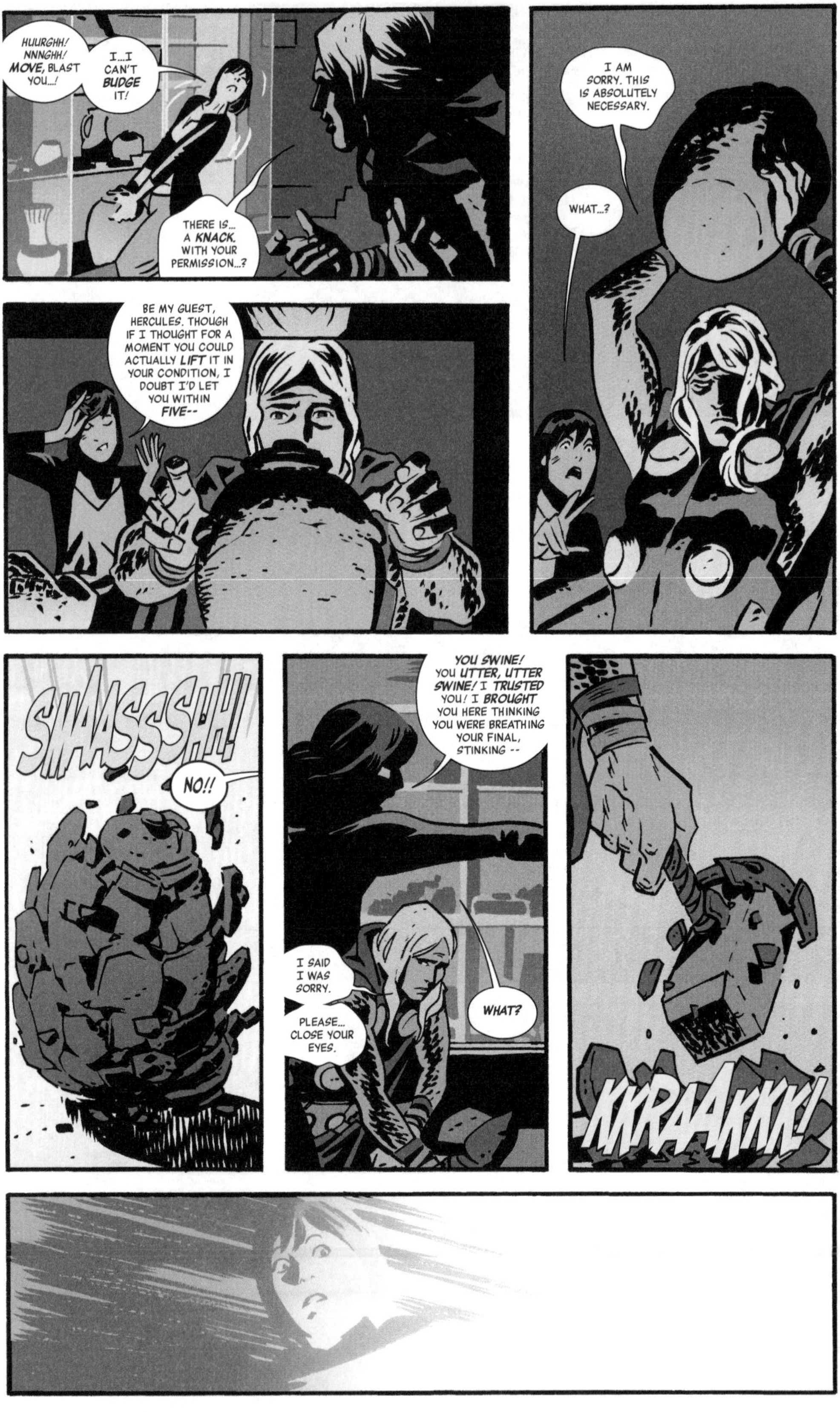
HUURGHH! NNNGHH! MOVE, BLAST YOU...!
I...I CAN'T BUDGE IT!
THERE IS... A KNACK. WITH YOUR PERMISSION...?
I AM SORRY. THIS IS ABSOLUTELY NECESSARY.
WHAT...?
BE MY GUEST, HERCULES. THOUGH IF I THOUGHT FOR A MOMENT YOU COULD ACTUALLY LIFT IT IN YOUR CONDITION, I DOUBT I'D LET YOU WITHIN FIVE--
SHAASSSHH!
NO!!
YOU SWINE! YOU UTTER, UTTER SWINE! I TRUSTED YOU! I BROUGHT YOU HERE THINKING YOU WERE BREATHING YOUR FINAL, STINKING --
I SAID I WAS SORRY.
PLEASE... CLOSE YOUR EYES.
WHAT?
KKRAAKKK!

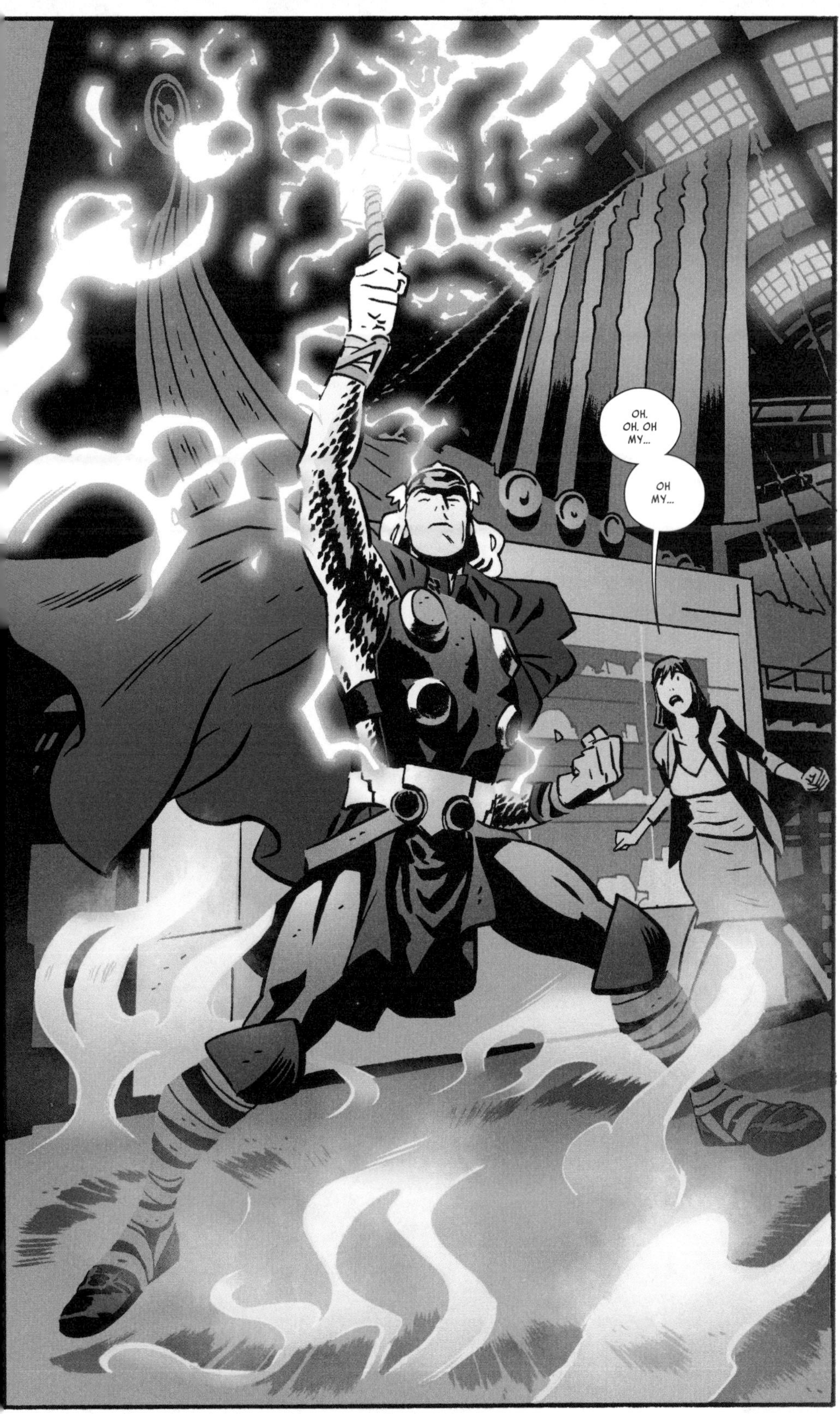
OH.
OH. OH
MY...
OH
MY...

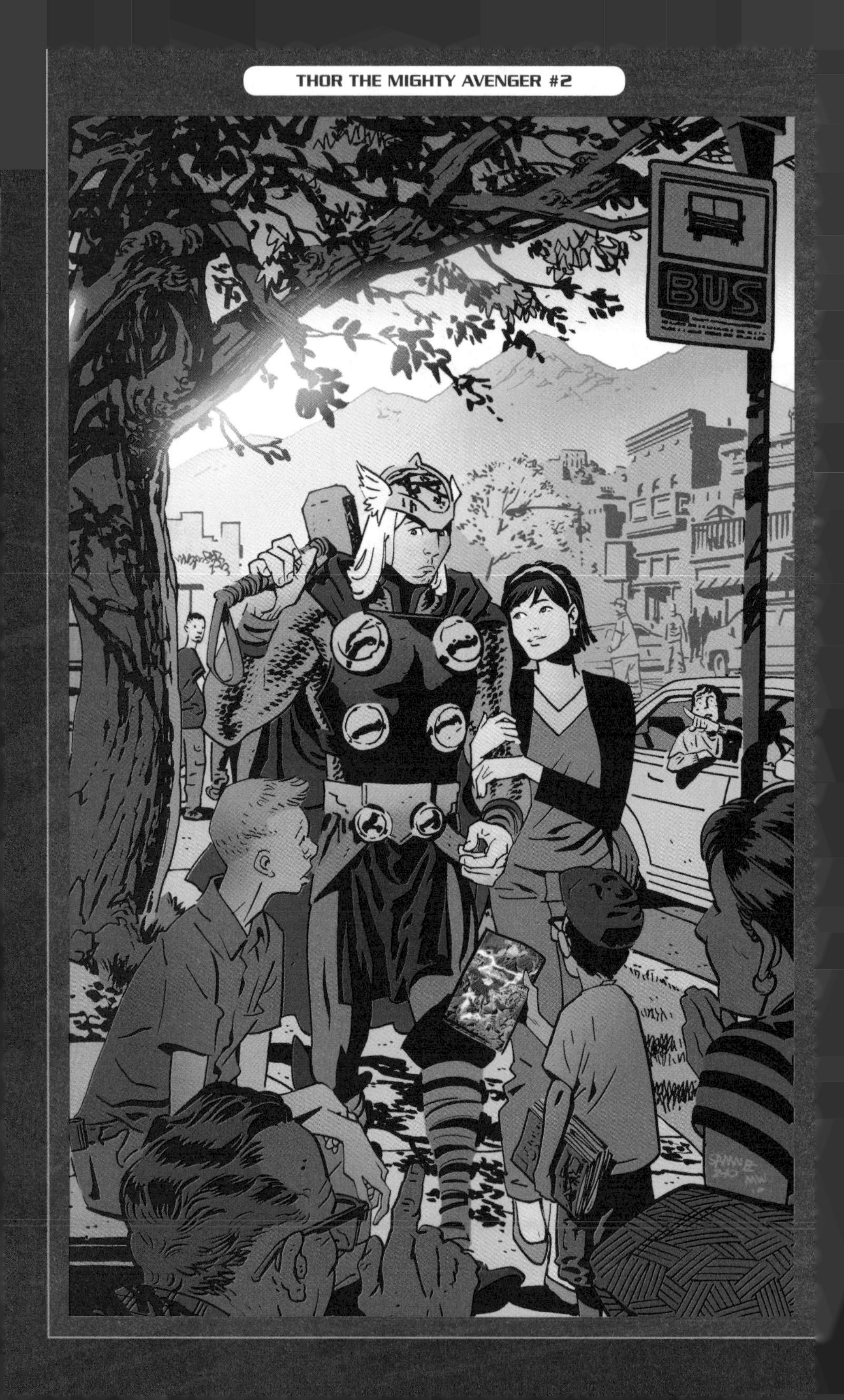
BUS

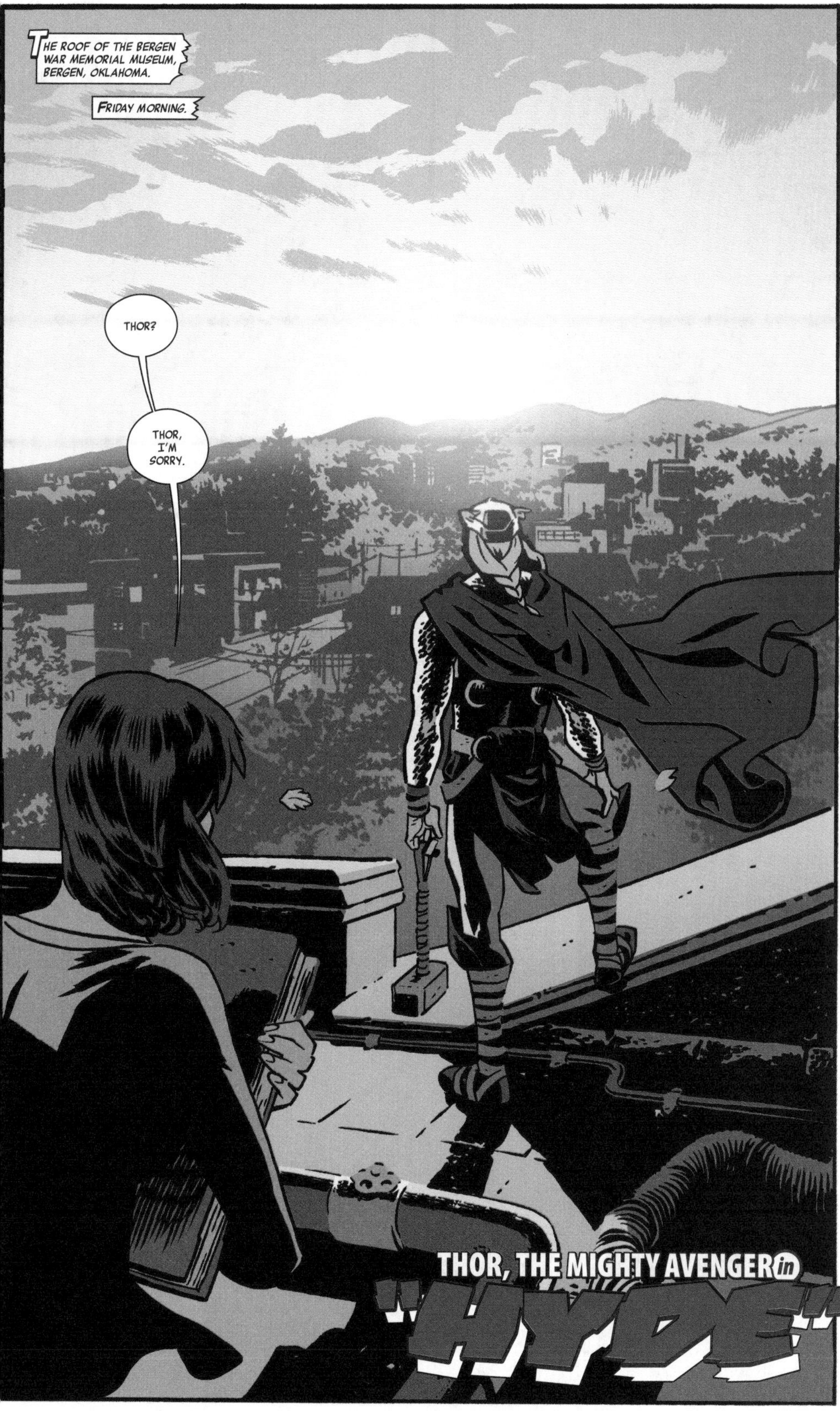
THE ROOF OF THE BERGEN WAR MEMORIAL MUSEUM, BERGEN, OKLAHOMA.
FRIDAY MORNING.
THOR?
THOR, I'M SORRY.
THOR, THE MIGHTY AVENGER in
"HYDE"

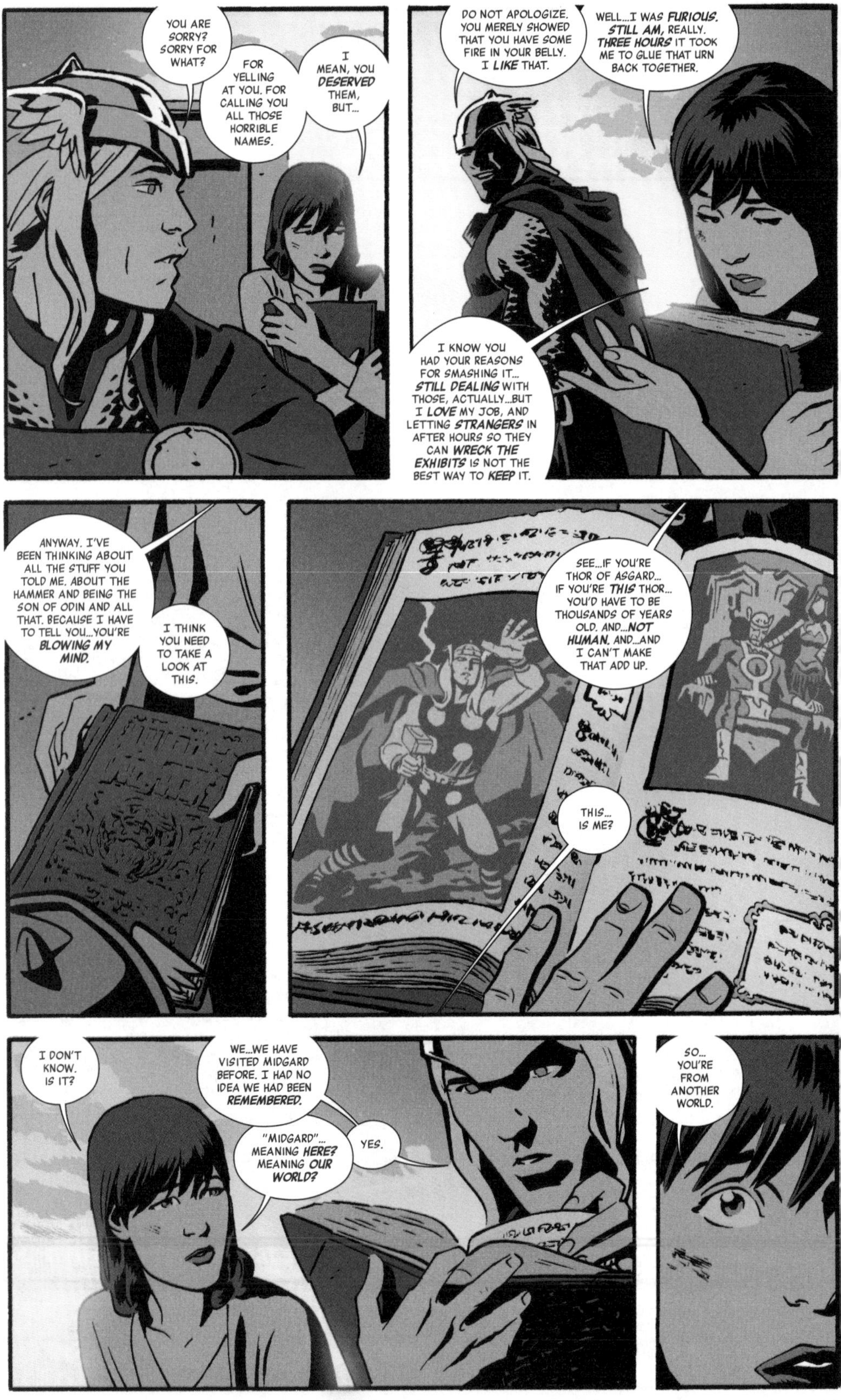
YOU ARE SORRY? SORRY FOR WHAT?
FOR YELLING AT YOU. FOR CALLING YOU ALL THOSE HORRIBLE NAMES.
I MEAN, YOU DESERVED THEM, BUT...
DO NOT APOLOGIZE. YOU MERELY SHOWED THAT YOU HAVE SOME FIRE IN YOUR BELLY. I LIKE THAT.
WELL...I WAS FURIOUS. STILL AM, REALLY. THREE HOURS IT TOOK ME TO GLUE THAT URN BACK TOGETHER.
I KNOW YOU HAD YOUR REASONS FOR SMASHING IT... STILL DEALING WITH THOSE, ACTUALLY...BUT I LOVE MY JOB, AND LETTING STRANGERS IN AFTER HOURS SO THEY CAN WRECK THE EXHIBITS IS NOT THE BEST WAY TO KEEP IT.
ANYWAY. I'VE BEEN THINKING ABOUT ALL THE STUFF YOU TOLD ME. ABOUT THE HAMMER AND BEING THE SON OF ODIN AND ALL THAT. BECAUSE I HAVE TO TELL YOU...YOU'RE BLOWING MY MIND.
I THINK YOU NEED TO TAKE A LOOK AT THIS.
SEE...IF YOU'RE THOR OF ASGARD... IF YOU'RE THIS THOR... YOU'D HAVE TO BE THOUSANDS OF YEARS OLD. AND...NOT HUMAN. AND...AND I CAN'T MAKE THAT ADD UP.
THIS... IS ME?
I DON'T KNOW. IS IT?
WE...WE HAVE VISITED MIDGARD BEFORE. I HAD NO IDEA WE HAD BEEN REMEMBERED.
"MIDGARD"... MEANING HERE? MEANING OUR WORLD?
YES.
SO... YOU'RE FROM ANOTHER WORLD.

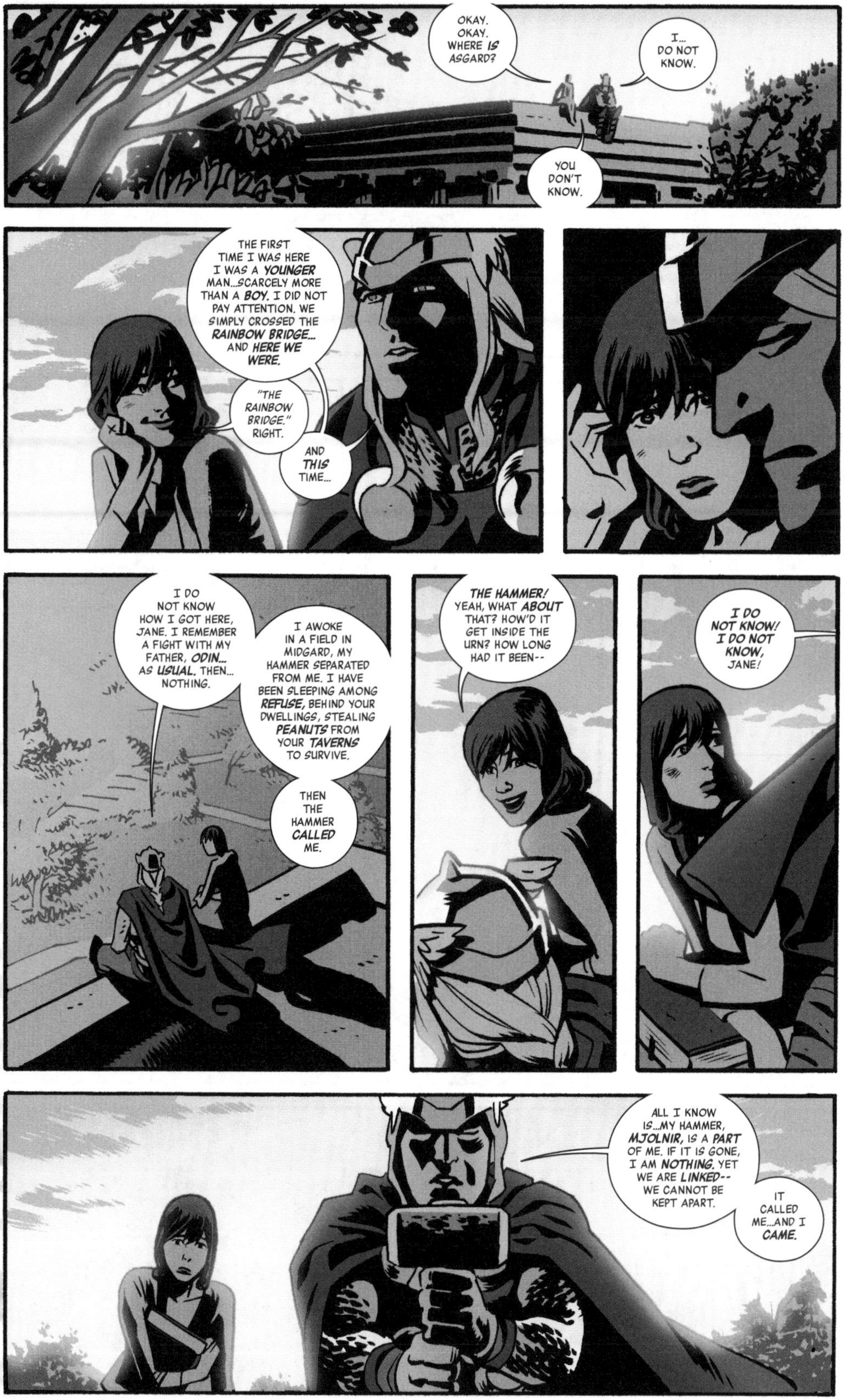
OKAY. OKAY. WHERE IS ASGARD?
I... DO NOT KNOW.
YOU DON'T KNOW.
THE FIRST TIME I WAS HERE I WAS A YOUNGER MAN...SCARCELY MORE THAN A BOY. I DID NOT PAY ATTENTION. WE SIMPLY CROSSED THE RAINBOW BRIDGE... AND HERE WE WERE.
"THE RAINBOW BRIDGE." RIGHT.
AND THIS TIME...
I DO NOT KNOW HOW I GOT HERE, JANE. I REMEMBER A FIGHT WITH MY FATHER, ODIN... AS USUAL. THEN... NOTHING.
I AWOKE IN A FIELD IN MIDGARD, MY HAMMER SEPARATED FROM ME. I HAVE BEEN SLEEPING AMONG REFUSE, BEHIND YOUR DWELLINGS, STEALING PEANUTS FROM YOUR TAVERNS TO SURVIVE.
THEN THE HAMMER CALLED ME.
THE HAMMER! YEAH, WHAT ABOUT THAT? HOW'D IT GET INSIDE THE URN? HOW LONG HAD IT BEEN--
I DO NOT KNOW! I DO NOT KNOW, JANE!
ALL I KNOW IS...MY HAMMER, MJOLNIR, IS A PART OF ME. IF IT IS GONE, I AM NOTHING. YET WE ARE LINKED-- WE CANNOT BE KEPT APART.
IT CALLED ME...AND I CAME.

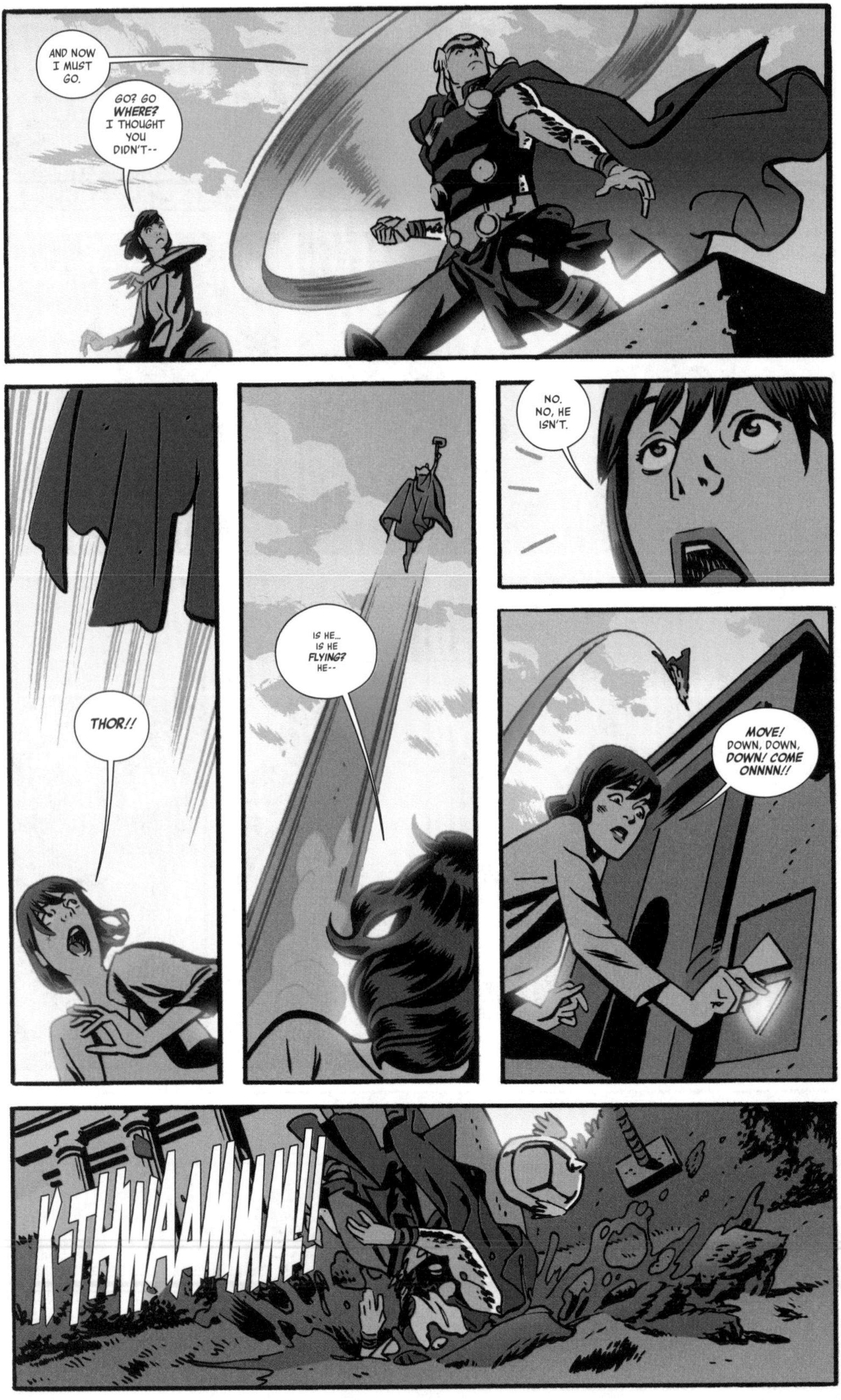
AND NOW I MUST GO.
GO? GO WHERE? I THOUGHT YOU DIDN'T--
THOR!!
IS HE... IS HE FLYING? HE--
NO. NO, HE ISN'T.
MOVE! DOWN, DOWN, DOWN! COME ONNNN!!
K-THWAAMMM!!

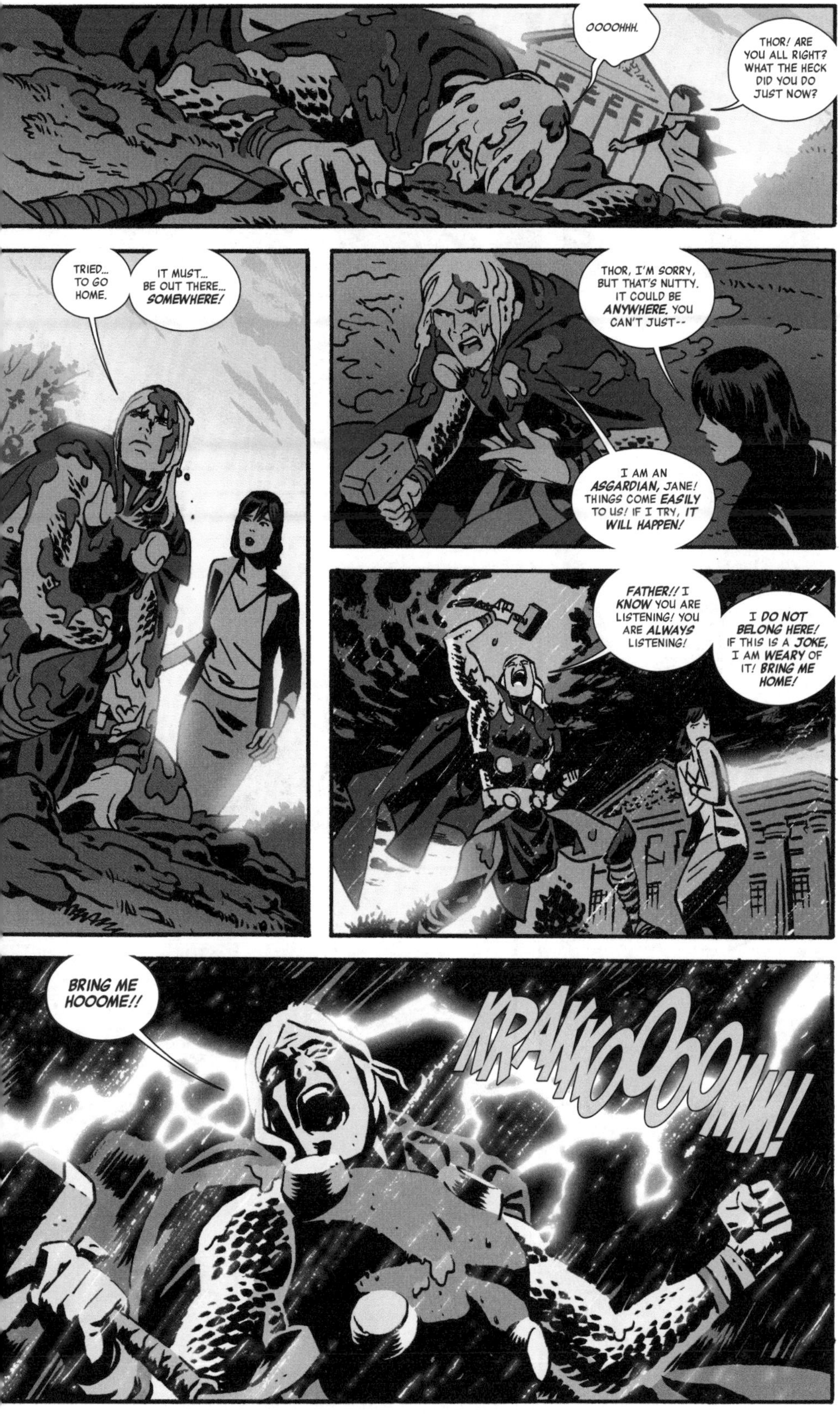
OOOOHHH.
THOR! ARE YOU ALL RIGHT? WHAT THE HECK DID YOU DO JUST NOW?
TRIED... TO GO HOME.
IT MUST... BE OUT THERE... SOMEWHERE!
THOR, I'M SORRY, BUT THAT'S NUTTY. IT COULD BE ANYWHERE. YOU CAN'T JUST--
I AM AN ASGARDIAN, JANE! THINGS COME EASILY TO US! IF I TRY, IT WILL HAPPEN!
FATHER!! I KNOW YOU ARE LISTENING! YOU ARE ALWAYS LISTENING!
I DO NOT BELONG HERE! IF THIS IS A JOKE, I AM WEARY OF IT! BRING ME HOME!
BRING ME HOOOME!!
KRAKOOOOMM!

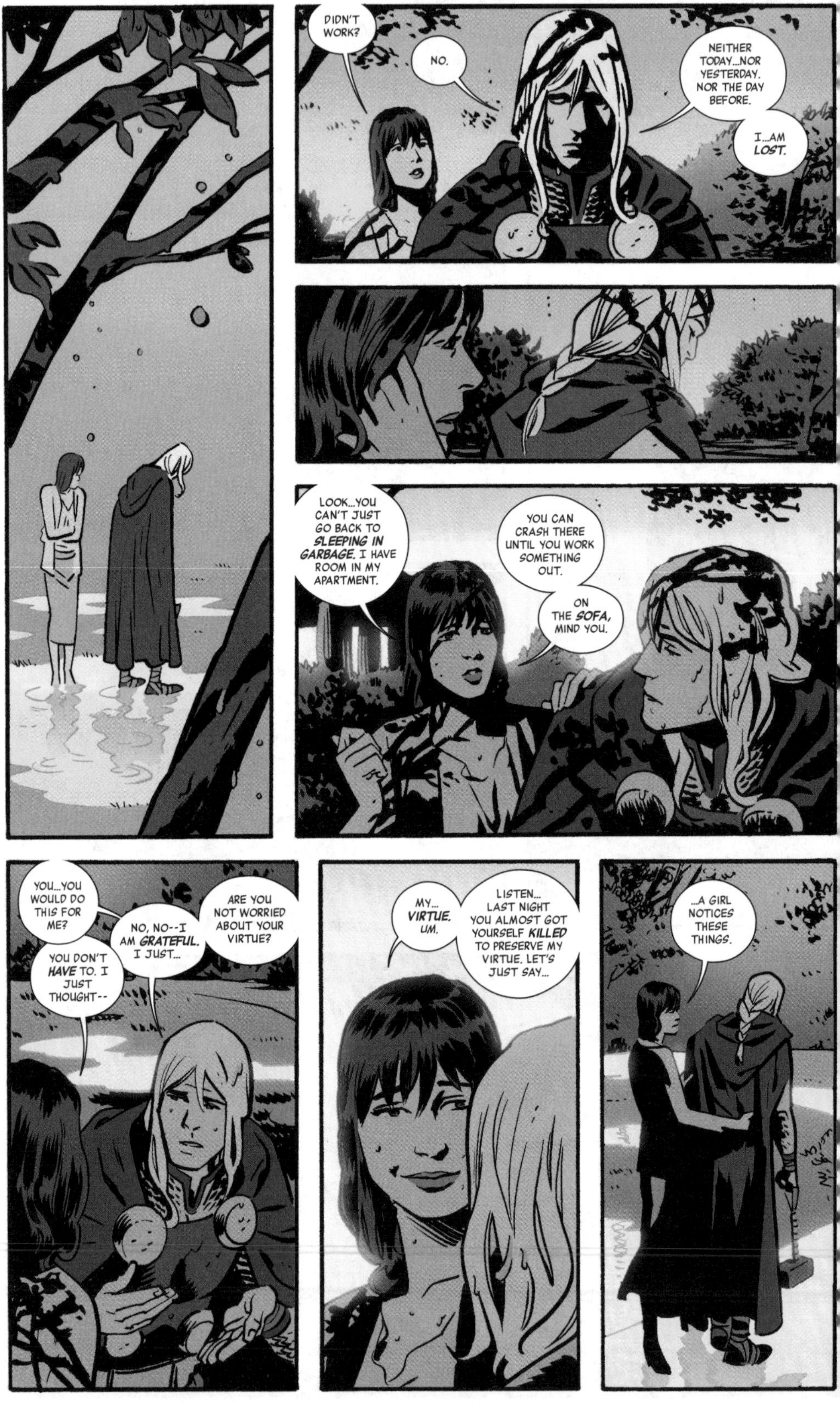
DIDN'T WORK?
NO.
NEITHER TODAY...NOR YESTERDAY. NOR THE DAY BEFORE.
I...AM LOST.
LOOK...YOU CAN'T JUST GO BACK TO SLEEPING IN GARBAGE. I HAVE ROOM IN MY APARTMENT.
YOU CAN CRASH THERE UNTIL YOU WORK SOMETHING OUT.
ON THE SOFA, MIND YOU.
YOU...YOU WOULD DO THIS FOR ME?
YOU DON'T HAVE TO. I JUST THOUGHT--
NO, NO--I AM GRATEFUL. I JUST...
ARE YOU NOT WORRIED ABOUT YOUR VIRTUE?
MY... VIRTUE. UM.
LISTEN... LAST NIGHT YOU ALMOST GOT YOURSELF KILLED TO PRESERVE MY VIRTUE. LET'S JUST SAY...
...A GIRL NOTICES THESE THINGS.

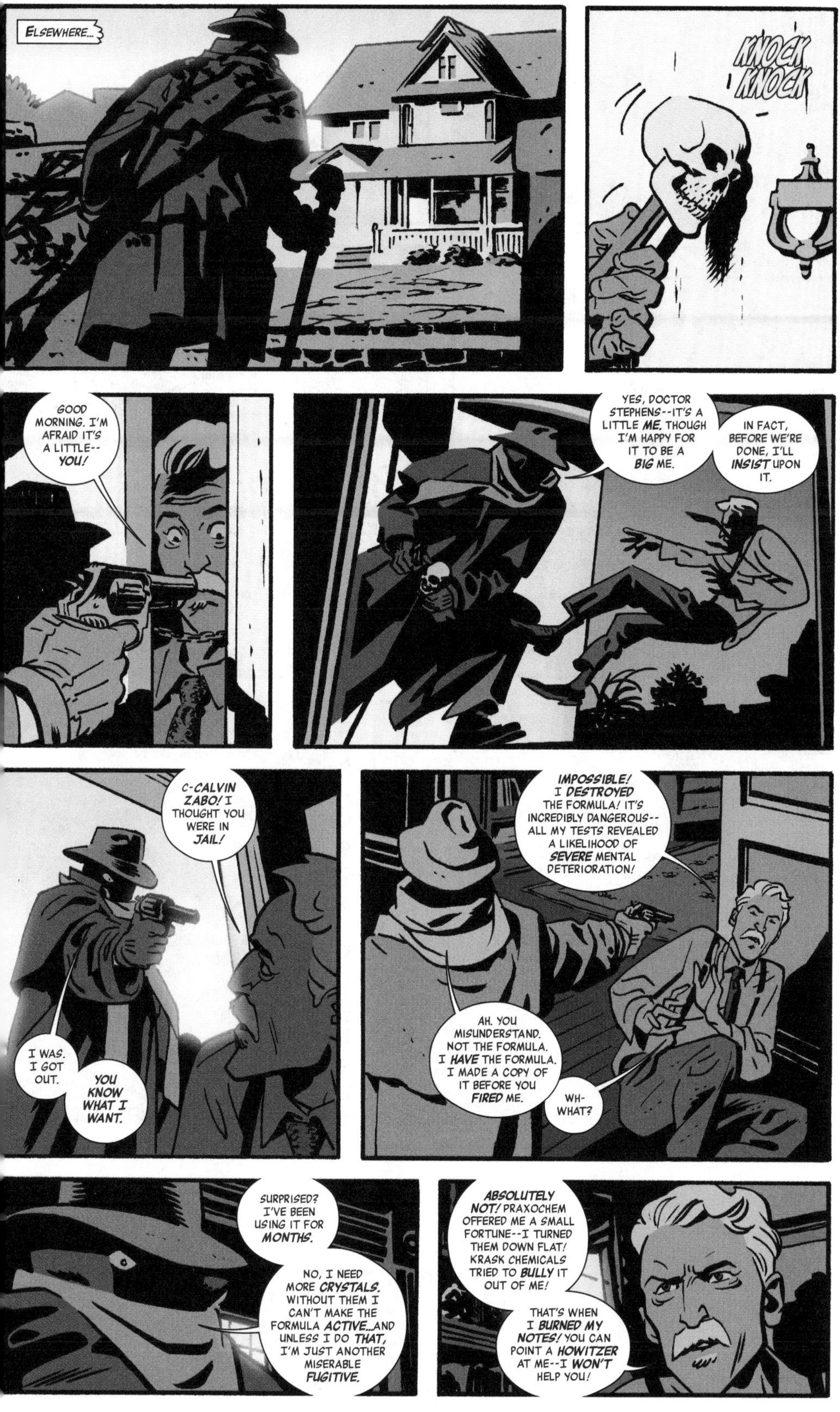
ELSEWHERE...
KNOCK KNOCK
GOOD MORNING. I'M AFRAID IT'S A LITTLE-- YOU!
YES, DOCTOR STEPHENS--IT'S A LITTLE ME. THOUGH I'M HAPPY FOR IT TO BE A BIG ME.
IN FACT, BEFORE WE'RE DONE, I'LL INSIST UPON IT.
C-CALVIN ZABO! I THOUGHT YOU WERE IN JAIL!
I WAS. I GOT OUT.
YOU KNOW WHAT I WANT.
IMPOSSIBLE! I DESTROYED THE FORMULA! IT'S INCREDIBLY DANGEROUS--ALL MY TESTS REVEALED A LIKELIHOOD OF SEVERE MENTAL DETERIORATION!
AH. YOU MISUNDERSTAND. NOT THE FORMULA. I HAVE THE FORMULA. I MADE A COPY OF IT BEFORE YOU FIRED ME.
WH-WHAT?
SURPRISED? I'VE BEEN USING IT FOR MONTHS.
NO, I NEED MORE CRYSTALS. WITHOUT THEM I CAN'T MAKE THE FORMULA ACTIVE...AND UNLESS I DO THAT, I'M JUST ANOTHER MISERABLE FUGITIVE.
ABSOLUTELY NOT! PRAXOCHEM OFFERED ME A SMALL FORTUNE--I TURNED THEM DOWN FLAT! KRASK CHEMICALS TRIED TO BULLY IT OUT OF ME!
THAT'S WHEN I BURNED MY NOTES! YOU CAN POINT A HOWITZER AT ME--I WON'T HELP YOU!

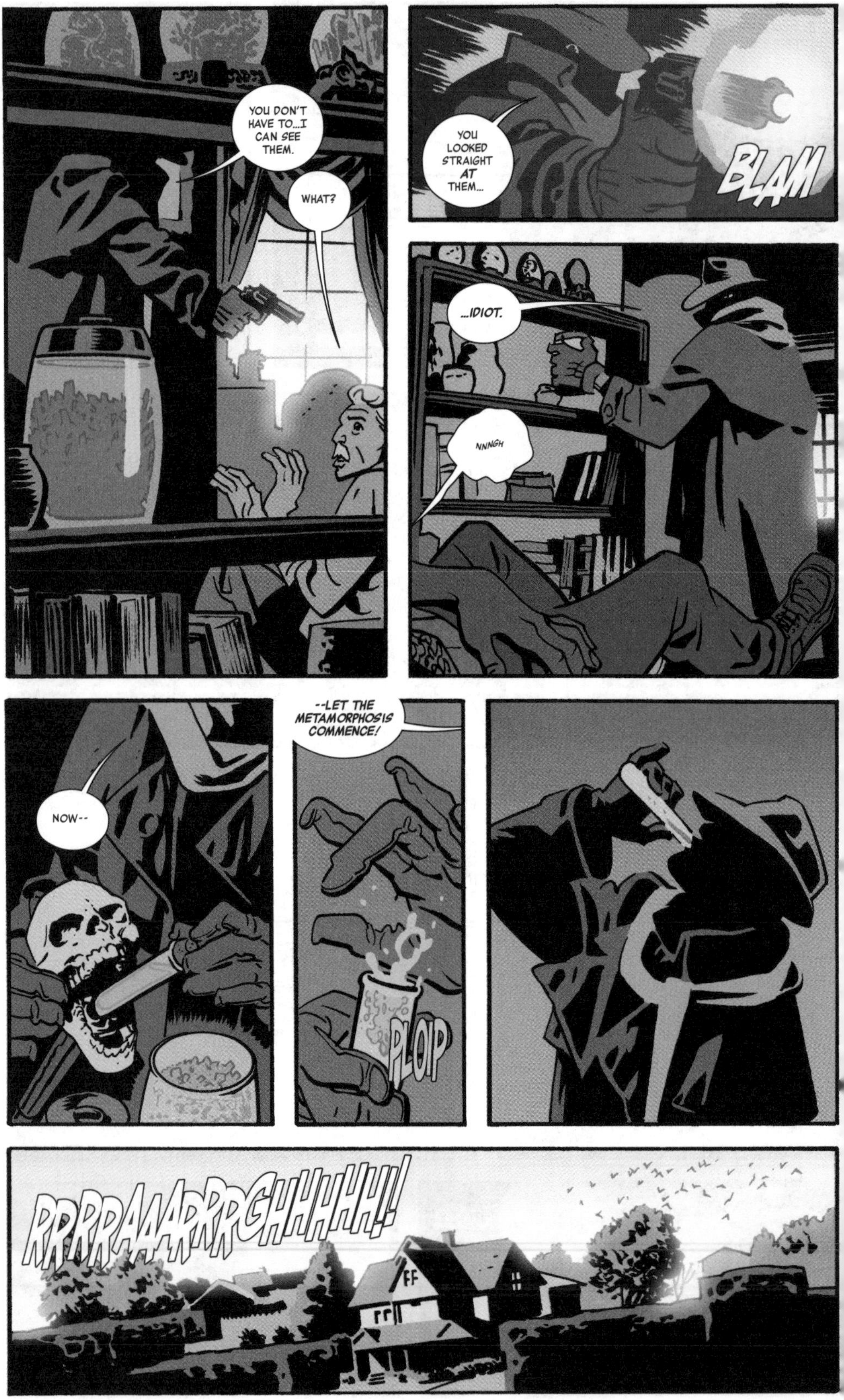
YOU DON'T HAVE TO...I CAN SEE THEM.
WHAT?
YOU LOOKED STRAIGHT AT THEM...
BLAM
...IDIOT.
NNNGH
NOW--
--LET THE METAMORPHOSIS COMMENCE!
PLOIP
RRRRAAAARRRGHHHHH!!

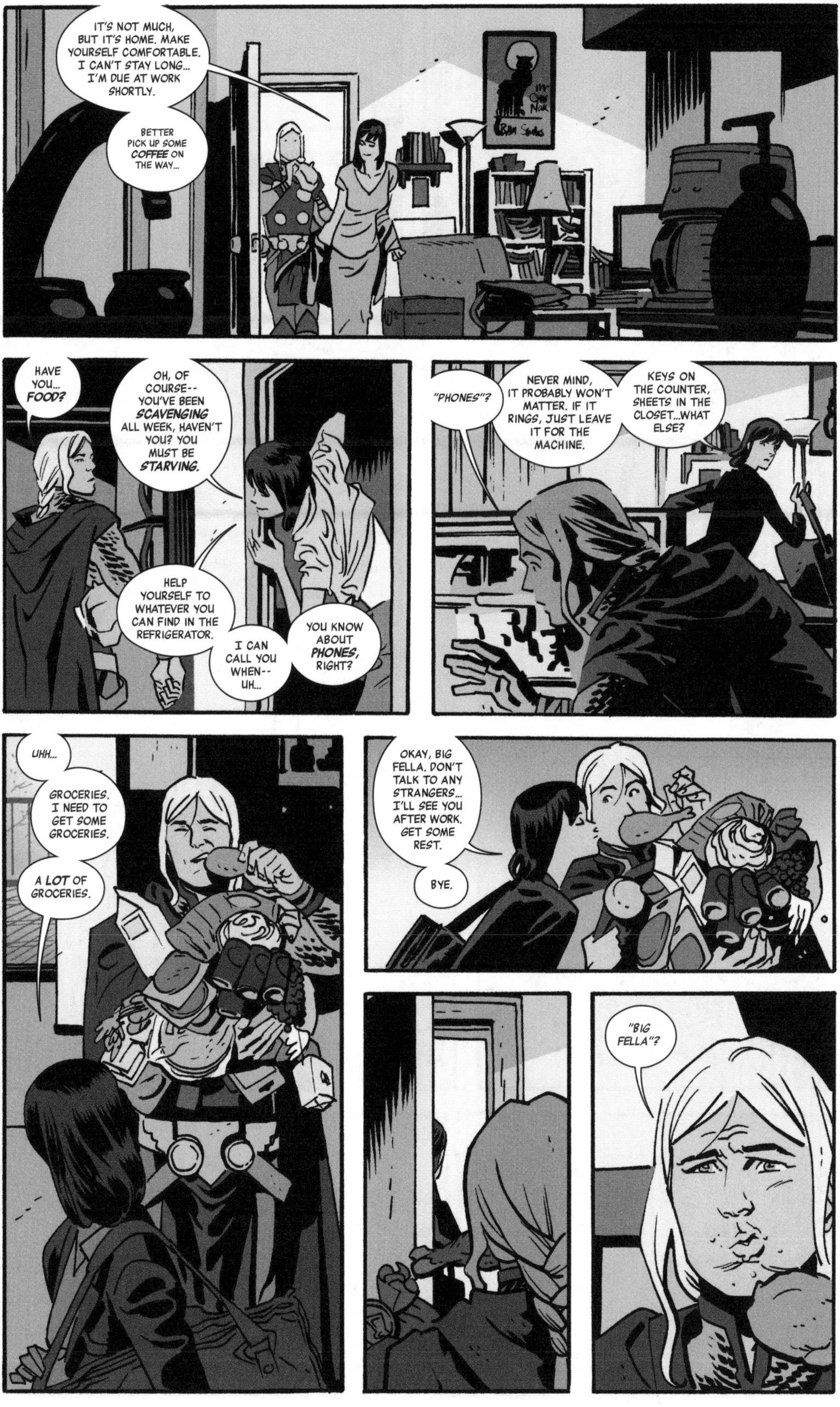
IT'S NOT MUCH, BUT IT'S HOME. MAKE YOURSELF COMFORTABLE. I CAN'T STAY LONG... I'M DUE AT WORK SHORTLY.
BETTER PICK UP SOME COFFEE ON THE WAY...
HAVE YOU... FOOD?
OH, OF COURSE-- YOU'VE BEEN SCAVENGING ALL WEEK, HAVEN'T YOU? YOU MUST BE STARVING.
HELP YOURSELF TO WHATEVER YOU CAN FIND IN THE REFRIGERATOR.
I CAN CALL YOU WHEN-- UH...
YOU KNOW ABOUT PHONES, RIGHT?
"PHONES"?
NEVER MIND, IT PROBABLY WON'T MATTER. IF IT RINGS, JUST LEAVE IT FOR THE MACHINE.
KEYS ON THE COUNTER, SHEETS IN THE CLOSET...WHAT ELSE?
UHH...
GROCERIES. I NEED TO GET SOME GROCERIES.
A LOT OF GROCERIES.
OKAY, BIG FELLA. DON'T TALK TO ANY STRANGERS... I'LL SEE YOU AFTER WORK. GET SOME REST.
BYE.
"BIG FELLA"?

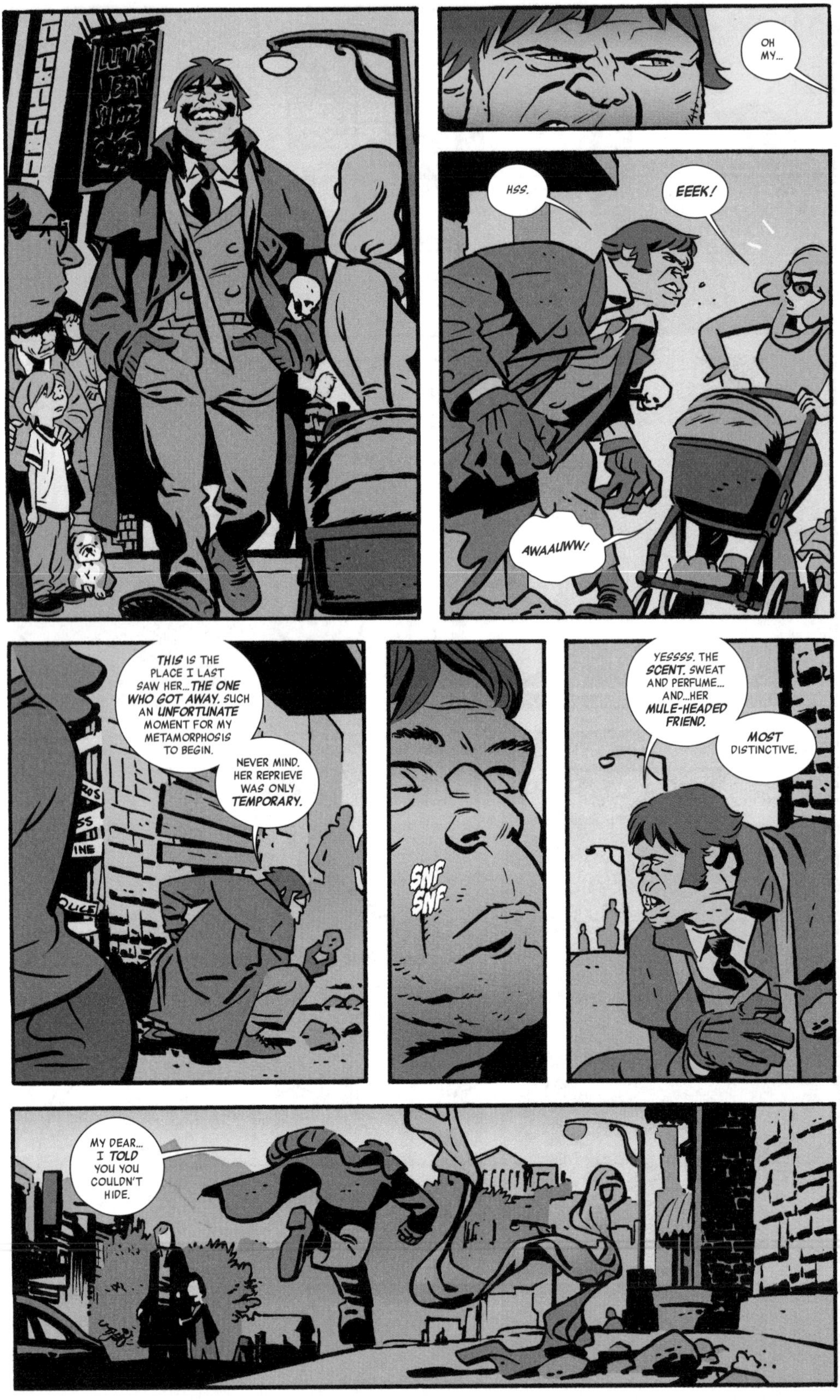

OH MY...
HSS.
EEEK!
AWAAUWW!
THIS IS THE PLACE I LAST SAW HER...THE ONE WHO GOT AWAY. SUCH AN UNFORTUNATE MOMENT FOR MY METAMORPHOSIS TO BEGIN.
NEVER MIND. HER REPRIEVE WAS ONLY TEMPORARY.
SNF SNF
YESSSS. THE SCENT. SWEAT AND PERFUME... AND...HER MULE-HEADED FRIEND.
MOST DISTINCTIVE.
MY DEAR... I TOLD YOU YOU COULDN'T HIDE.

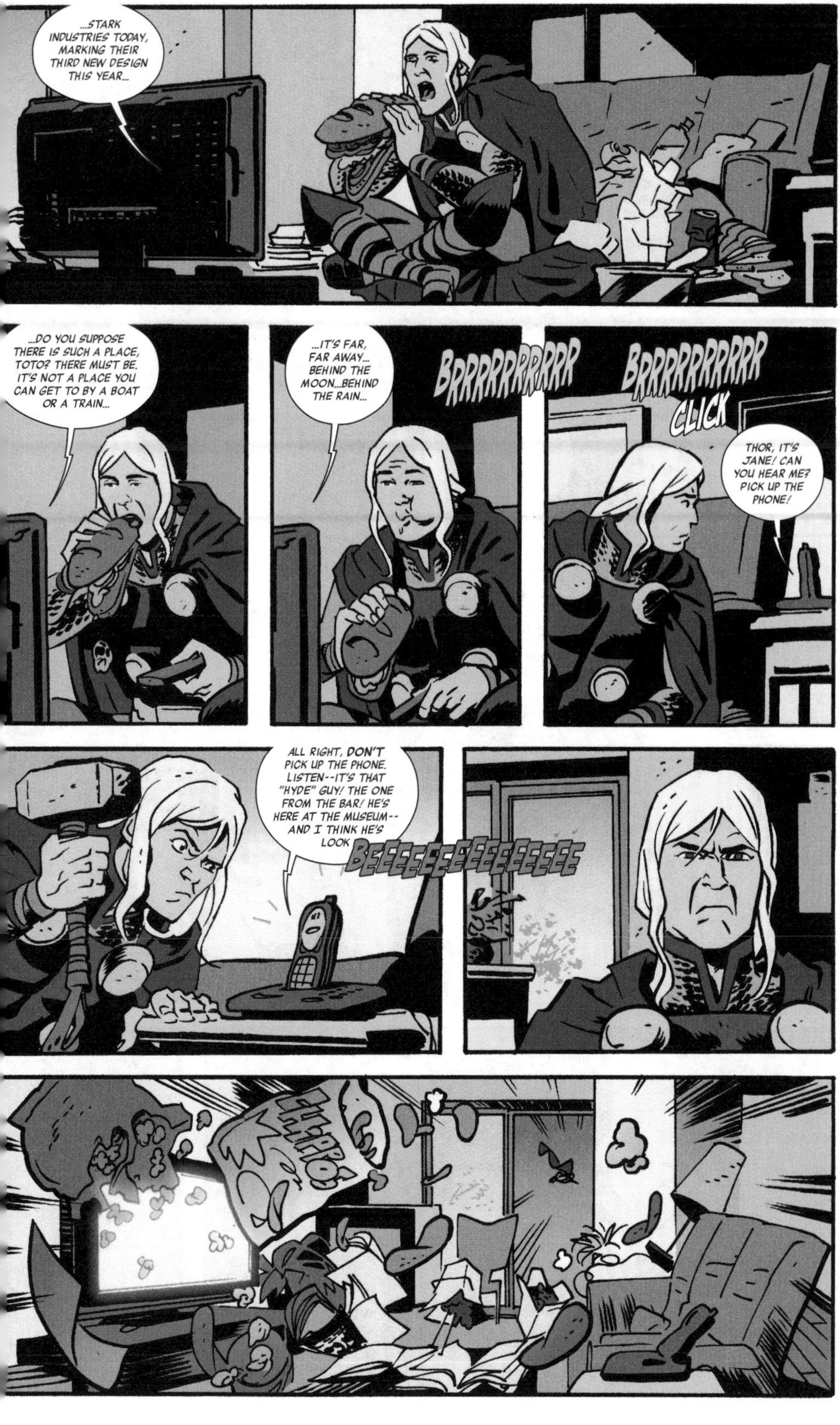
...STARK INDUSTRIES TODAY, MARKING THEIR THIRD NEW DESIGN THIS YEAR...
...DO YOU SUPPOSE THERE IS SUCH A PLACE, TOTO? THERE MUST BE. IT'S NOT A PLACE YOU CAN GET TO BY A BOAT OR A TRAIN...
...IT'S FAR, FAR AWAY... BEHIND THE MOON...BEHIND THE RAIN...
BRRRRRRRRRR
BRRRRRRRRRR
CLICK
THOR, IT'S JANE! CAN YOU HEAR ME? PICK UP THE PHONE!
ALL RIGHT, **DON'T** PICK UP THE PHONE. LISTEN--IT'S THAT "HYDE" GUY! THE ONE FROM THE BAR! HE'S HERE AT THE MUSEUM--AND I THINK HE'S LOOK
BEEEEEEEEEEEEEEE

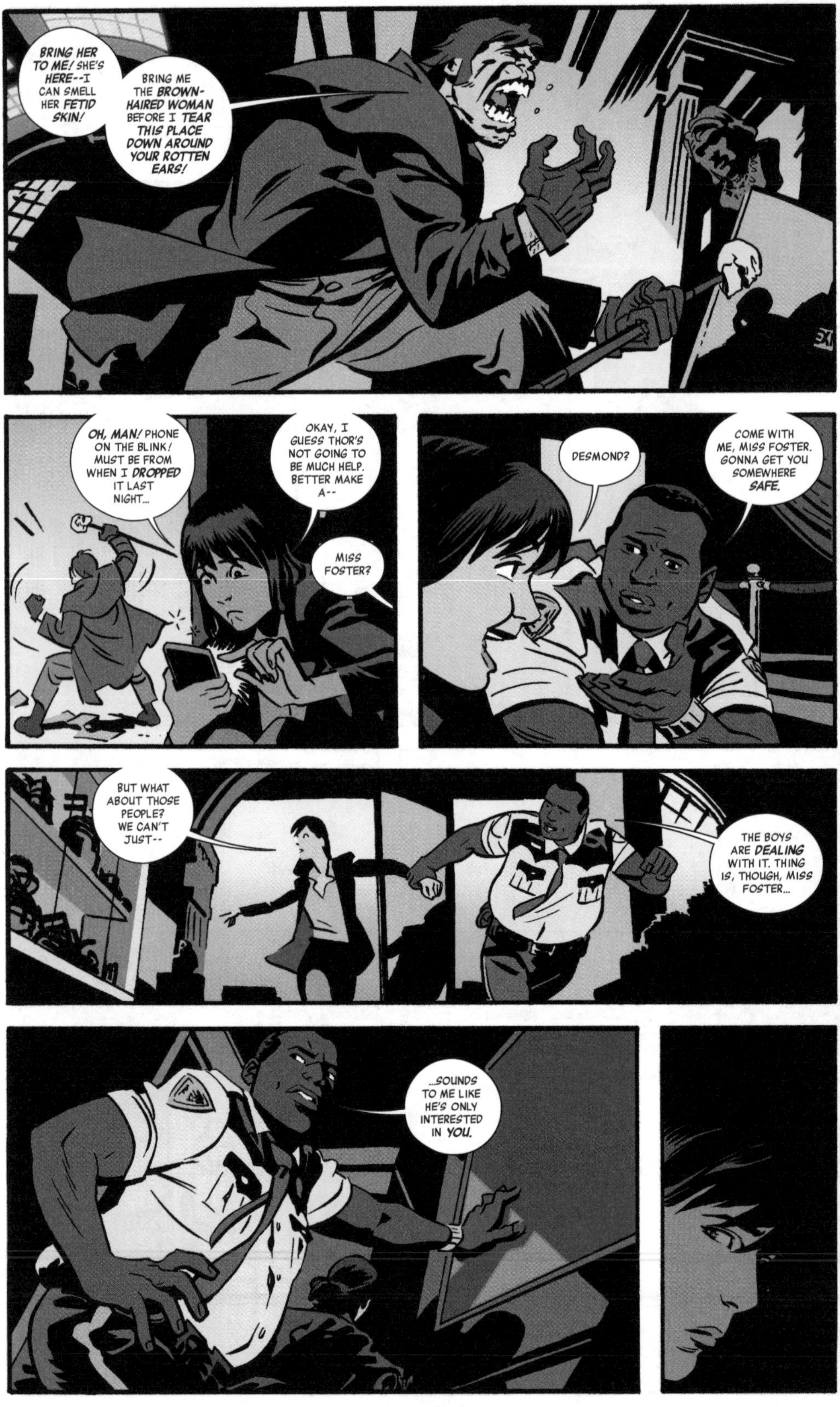

BRING HER TO ME! SHE'S HERE--I CAN SMELL HER FETID SKIN!
BRING ME THE BROWN-HAIRED WOMAN BEFORE I TEAR THIS PLACE DOWN AROUND YOUR ROTTEN EARS!
OH, MAN! PHONE ON THE BLINK! MUST BE FROM WHEN I DROPPED IT LAST NIGHT...
OKAY, I GUESS THOR'S NOT GOING TO BE MUCH HELP. BETTER MAKE A--
MISS FOSTER?
DESMOND?
COME WITH ME, MISS FOSTER. GONNA GET YOU SOMEWHERE SAFE.
BUT WHAT ABOUT THOSE PEOPLE? WE CAN'T JUST--
THE BOYS ARE DEALING WITH IT. THING IS, THOUGH, MISS FOSTER...
...SOUNDS TO ME LIKE HE'S ONLY INTERESTED IN YOU.

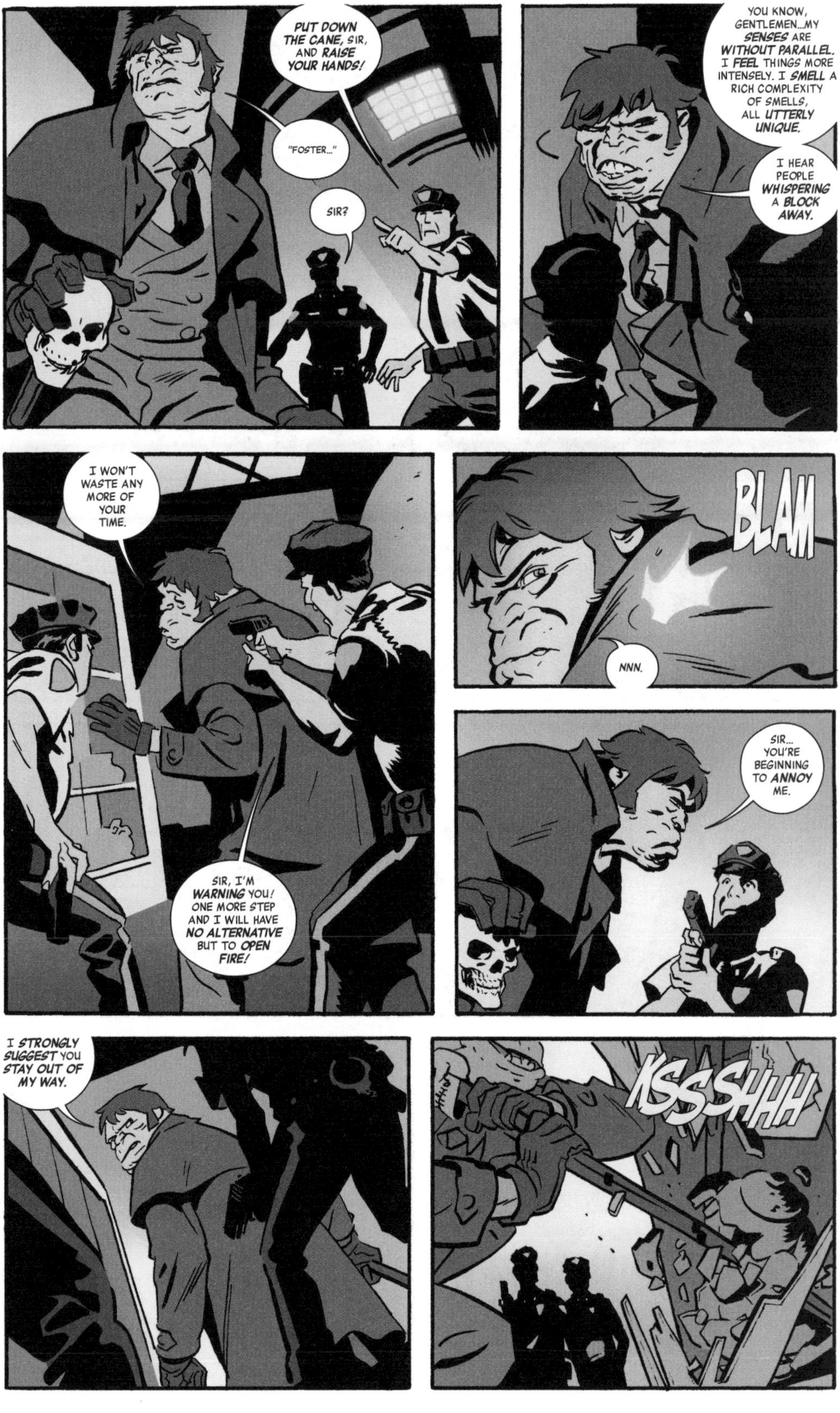

PUT DOWN THE CANE, SIR, AND RAISE YOUR HANDS!
"FOSTER..."
SIR?
YOU KNOW, GENTLEMEN...MY SENSES ARE WITHOUT PARALLEL. I FEEL THINGS MORE INTENSELY. I SMELL A RICH COMPLEXITY OF SMELLS, ALL UTTERLY UNIQUE.
I HEAR PEOPLE WHISPERING A BLOCK AWAY.
I WON'T WASTE ANY MORE OF YOUR TIME.
SIR, I'M WARNING YOU! ONE MORE STEP AND I WILL HAVE NO ALTERNATIVE BUT TO OPEN FIRE!
BLAM
NNN.
SIR... YOU'RE BEGINNING TO ANNOY ME.
I STRONGLY SUGGEST YOU STAY OUT OF MY WAY.
KSSSHHH

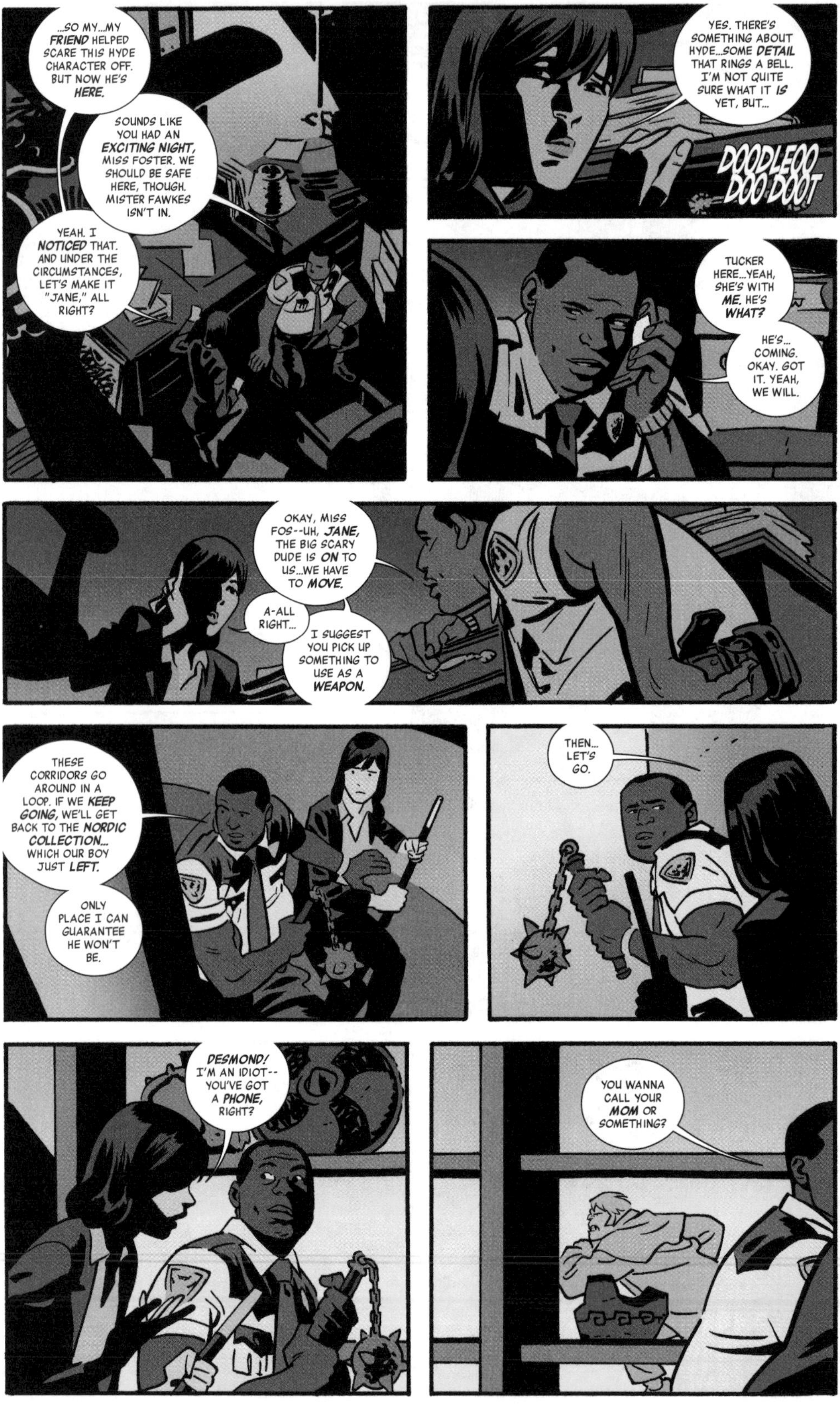
...SO MY...MY FRIEND HELPED SCARE THIS HYDE CHARACTER OFF. BUT NOW HE'S HERE.
SOUNDS LIKE YOU HAD AN EXCITING NIGHT, MISS FOSTER. WE SHOULD BE SAFE HERE, THOUGH. MISTER FAWKES ISN'T IN.
YEAH. I NOTICED THAT. AND UNDER THE CIRCUMSTANCES, LET'S MAKE IT "JANE," ALL RIGHT?
YES. THERE'S SOMETHING ABOUT HYDE...SOME DETAIL THAT RINGS A BELL. I'M NOT QUITE SURE WHAT IT IS YET, BUT...
DOODLEOO DOO DOOT
TUCKER HERE...YEAH, SHE'S WITH ME. HE'S WHAT?
HE'S... COMING. OKAY. GOT IT. YEAH, WE WILL.
OKAY, MISS FOS--UH, JANE, THE BIG SCARY DUDE IS ON TO US...WE HAVE TO MOVE.
A-ALL RIGHT...
I SUGGEST YOU PICK UP SOMETHING TO USE AS A WEAPON.
THESE CORRIDORS GO AROUND IN A LOOP. IF WE KEEP GOING, WE'LL GET BACK TO THE NORDIC COLLECTION... WHICH OUR BOY JUST LEFT.
ONLY PLACE I CAN GUARANTEE HE WON'T BE.
THEN... LET'S GO.
DESMOND! I'M AN IDIOT-- YOU'VE GOT A PHONE, RIGHT?
YOU WANNA CALL YOUR MOM OR SOMETHING?

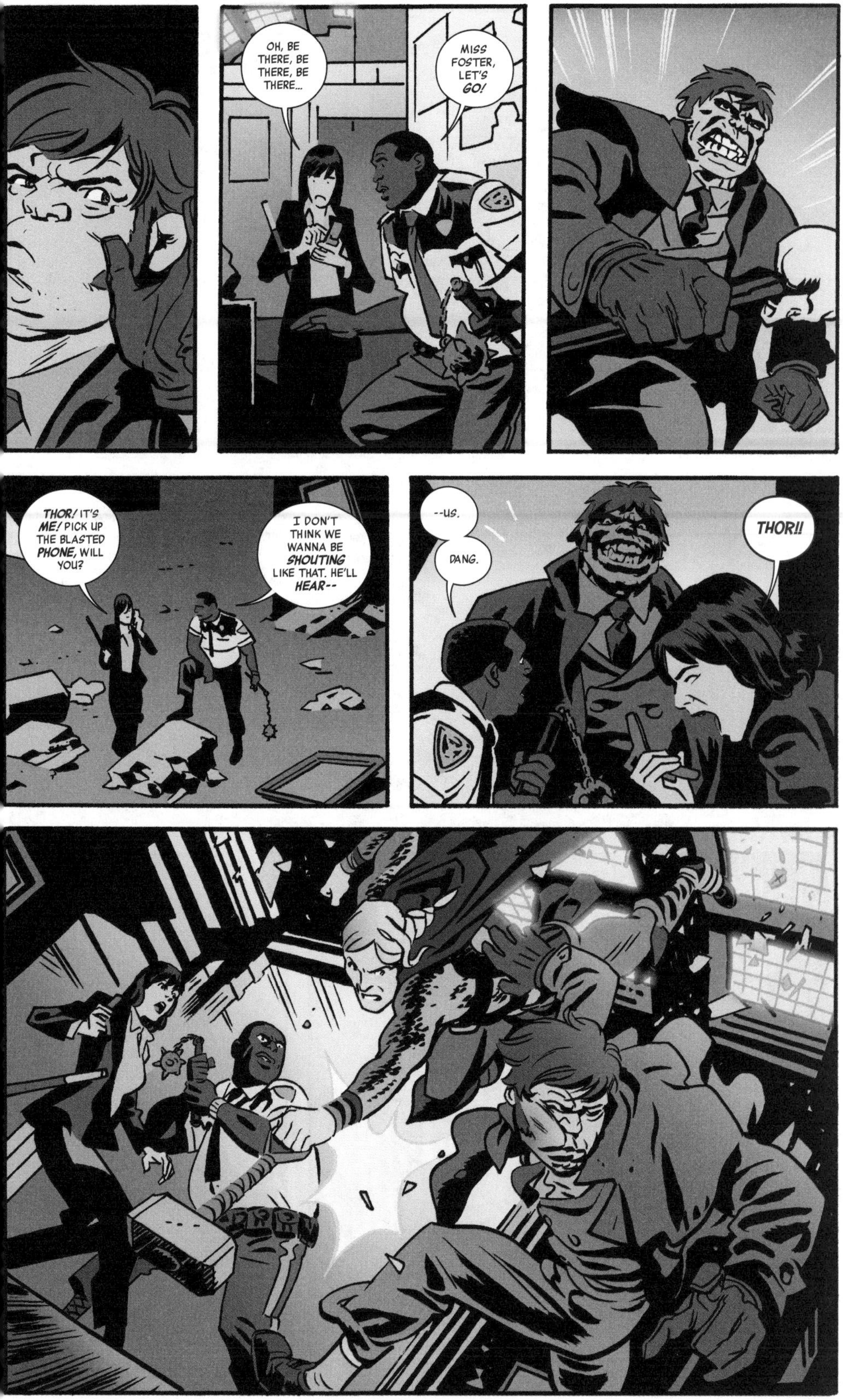

OH, BE THERE, BE THERE, BE THERE...
MISS FOSTER, LET'S GO!
THOR! IT'S ME! PICK UP THE BLASTED PHONE, WILL YOU?
I DON'T THINK WE WANNA BE SHOUTING LIKE THAT. HE'LL HEAR--
--US.
DANG.
THOR!!

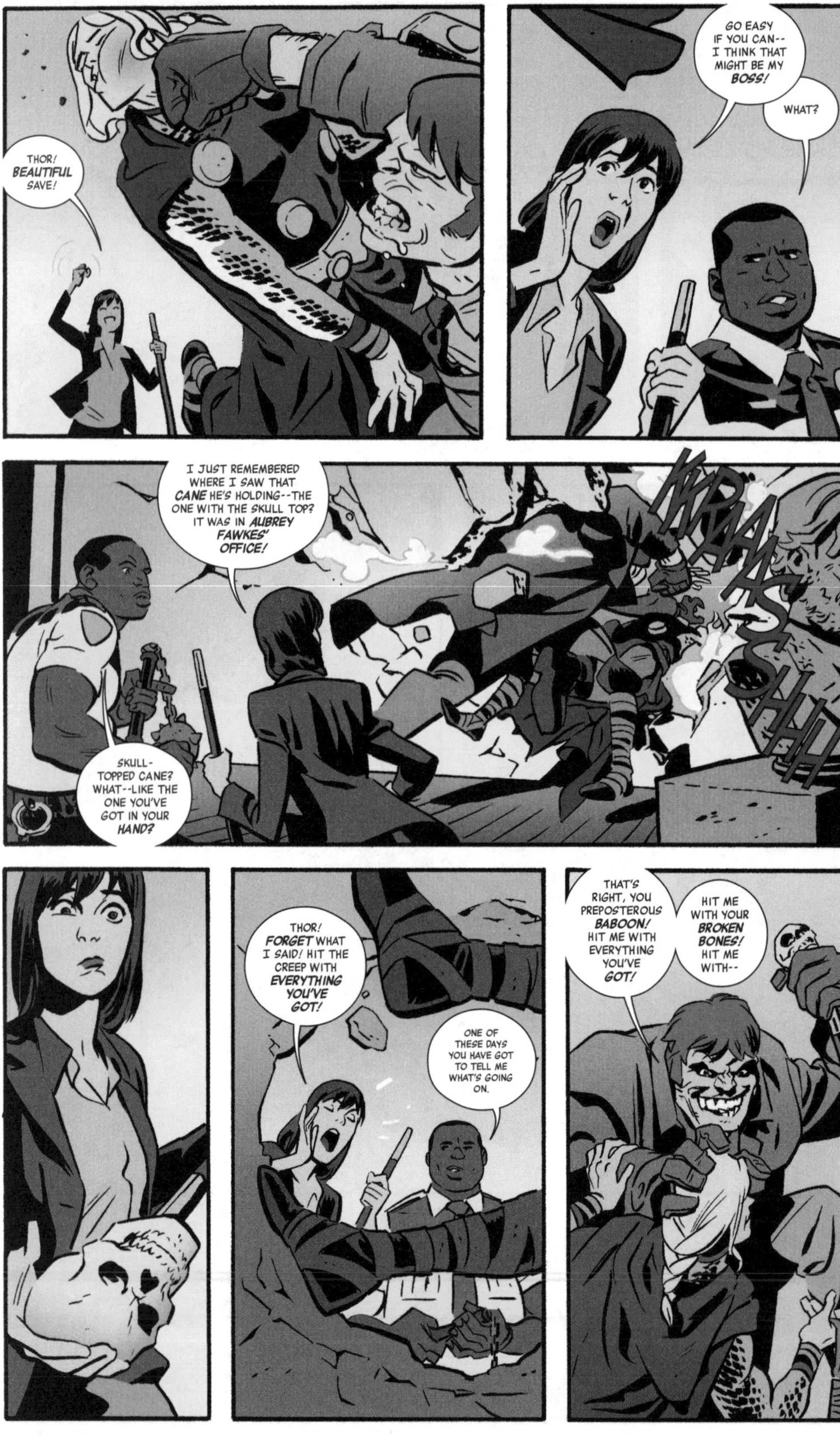

THOR! BEAUTIFUL SAVE!
GO EASY IF YOU CAN-- I THINK THAT MIGHT BE MY BOSS!
WHAT?
I JUST REMEMBERED WHERE I SAW THAT CANE HE'S HOLDING--THE ONE WITH THE SKULL TOP? IT WAS IN AUBREY FAWKES' OFFICE!
KKRAAASHHH
SKULL-TOPPED CANE? WHAT--LIKE THE ONE YOU'VE GOT IN YOUR HAND?
THOR! FORGET WHAT I SAID! HIT THE CREEP WITH EVERYTHING YOU'VE GOT!
ONE OF THESE DAYS YOU HAVE GOT TO TELL ME WHAT'S GOING ON.
THAT'S RIGHT, YOU PREPOSTEROUS BABOON! HIT ME WITH EVERYTHING YOU'VE GOT!
HIT ME WITH YOUR BROKEN BONES! HIT ME WITH--

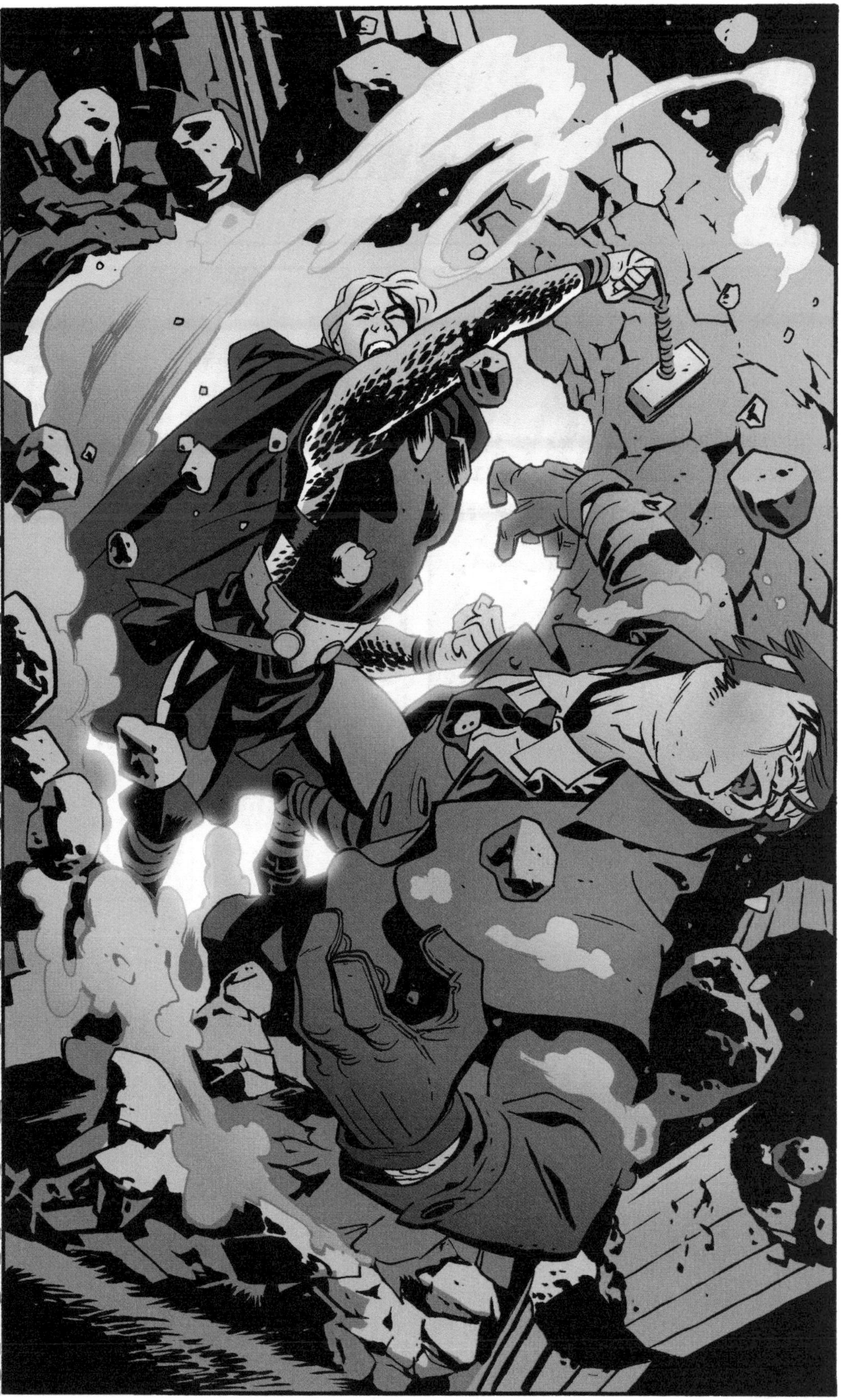

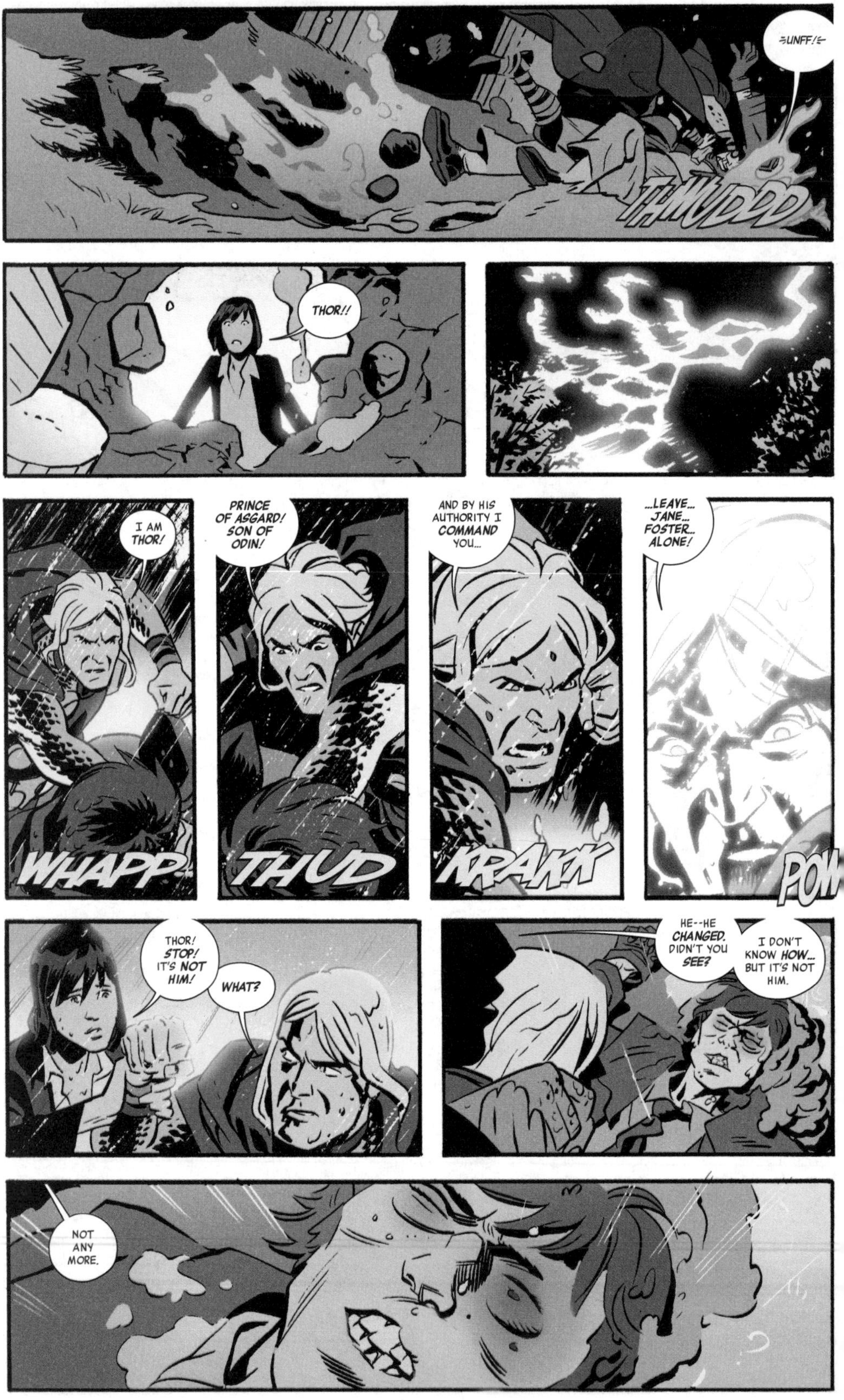
UNFF!
THUDDD
THOR!!
I AM THOR!
PRINCE OF ASGARD! SON OF ODIN!
AND BY HIS AUTHORITY I COMMAND YOU...
...LEAVE... JANE... FOSTER... ALONE!
WHAPP
THUD
KRAKK
POW
THOR! STOP! IT'S NOT HIM!
WHAT?
HE--HE CHANGED. DIDN'T YOU SEE?
I DON'T KNOW HOW... BUT IT'S NOT HIM.
NOT ANY MORE.

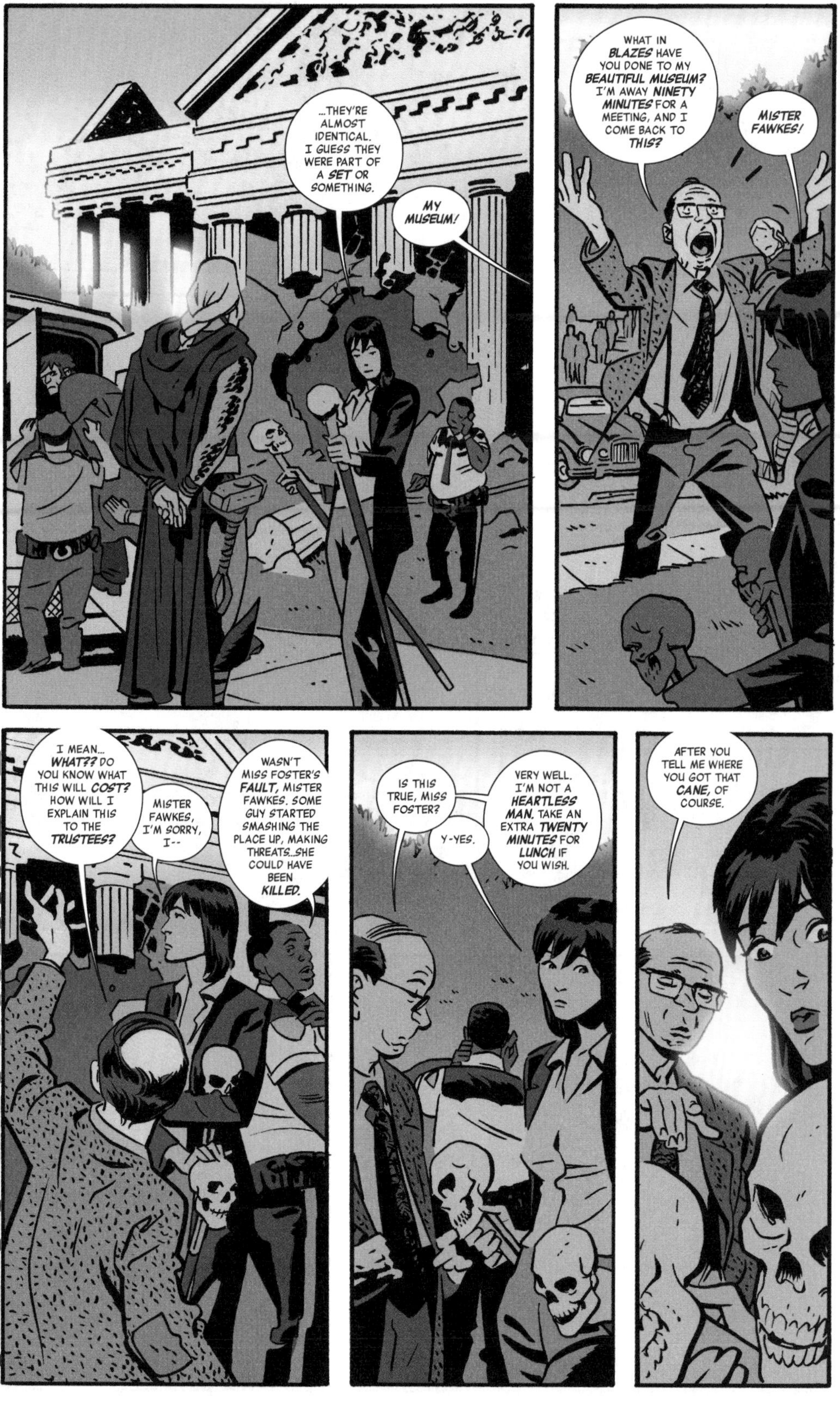
...THEY'RE ALMOST IDENTICAL. I GUESS THEY WERE PART OF A SET OR SOMETHING.
MY MUSEUM!
WHAT IN BLAZES HAVE YOU DONE TO MY BEAUTIFUL MUSEUM? I'M AWAY NINETY MINUTES FOR A MEETING, AND I COME BACK TO THIS?
MISTER FAWKES!
I MEAN... WHAT?? DO YOU KNOW WHAT THIS WILL COST? HOW WILL I EXPLAIN THIS TO THE TRUSTEES?
MISTER FAWKES, I'M SORRY, I--
WASN'T MISS FOSTER'S FAULT, MISTER FAWKES. SOME GUY STARTED SMASHING THE PLACE UP, MAKING THREATS...SHE COULD HAVE BEEN KILLED.
IS THIS TRUE, MISS FOSTER?
Y-YES.
VERY WELL. I'M NOT A HEARTLESS MAN. TAKE AN EXTRA TWENTY MINUTES FOR LUNCH IF YOU WISH.
AFTER YOU TELL ME WHERE YOU GOT THAT CANE, OF COURSE.

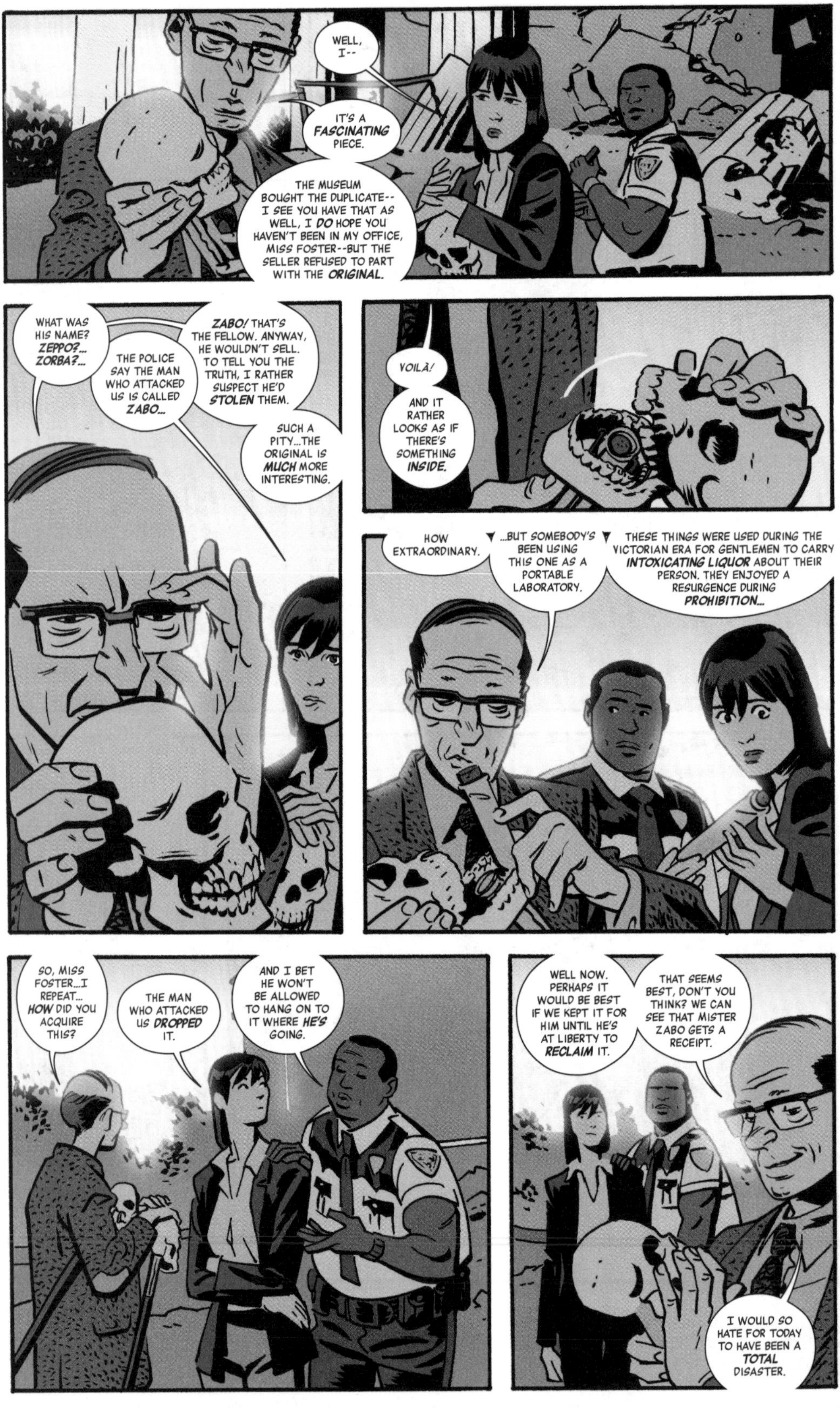
WELL, I--
IT'S A FASCINATING PIECE.
THE MUSEUM BOUGHT THE DUPLICATE-- I SEE YOU HAVE THAT AS WELL, I DO HOPE YOU HAVEN'T BEEN IN MY OFFICE, MISS FOSTER--BUT THE SELLER REFUSED TO PART WITH THE ORIGINAL.
WHAT WAS HIS NAME? ZEPPO?... ZORBA?...
THE POLICE SAY THE MAN WHO ATTACKED US IS CALLED ZABO...
ZABO! THAT'S THE FELLOW. ANYWAY, HE WOULDN'T SELL. TO TELL YOU THE TRUTH, I RATHER SUSPECT HE'D STOLEN THEM.
SUCH A PITY...THE ORIGINAL IS MUCH MORE INTERESTING.
VOILÀ!
AND IT RATHER LOOKS AS IF THERE'S SOMETHING INSIDE.
HOW EXTRAORDINARY.
...BUT SOMEBODY'S BEEN USING THIS ONE AS A PORTABLE LABORATORY.
THESE THINGS WERE USED DURING THE VICTORIAN ERA FOR GENTLEMEN TO CARRY INTOXICATING LIQUOR ABOUT THEIR PERSON. THEY ENJOYED A RESURGENCE DURING PROHIBITION...
SO, MISS FOSTER...I REPEAT... HOW DID YOU ACQUIRE THIS?
THE MAN WHO ATTACKED US DROPPED IT.
AND I BET HE WON'T BE ALLOWED TO HANG ON TO IT WHERE HE'S GOING.
WELL NOW. PERHAPS IT WOULD BE BEST IF WE KEPT IT FOR HIM UNTIL HE'S AT LIBERTY TO RECLAIM IT.
THAT SEEMS BEST, DON'T YOU THINK? WE CAN SEE THAT MISTER ZABO GETS A RECEIPT.
I WOULD SO HATE FOR TODAY TO HAVE BEEN A TOTAL DISASTER.

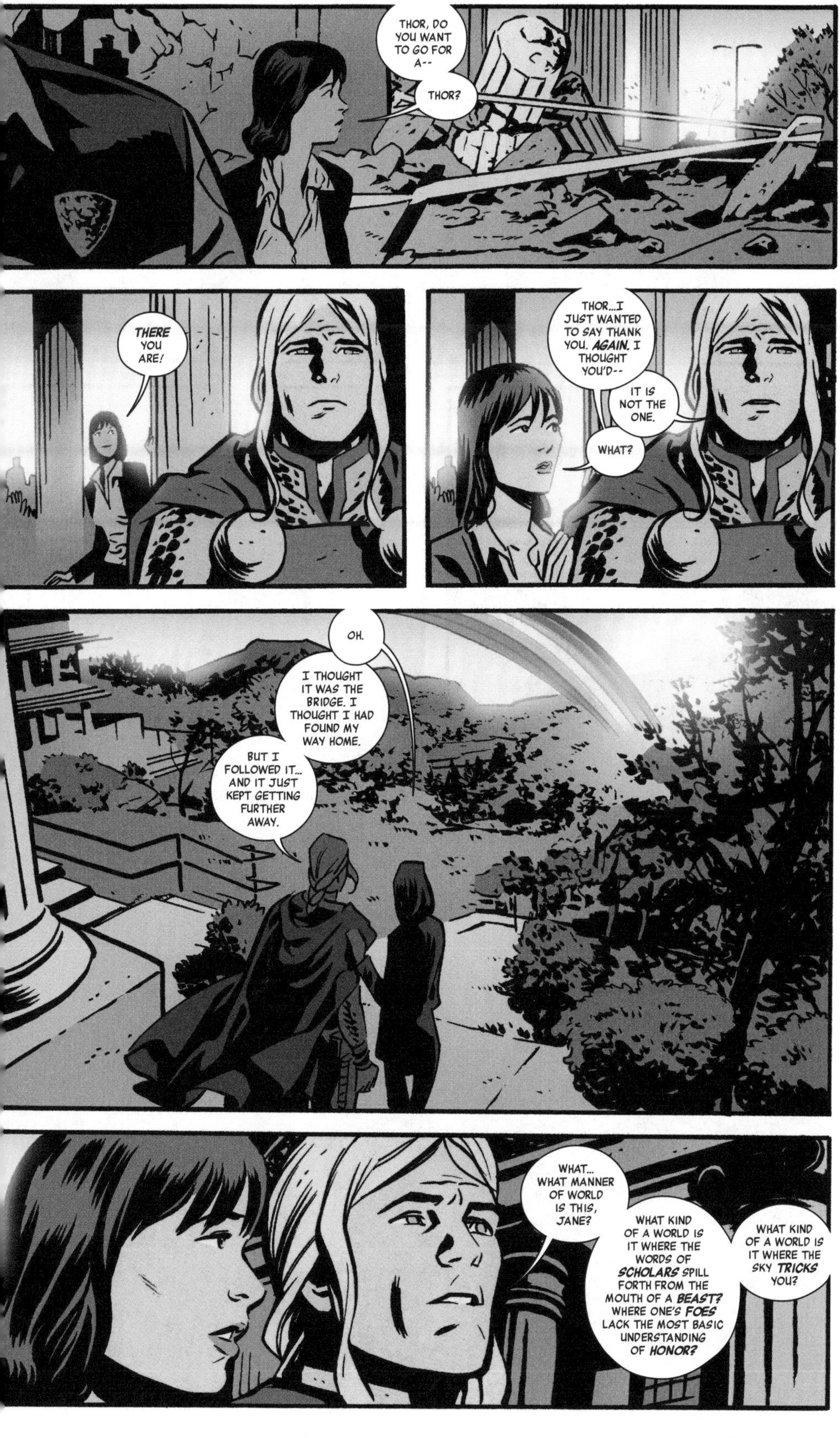

THOR, DO YOU WANT TO GO FOR A--
THOR?
THERE YOU ARE!
THOR...I JUST WANTED TO SAY THANK YOU. AGAIN. I THOUGHT YOU'D--
IT IS NOT THE ONE.
WHAT?
OH.
I THOUGHT IT WAS THE BRIDGE. I THOUGHT I HAD FOUND MY WAY HOME.
BUT I FOLLOWED IT... AND IT JUST KEPT GETTING FURTHER AWAY.
WHAT... WHAT MANNER OF WORLD IS THIS, JANE?
WHAT KIND OF A WORLD IS IT WHERE THE WORDS OF SCHOLARS SPILL FORTH FROM THE MOUTH OF A BEAST? WHERE ONE'S FOES LACK THE MOST BASIC UNDERSTANDING OF HONOR?
WHAT KIND OF A WORLD IS IT WHERE THE SKY TRICKS YOU?

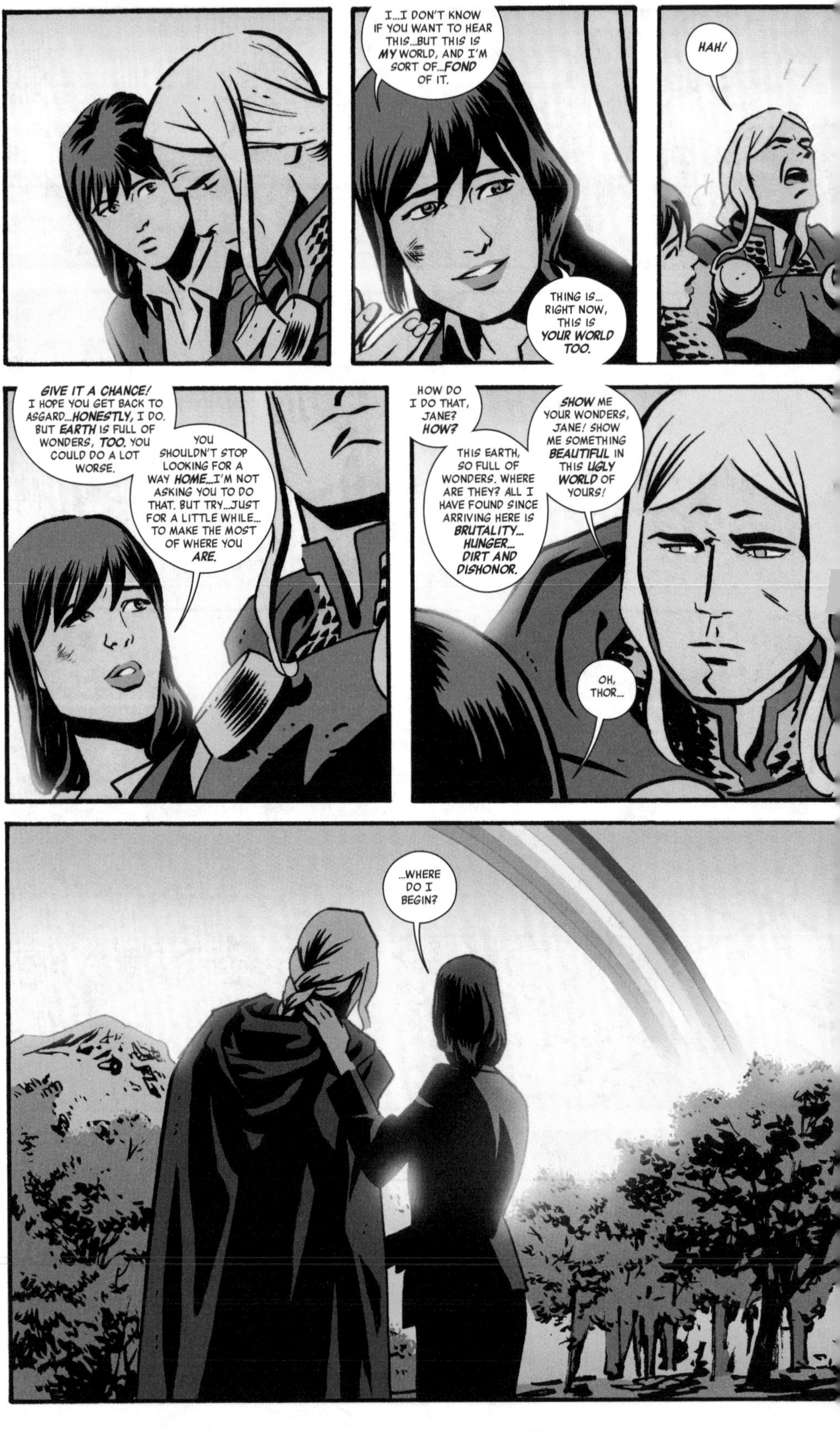

I...I DON'T KNOW IF YOU WANT TO HEAR THIS...BUT THIS IS MY WORLD, AND I'M SORT OF...FOND OF IT.
THING IS... RIGHT NOW, THIS IS YOUR WORLD TOO.
HAH!
GIVE IT A CHANCE! I HOPE YOU GET BACK TO ASGARD...HONESTLY, I DO. BUT EARTH IS FULL OF WONDERS, TOO. YOU COULD DO A LOT WORSE.
YOU SHOULDN'T STOP LOOKING FOR A WAY HOME...I'M NOT ASKING YOU TO DO THAT. BUT TRY...JUST FOR A LITTLE WHILE... TO MAKE THE MOST OF WHERE YOU ARE.
HOW DO I DO THAT, JANE? HOW?
THIS EARTH, SO FULL OF WONDERS. WHERE ARE THEY? ALL I HAVE FOUND SINCE ARRIVING HERE IS BRUTALITY... HUNGER... DIRT AND DISHONOR.
SHOW ME YOUR WONDERS, JANE! SHOW ME SOMETHING BEAUTIFUL IN THIS UGLY WORLD OF YOURS!
OH, THOR...
...WHERE DO I BEGIN?

THOR THE MIGHTY AVENGER #3

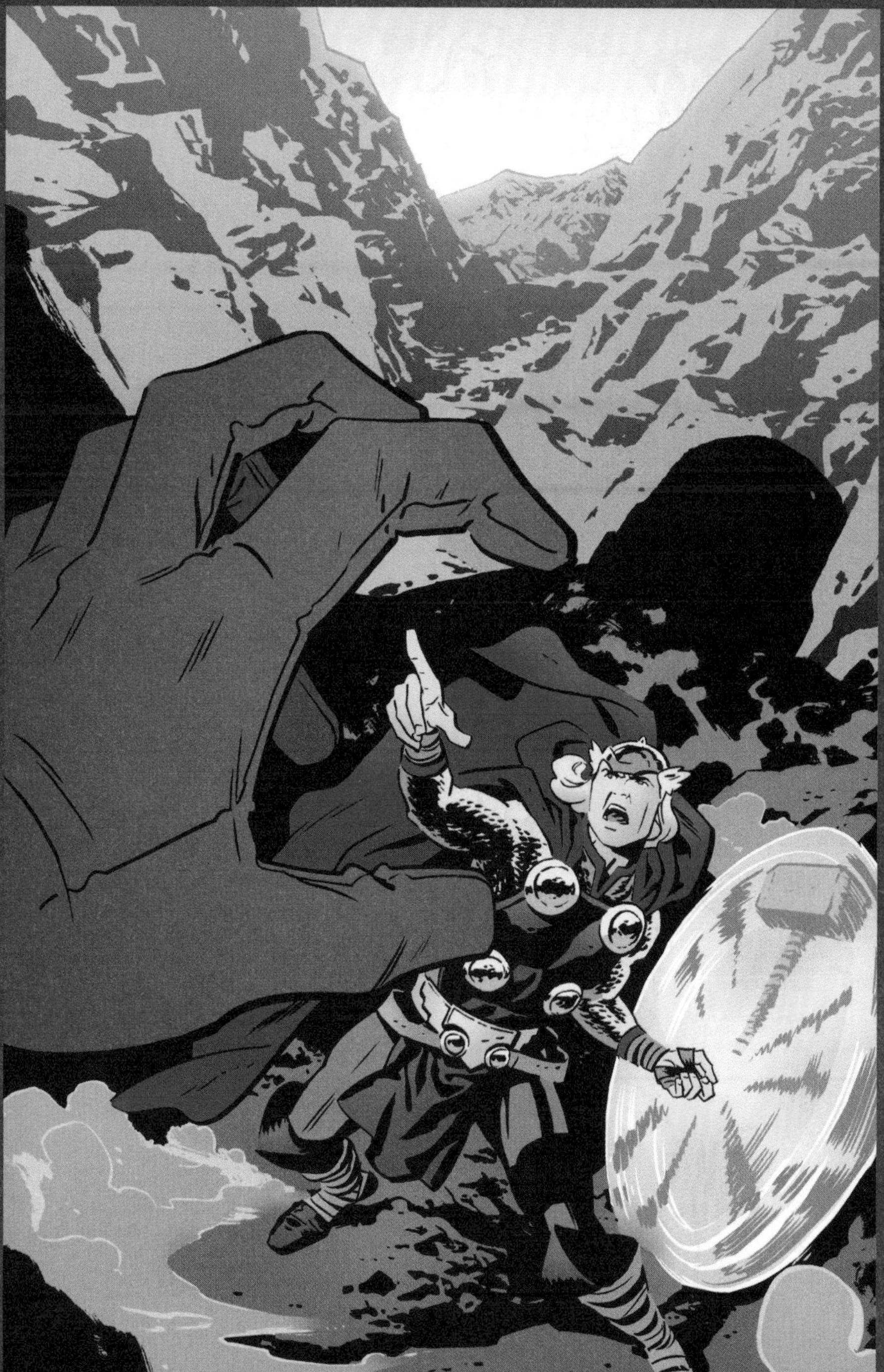

MW 10

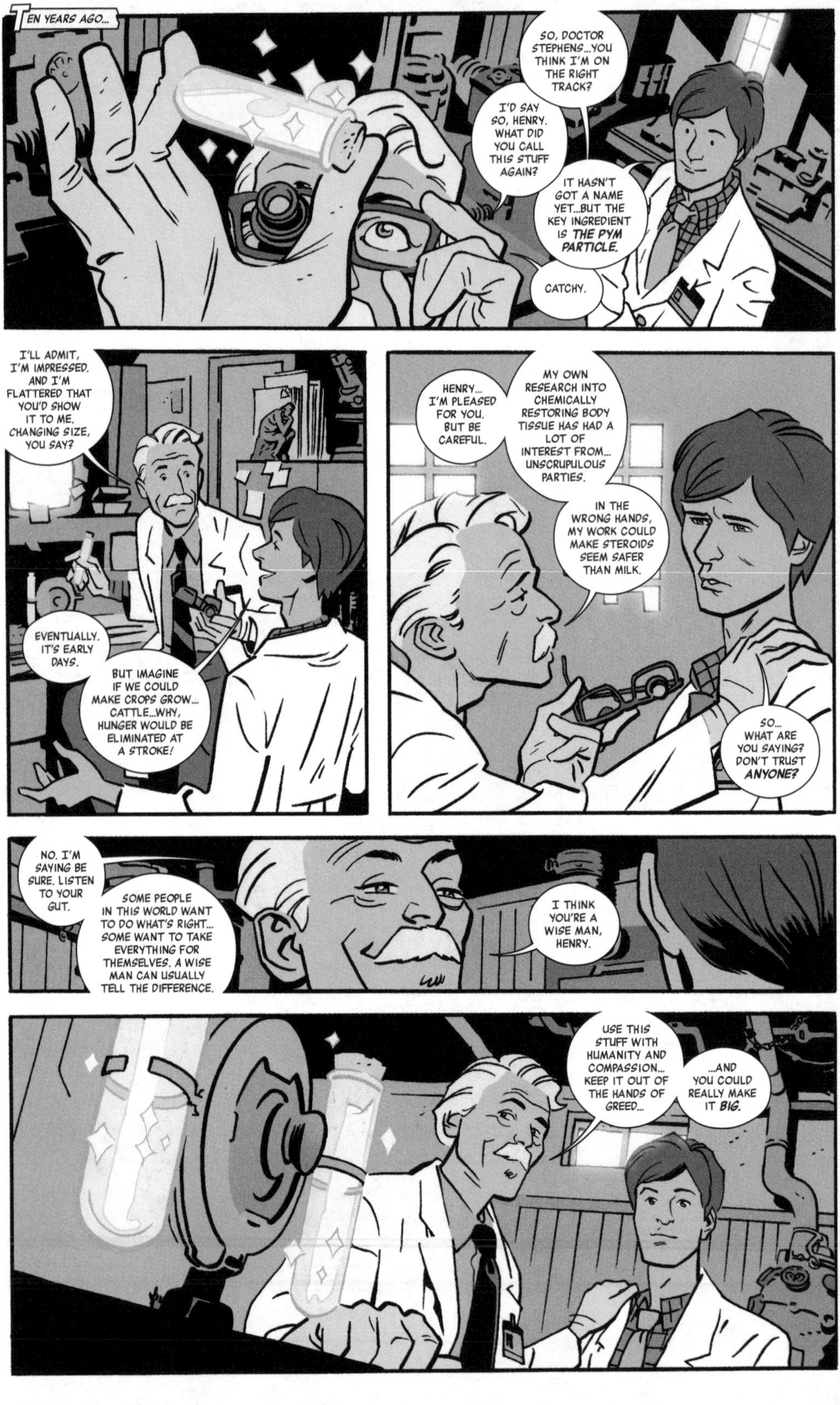
TEN YEARS AGO...
SO, DOCTOR STEPHENS...YOU THINK I'M ON THE RIGHT TRACK?
I'D SAY SO, HENRY. WHAT DID YOU CALL THIS STUFF AGAIN?
IT HASN'T GOT A NAME YET...BUT THE KEY INGREDIENT IS THE PYM PARTICLE.
CATCHY.
I'LL ADMIT, I'M IMPRESSED. AND I'M FLATTERED THAT YOU'D SHOW IT TO ME. CHANGING SIZE, YOU SAY?
EVENTUALLY. IT'S EARLY DAYS.
BUT IMAGINE IF WE COULD MAKE CROPS GROW... CATTLE...WHY, HUNGER WOULD BE ELIMINATED AT A STROKE!
HENRY... I'M PLEASED FOR YOU. BUT BE CAREFUL.
MY OWN RESEARCH INTO CHEMICALLY RESTORING BODY TISSUE HAS HAD A LOT OF INTEREST FROM... UNSCRUPULOUS PARTIES.
IN THE WRONG HANDS, MY WORK COULD MAKE STEROIDS SEEM SAFER THAN MILK.
SO... WHAT ARE YOU SAYING? DON'T TRUST ANYONE?
NO. I'M SAYING BE SURE. LISTEN TO YOUR GUT.
SOME PEOPLE IN THIS WORLD WANT TO DO WHAT'S RIGHT... SOME WANT TO TAKE EVERYTHING FOR THEMSELVES. A WISE MAN CAN USUALLY TELL THE DIFFERENCE.
I THINK YOU'RE A WISE MAN, HENRY.
USE THIS STUFF WITH HUMANITY AND COMPASSION... KEEP IT OUT OF THE HANDS OF GREED...
...AND YOU COULD REALLY MAKE IT BIG.

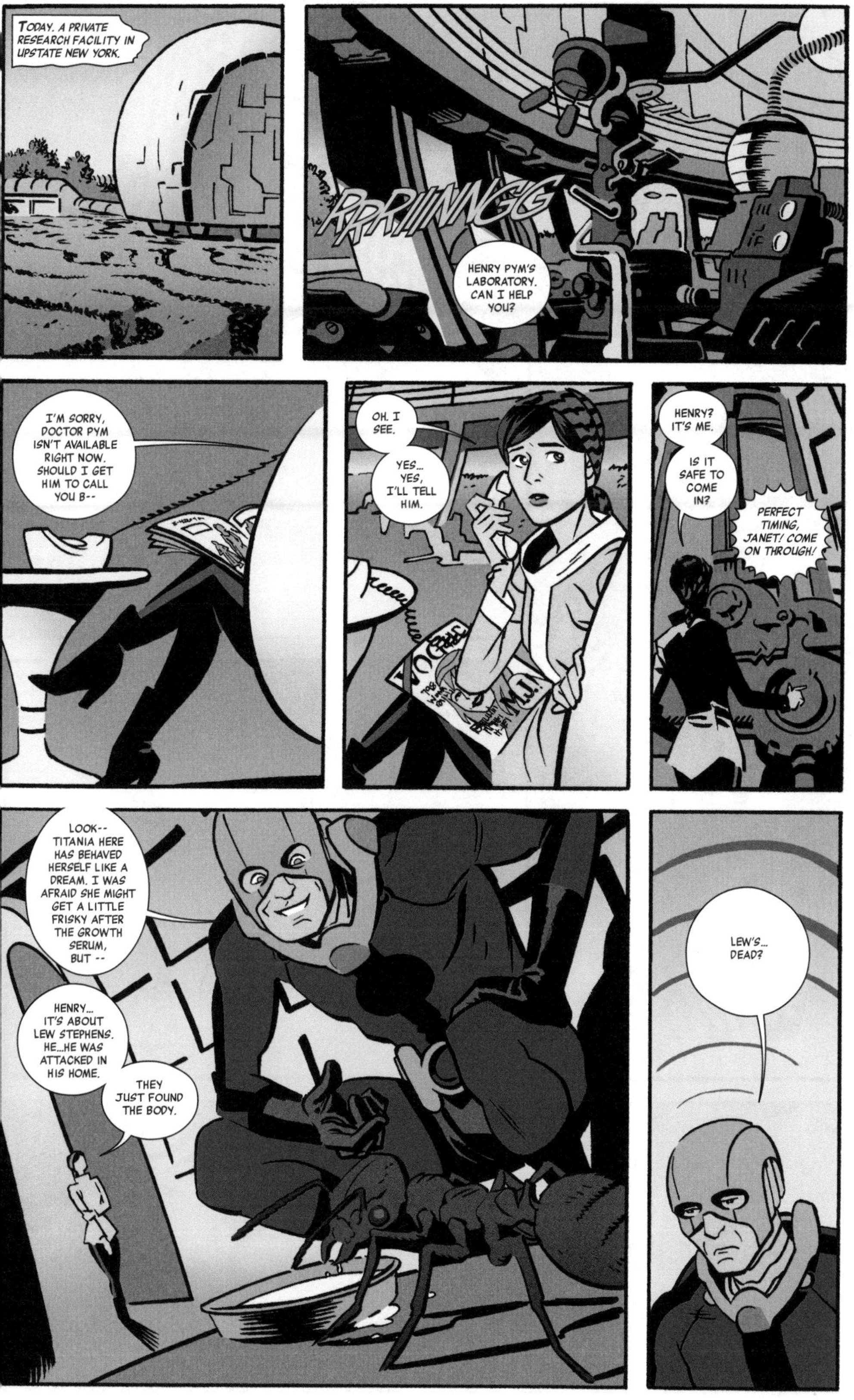
TODAY. A PRIVATE RESEARCH FACILITY IN UPSTATE NEW YORK.
RRRIINNGG
HENRY PYM'S LABORATORY. CAN I HELP YOU?
I'M SORRY, DOCTOR PYM ISN'T AVAILABLE RIGHT NOW. SHOULD I GET HIM TO CALL YOU B--
OH. I SEE.
YES... YES, I'LL TELL HIM.
HENRY? IT'S ME.
IS IT SAFE TO COME IN?
PERFECT TIMING, JANET! COME ON THROUGH!
LOOK-- TITANIA HERE HAS BEHAVED HERSELF LIKE A DREAM. I WAS AFRAID SHE MIGHT GET A LITTLE FRISKY AFTER THE GROWTH SERUM, BUT --
HENRY... IT'S ABOUT LEW STEPHENS. HE...HE WAS ATTACKED IN HIS HOME.
THEY JUST FOUND THE BODY.
LEW'S... DEAD?

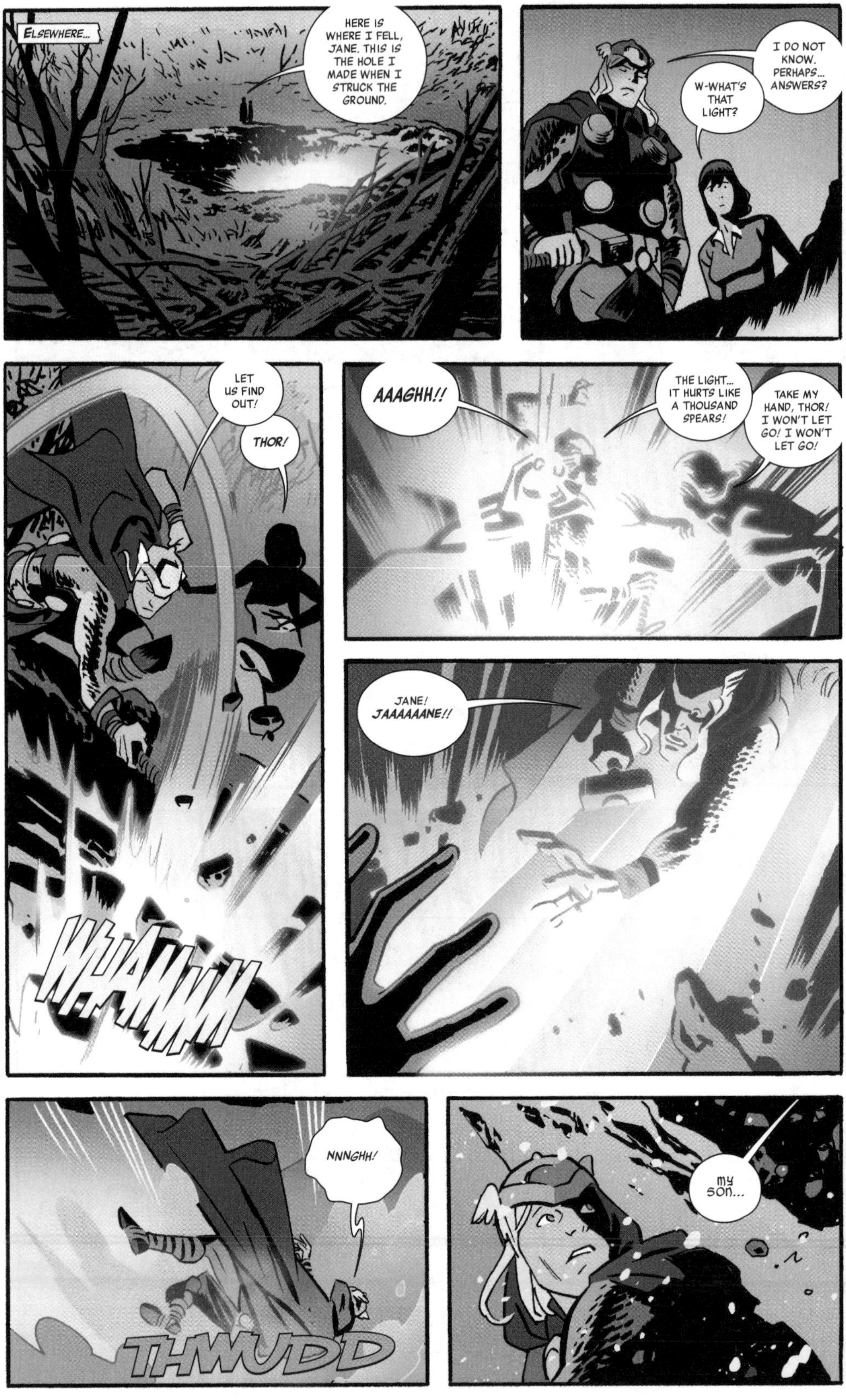
ELSEWHERE...
HERE IS WHERE I FELL, JANE. THIS IS THE HOLE I MADE WHEN I STRUCK THE GROUND.
W-WHAT'S THAT LIGHT?
I DO NOT KNOW. PERHAPS... ANSWERS?
LET US FIND OUT!
THOR!
WHAMMM
AAAGHH!!
THE LIGHT... IT HURTS LIKE A THOUSAND SPEARS!
TAKE MY HAND, THOR! I WON'T LET GO! I WON'T LET GO!
JANE! JAAAAAANE!!
NNNGHH!
THWUDD
MY SON...

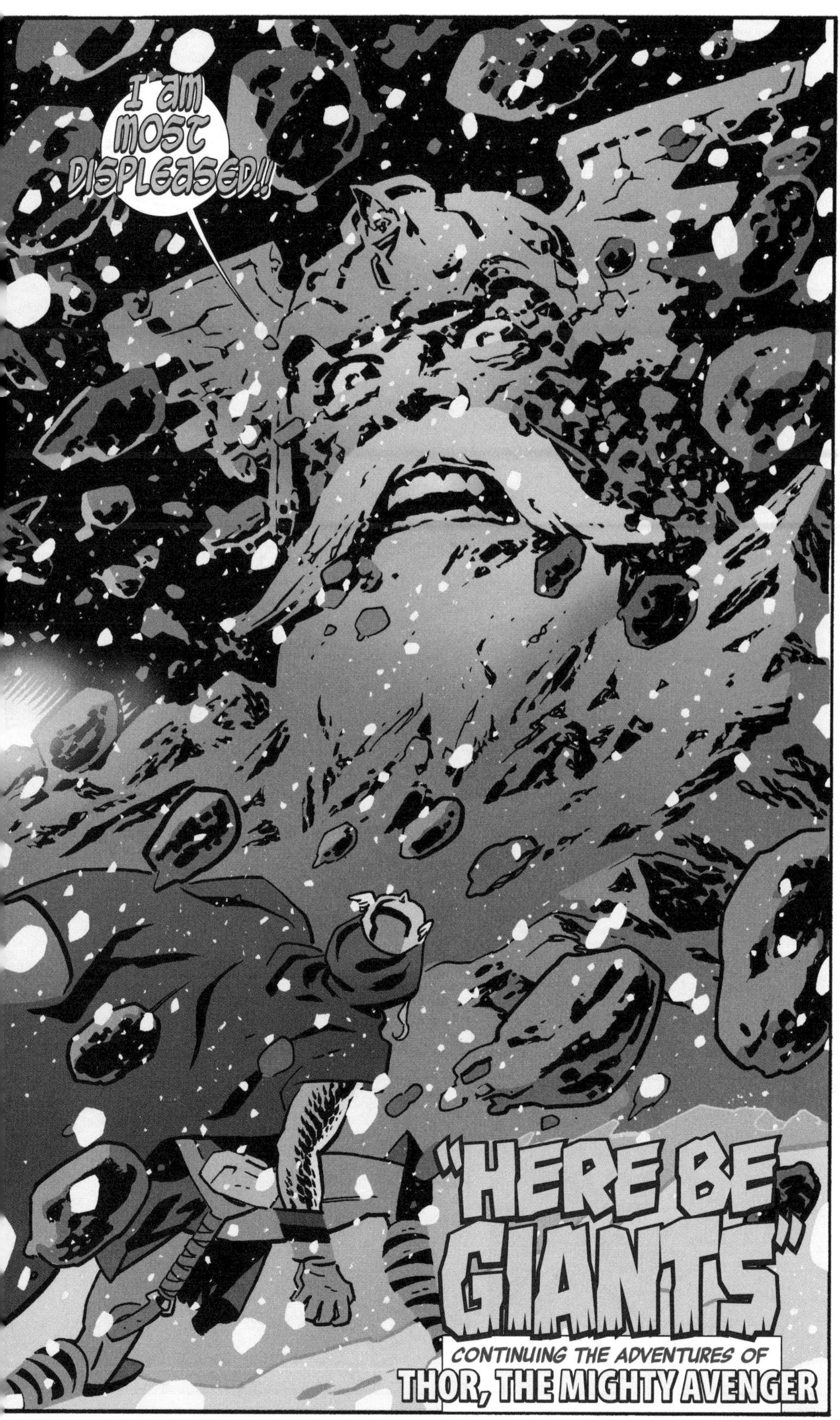
I am most displeased!!
"HERE BE GIANTS"
CONTINUING THE ADVENTURES OF
THOR, THE MIGHTY AVENGER

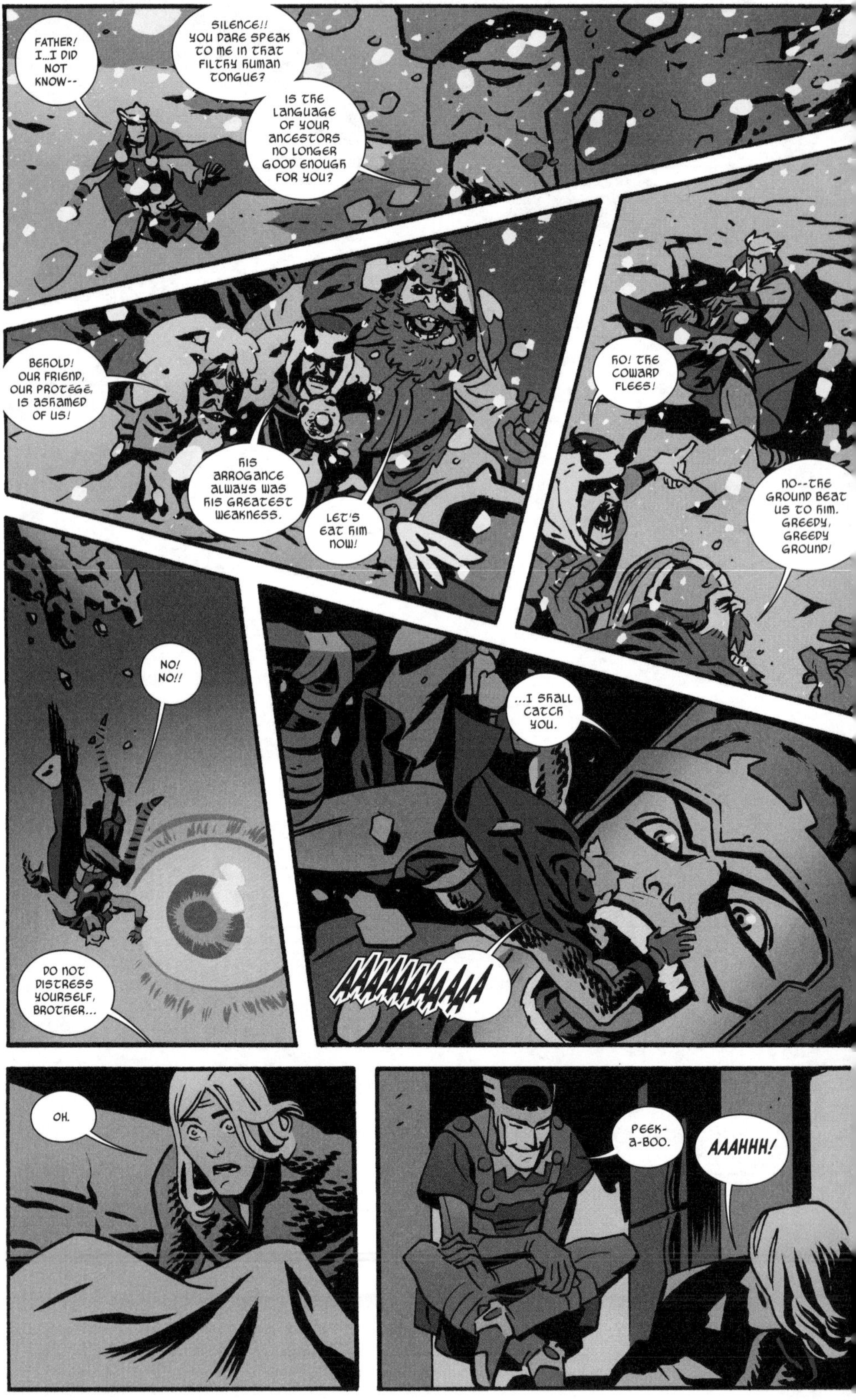

FATHER! I...I DID NOT KNOW--
SILENCE!! YOU DARE SPEAK TO ME IN THAT FILTHY HUMAN TONGUE?
IS THE LANGUAGE OF YOUR ANCESTORS NO LONGER GOOD ENOUGH FOR YOU?
BEHOLD! OUR FRIEND, OUR PROTÉGÉ, IS ASHAMED OF US!
HIS ARROGANCE ALWAYS WAS HIS GREATEST WEAKNESS.
LET'S EAT HIM NOW!
HO! THE COWARD FLEES!
NO--THE GROUND BEAT US TO HIM. GREEDY, GREEDY GROUND!
NO! NO!!
DO NOT DISTRESS YOURSELF, BROTHER...
...I SHALL CATCH YOU.
AAAAAAAAAAA
OH.
PEEK-A-BOO.
AAAHHH!

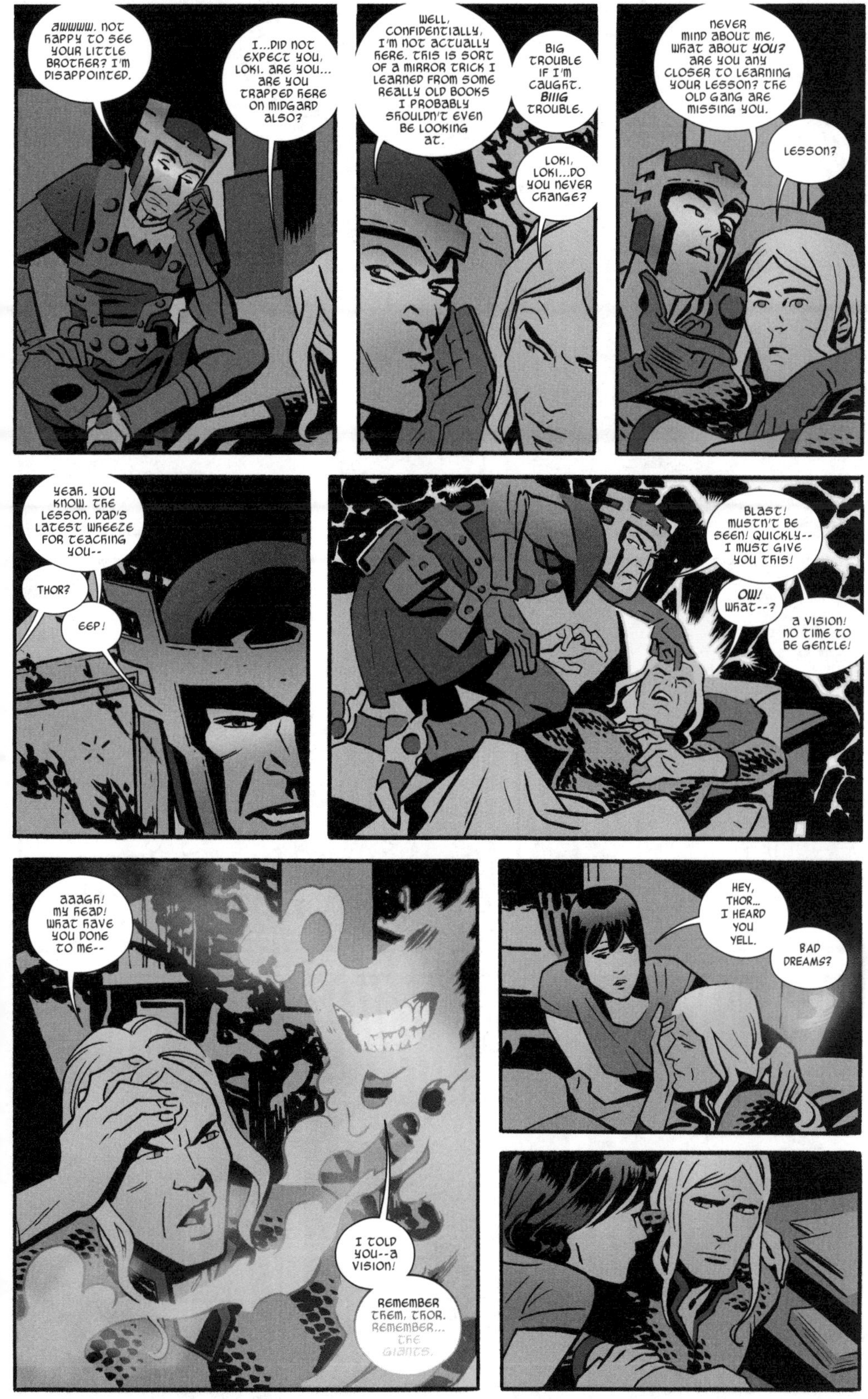
AWWWW. NOT HAPPY TO SEE YOUR LITTLE BROTHER? I'M DISAPPOINTED.
I...DID NOT EXPECT YOU, LOKI. ARE YOU... ARE YOU TRAPPED HERE ON MIDGARD ALSO?
WELL, CONFIDENTIALLY, I'M NOT ACTUALLY HERE. THIS IS SORT OF A MIRROR TRICK I LEARNED FROM SOME REALLY OLD BOOKS I PROBABLY SHOULDN'T EVEN BE LOOKING AT.
BIG TROUBLE IF I'M CAUGHT. BIIIG TROUBLE.
LOKI, LOKI...DO YOU NEVER CHANGE?
NEVER MIND ABOUT ME, WHAT ABOUT YOU? ARE YOU ANY CLOSER TO LEARNING YOUR LESSON? THE OLD GANG ARE MISSING YOU.
LESSON?
YEAH. YOU KNOW. THE LESSON. DAD'S LATEST WHEEZE FOR TEACHING YOU--
THOR?
EEP!
BLAST! MUSTN'T BE SEEN! QUICKLY-- I MUST GIVE YOU THIS!
OW! WHAT--?
A VISION! NO TIME TO BE GENTLE!
AAAGH! MY HEAD! WHAT HAVE YOU DONE TO ME--
I TOLD YOU--A VISION!
REMEMBER THEM, THOR. REMEMBER... THE GIANTS.
HEY, THOR... I HEARD YOU YELL.
BAD DREAMS?

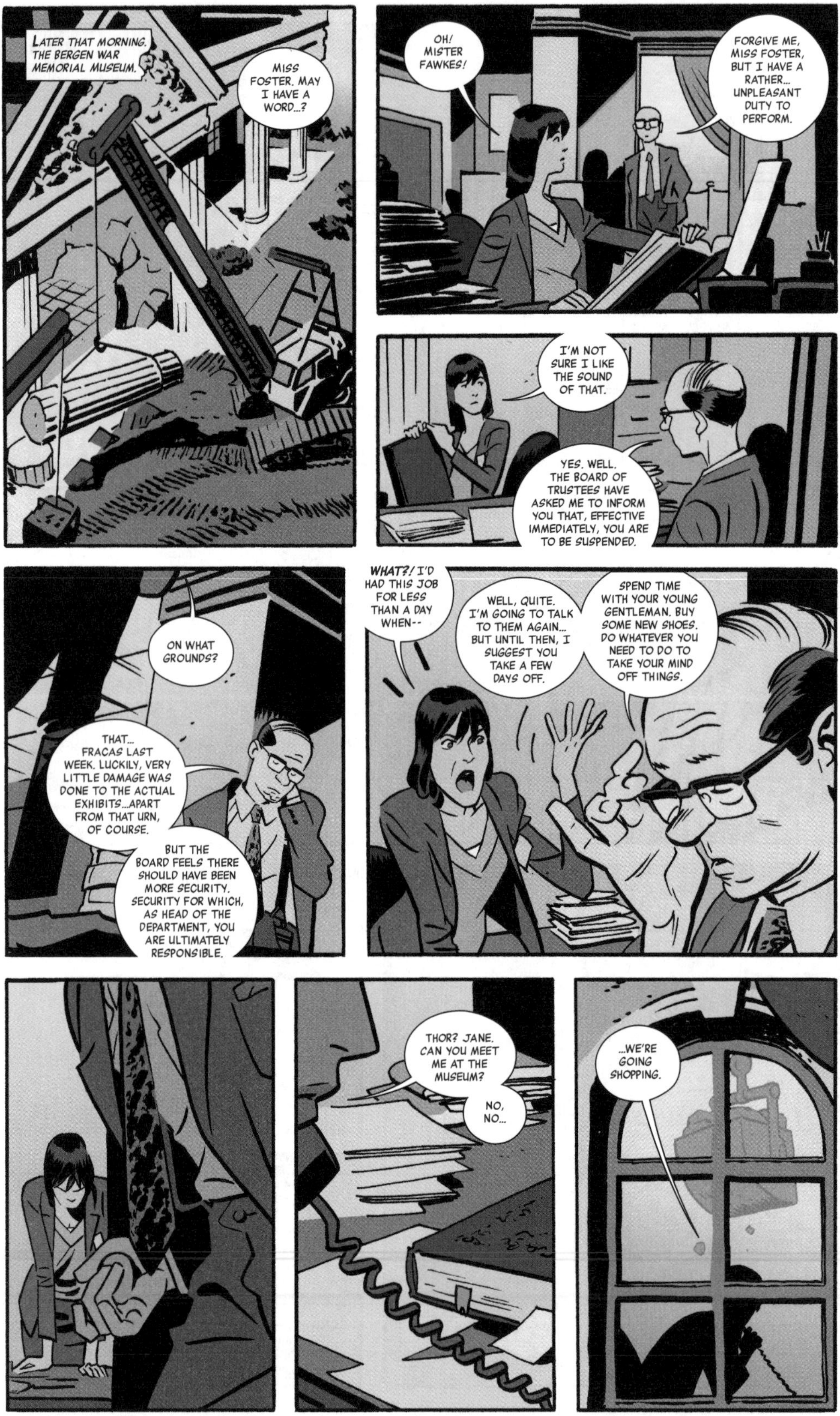
LATER THAT MORNING, THE BERGEN WAR MEMORIAL MUSEUM.
MISS FOSTER. MAY I HAVE A WORD...?
OH! MISTER FAWKES!
FORGIVE ME, MISS FOSTER, BUT I HAVE A RATHER... UNPLEASANT DUTY TO PERFORM.
I'M NOT SURE I LIKE THE SOUND OF THAT.
YES. WELL. THE BOARD OF TRUSTEES HAVE ASKED ME TO INFORM YOU THAT, EFFECTIVE IMMEDIATELY, YOU ARE TO BE SUSPENDED.
ON WHAT GROUNDS?
THAT... FRACAS LAST WEEK. LUCKILY, VERY LITTLE DAMAGE WAS DONE TO THE ACTUAL EXHIBITS...APART FROM THAT URN, OF COURSE.
BUT THE BOARD FEELS THERE SHOULD HAVE BEEN MORE SECURITY. SECURITY FOR WHICH, AS HEAD OF THE DEPARTMENT, YOU ARE ULTIMATELY RESPONSIBLE.
WHAT?! I'D HAD THIS JOB FOR LESS THAN A DAY WHEN--
WELL, QUITE. I'M GOING TO TALK TO THEM AGAIN... BUT UNTIL THEN, I SUGGEST YOU TAKE A FEW DAYS OFF.
SPEND TIME WITH YOUR YOUNG GENTLEMAN. BUY SOME NEW SHOES. DO WHATEVER YOU NEED TO DO TO TAKE YOUR MIND OFF THINGS.
THOR? JANE. CAN YOU MEET ME AT THE MUSEUM?
NO, NO...
...WE'RE GOING SHOPPING.

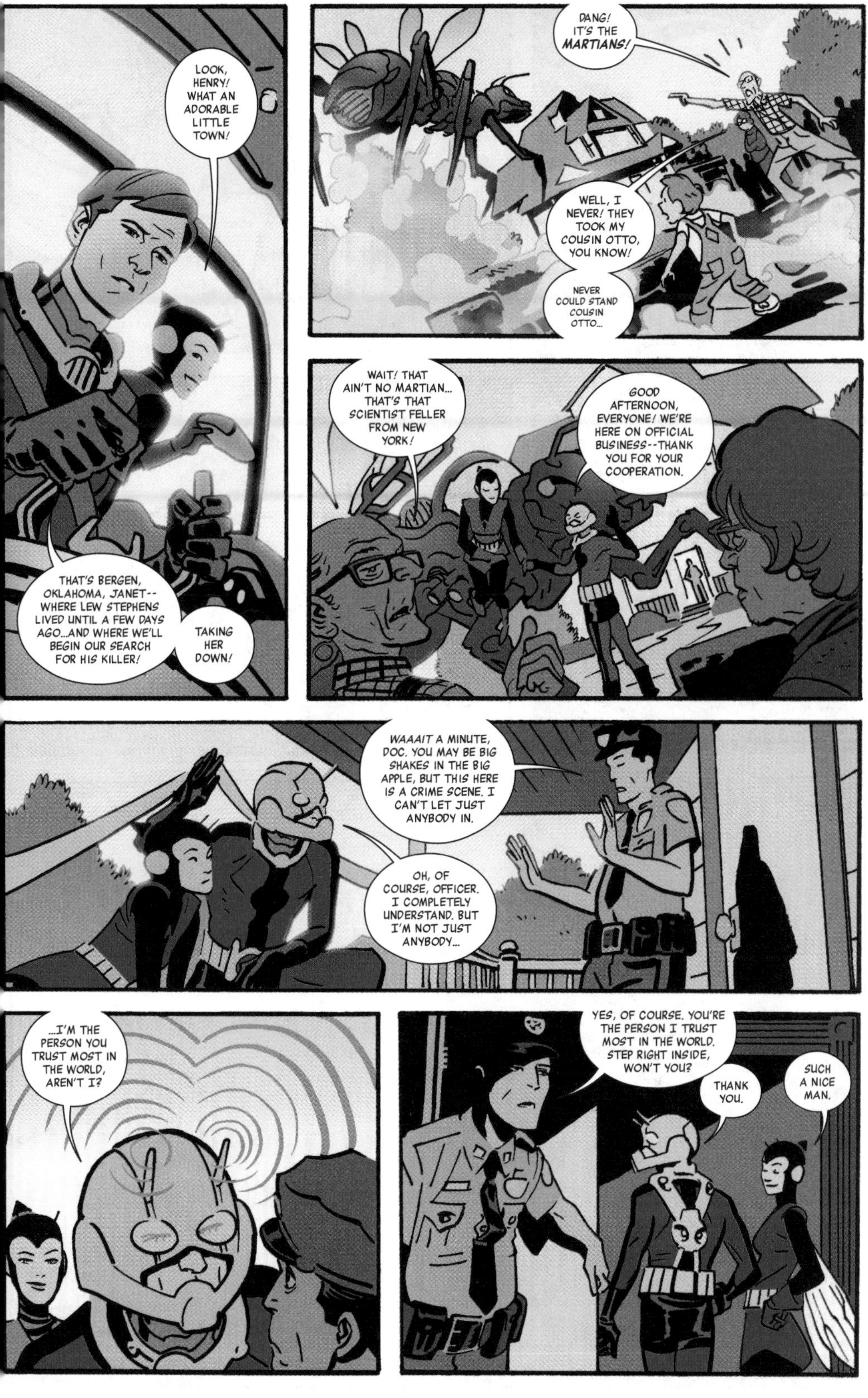
LOOK, HENRY! WHAT AN ADORABLE LITTLE TOWN!
THAT'S BERGEN, OKLAHOMA, JANET--WHERE LEW STEPHENS LIVED UNTIL A FEW DAYS AGO...AND WHERE WE'LL BEGIN OUR SEARCH FOR HIS KILLER!
TAKING HER DOWN!
DANG! IT'S THE MARTIANS!
WELL, I NEVER! THEY TOOK MY COUSIN OTTO, YOU KNOW!
NEVER COULD STAND COUSIN OTTO...
WAIT! THAT AIN'T NO MARTIAN... THAT'S THAT SCIENTIST FELLER FROM NEW YORK!
GOOD AFTERNOON, EVERYONE! WE'RE HERE ON OFFICIAL BUSINESS--THANK YOU FOR YOUR COOPERATION.
WAAAIT A MINUTE, DOC. YOU MAY BE BIG SHAKES IN THE BIG APPLE, BUT THIS HERE IS A CRIME SCENE. I CAN'T LET JUST ANYBODY IN.
OH, OF COURSE, OFFICER. I COMPLETELY UNDERSTAND. BUT I'M NOT JUST ANYBODY...
...I'M THE PERSON YOU TRUST MOST IN THE WORLD, AREN'T I?
YES, OF COURSE. YOU'RE THE PERSON I TRUST MOST IN THE WORLD. STEP RIGHT INSIDE, WON'T YOU?
THANK YOU.
SUCH A NICE MAN.

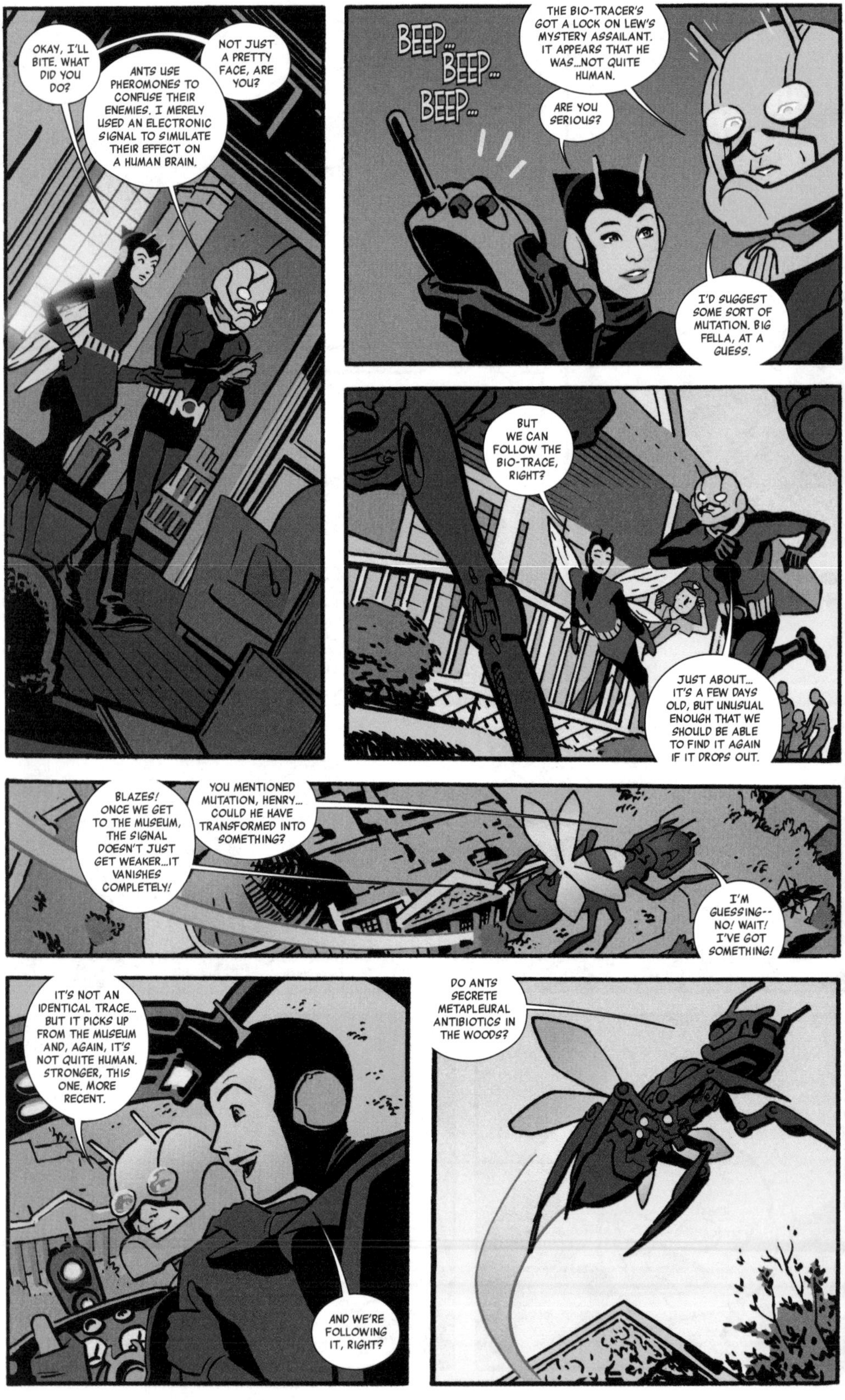
OKAY, I'LL BITE. WHAT DID YOU DO?
ANTS USE PHEROMONES TO CONFUSE THEIR ENEMIES. I MERELY USED AN ELECTRONIC SIGNAL TO SIMULATE THEIR EFFECT ON A HUMAN BRAIN.
NOT JUST A PRETTY FACE, ARE YOU?
BEEP... BEEP... BEEP...
THE BIO-TRACER'S GOT A LOCK ON LEW'S MYSTERY ASSAILANT. IT APPEARS THAT HE WAS...NOT QUITE HUMAN.
ARE YOU SERIOUS?
I'D SUGGEST SOME SORT OF MUTATION. BIG FELLA, AT A GUESS.
BUT WE CAN FOLLOW THE BIO-TRACE, RIGHT?
JUST ABOUT... IT'S A FEW DAYS OLD, BUT UNUSUAL ENOUGH THAT WE SHOULD BE ABLE TO FIND IT AGAIN IF IT DROPS OUT.
BLAZES! ONCE WE GET TO THE MUSEUM, THE SIGNAL DOESN'T JUST GET WEAKER...IT VANISHES COMPLETELY!
YOU MENTIONED MUTATION, HENRY... COULD HE HAVE TRANSFORMED INTO SOMETHING?
I'M GUESSING-- NO! WAIT! I'VE GOT SOMETHING!
IT'S NOT AN IDENTICAL TRACE... BUT IT PICKS UP FROM THE MUSEUM AND, AGAIN, IT'S NOT QUITE HUMAN. STRONGER, THIS ONE. MORE RECENT.
AND WE'RE FOLLOWING IT, RIGHT?
DO ANTS SECRETE METAPLEURAL ANTIBIOTICS IN THE WOODS?

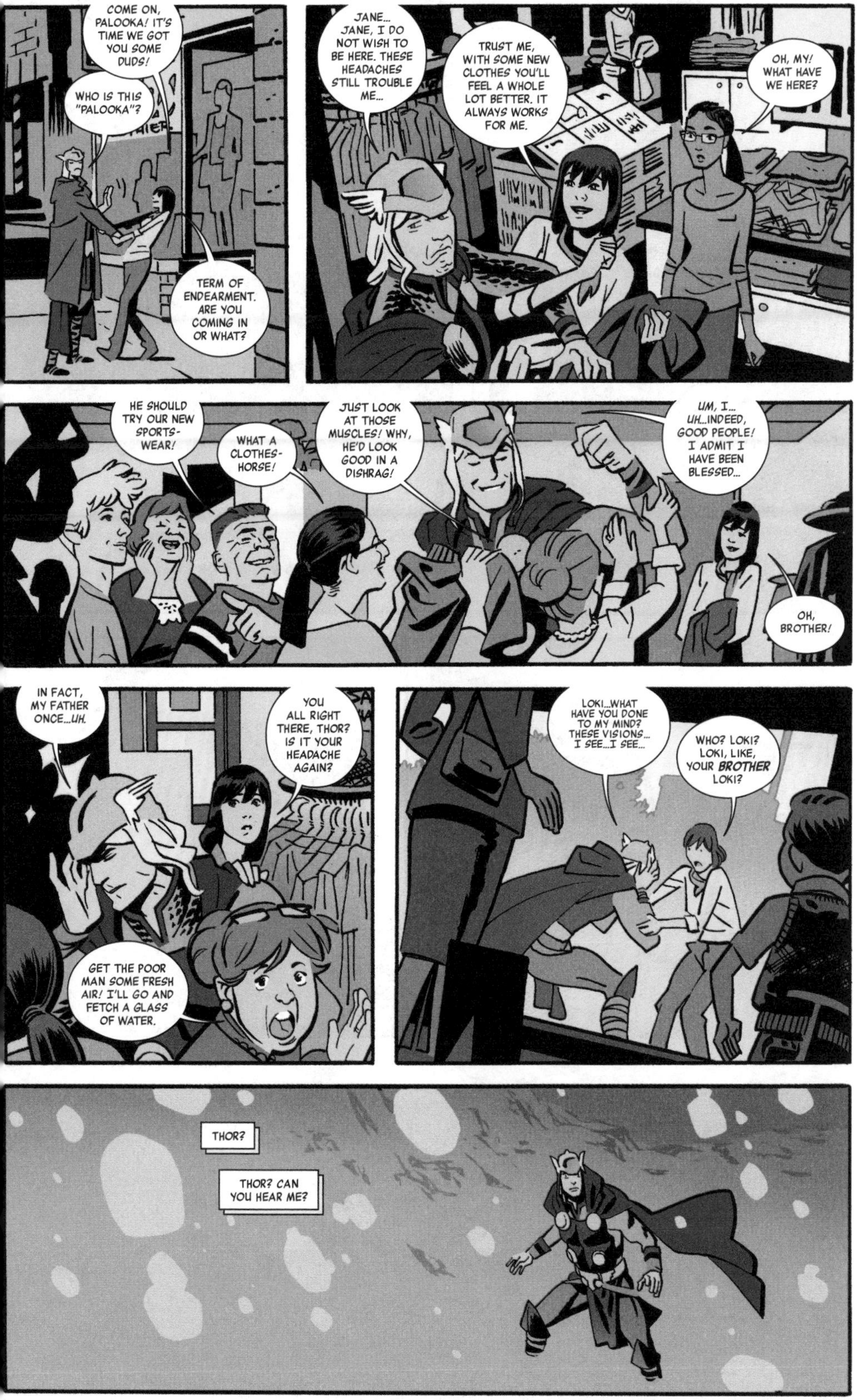
COME ON, PALOOKA! IT'S TIME WE GOT YOU SOME DUDS!
WHO IS THIS "PALOOKA"?
TERM OF ENDEARMENT. ARE YOU COMING IN OR WHAT?
JANE... JANE, I DO NOT WISH TO BE HERE. THESE HEADACHES STILL TROUBLE ME...
TRUST ME, WITH SOME NEW CLOTHES YOU'LL FEEL A WHOLE LOT BETTER. IT ALWAYS WORKS FOR ME.
OH, MY! WHAT HAVE WE HERE?
HE SHOULD TRY OUR NEW SPORTS-WEAR!
WHAT A CLOTHES-HORSE!
JUST LOOK AT THOSE MUSCLES! WHY, HE'D LOOK GOOD IN A DISHRAG!
UM, I... UH...INDEED, GOOD PEOPLE! I ADMIT I HAVE BEEN BLESSED...
OH, BROTHER!
IN FACT, MY FATHER ONCE...UH.
YOU ALL RIGHT THERE, THOR? IS IT YOUR HEADACHE AGAIN?
GET THE POOR MAN SOME FRESH AIR! I'LL GO AND FETCH A GLASS OF WATER.
LOKI...WHAT HAVE YOU DONE TO MY MIND? THESE VISIONS... I SEE...I SEE...
WHO? LOKI? LOKI, LIKE, YOUR BROTHER LOKI?
THOR?
THOR? CAN YOU HEAR ME?

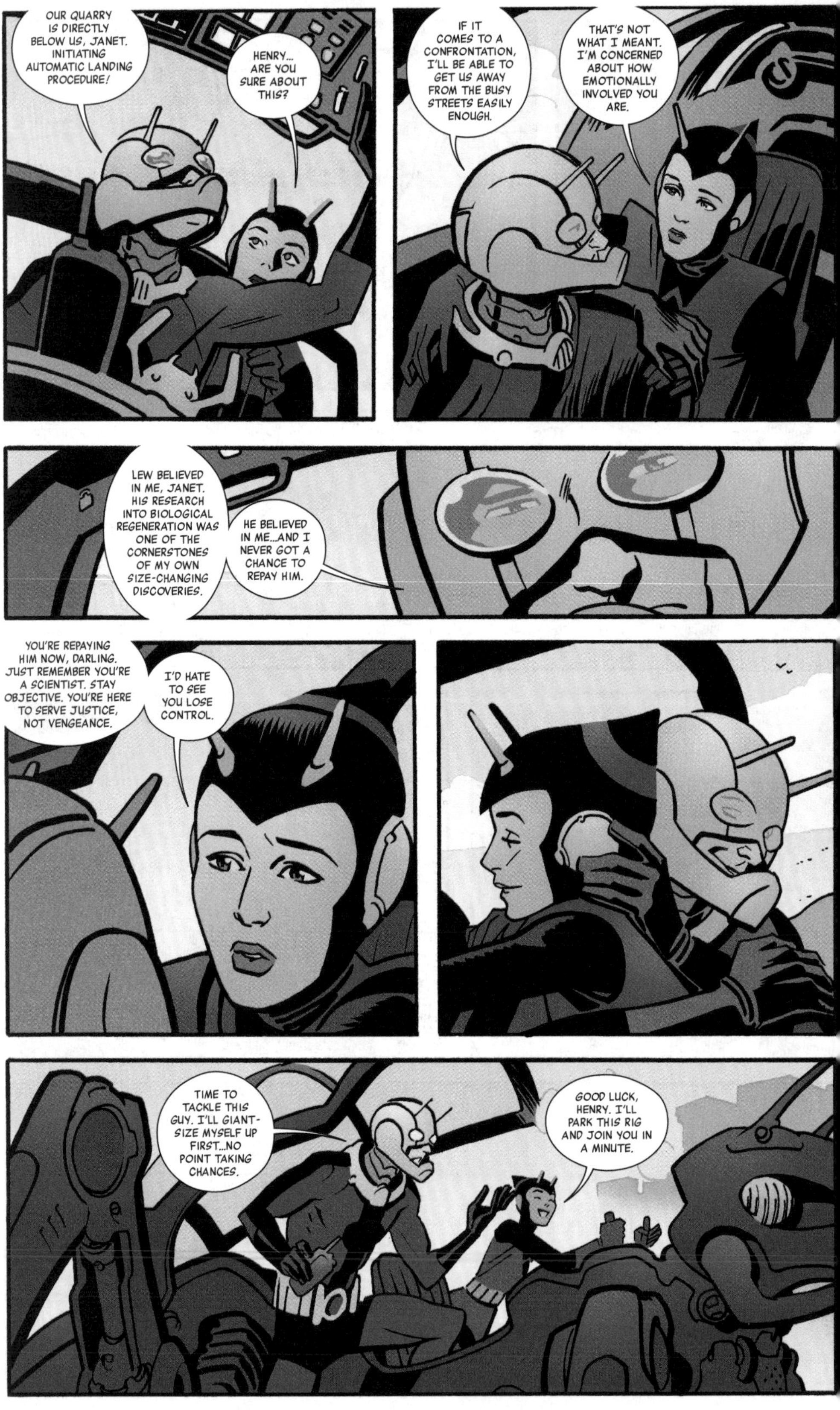
OUR QUARRY IS DIRECTLY BELOW US, JANET. INITIATING AUTOMATIC LANDING PROCEDURE!
HENRY... ARE YOU SURE ABOUT THIS?
IF IT COMES TO A CONFRONTATION, I'LL BE ABLE TO GET US AWAY FROM THE BUSY STREETS EASILY ENOUGH.
THAT'S NOT WHAT I MEANT. I'M CONCERNED ABOUT HOW EMOTIONALLY INVOLVED YOU ARE.
LEW BELIEVED IN ME, JANET. HIS RESEARCH INTO BIOLOGICAL REGENERATION WAS ONE OF THE CORNERSTONES OF MY OWN SIZE-CHANGING DISCOVERIES.
HE BELIEVED IN ME...AND I NEVER GOT A CHANCE TO REPAY HIM.
YOU'RE REPAYING HIM NOW, DARLING. JUST REMEMBER YOU'RE A SCIENTIST. STAY OBJECTIVE. YOU'RE HERE TO SERVE JUSTICE, NOT VENGEANCE.
I'D HATE TO SEE YOU LOSE CONTROL.
TIME TO TACKLE THIS GUY. I'LL GIANT-SIZE MYSELF UP FIRST...NO POINT TAKING CHANCES.
GOOD LUCK, HENRY. I'LL PARK THIS RIG AND JOIN YOU IN A MINUTE.

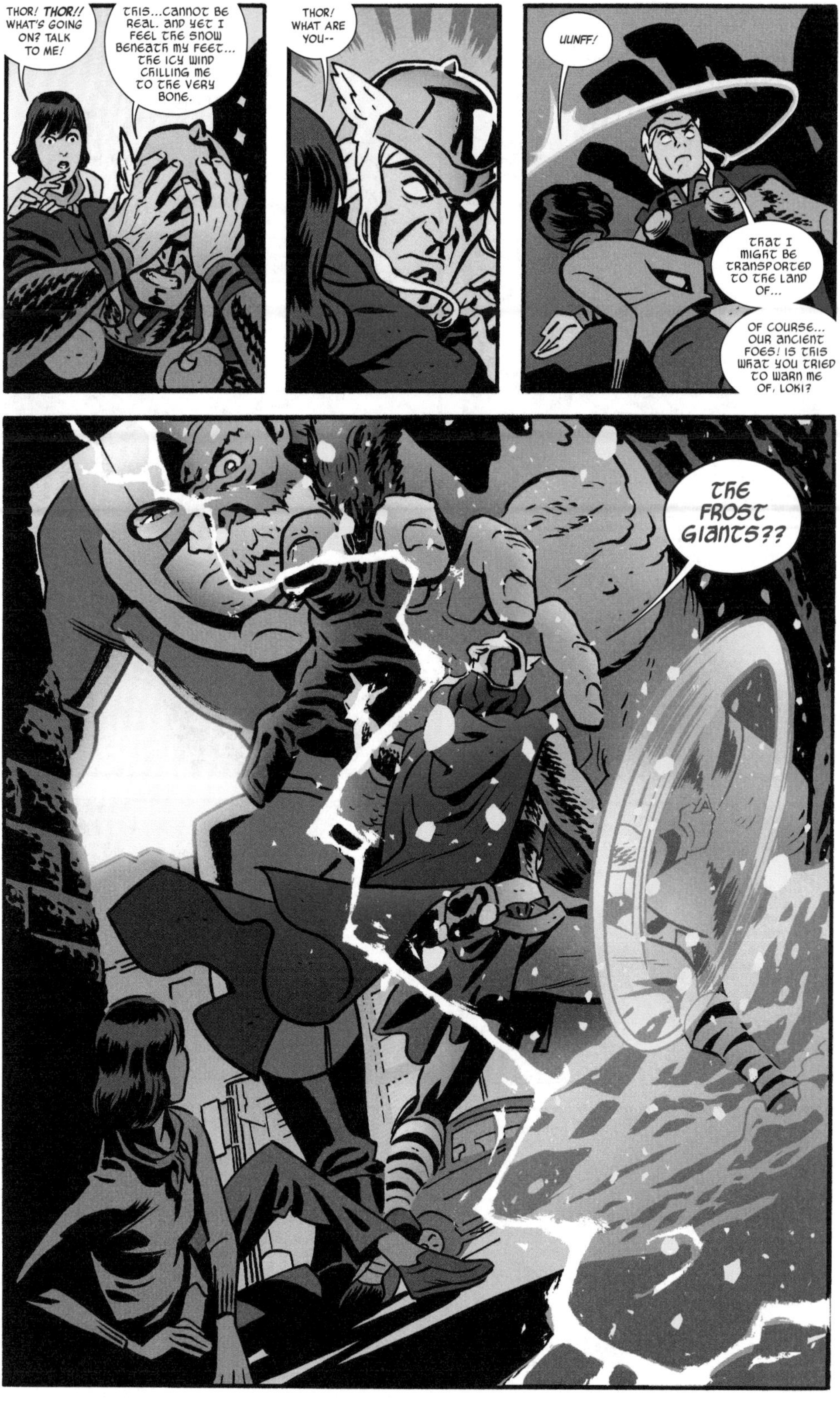
THOR! THOR!! WHAT'S GOING ON? TALK TO ME!
THIS...CANNOT BE REAL. AND YET I FEEL THE SNOW BENEATH MY FEET... THE ICY WIND CHILLING ME TO THE VERY BONE.
THOR! WHAT ARE YOU--
UUNFF!
THAT I MIGHT BE TRANSPORTED TO THE LAND OF...
OF COURSE... OUR ANCIENT FOES! IS THIS WHAT YOU TRIED TO WARN ME OF, LOKI?
THE FROST GIANTS??

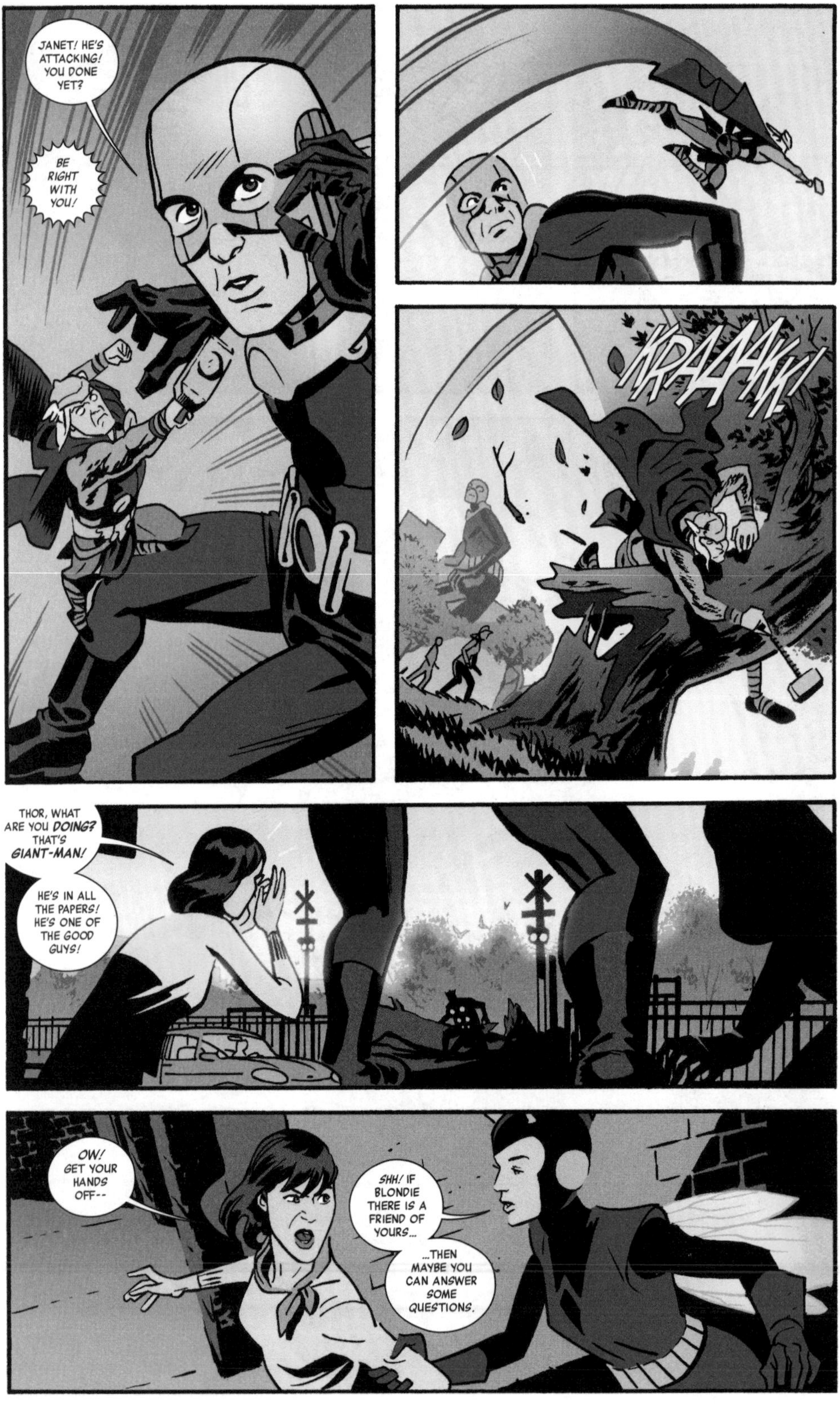
JANET! HE'S ATTACKING! YOU DONE YET?
BE RIGHT WITH YOU!
KRAAAKK!
THOR, WHAT ARE YOU DOING? THAT'S GIANT-MAN!
HE'S IN ALL THE PAPERS! HE'S ONE OF THE GOOD GUYS!
OW! GET YOUR HANDS OFF--
SHH! IF BLONDIE THERE IS A FRIEND OF YOURS...
...THEN MAYBE YOU CAN ANSWER SOME QUESTIONS.

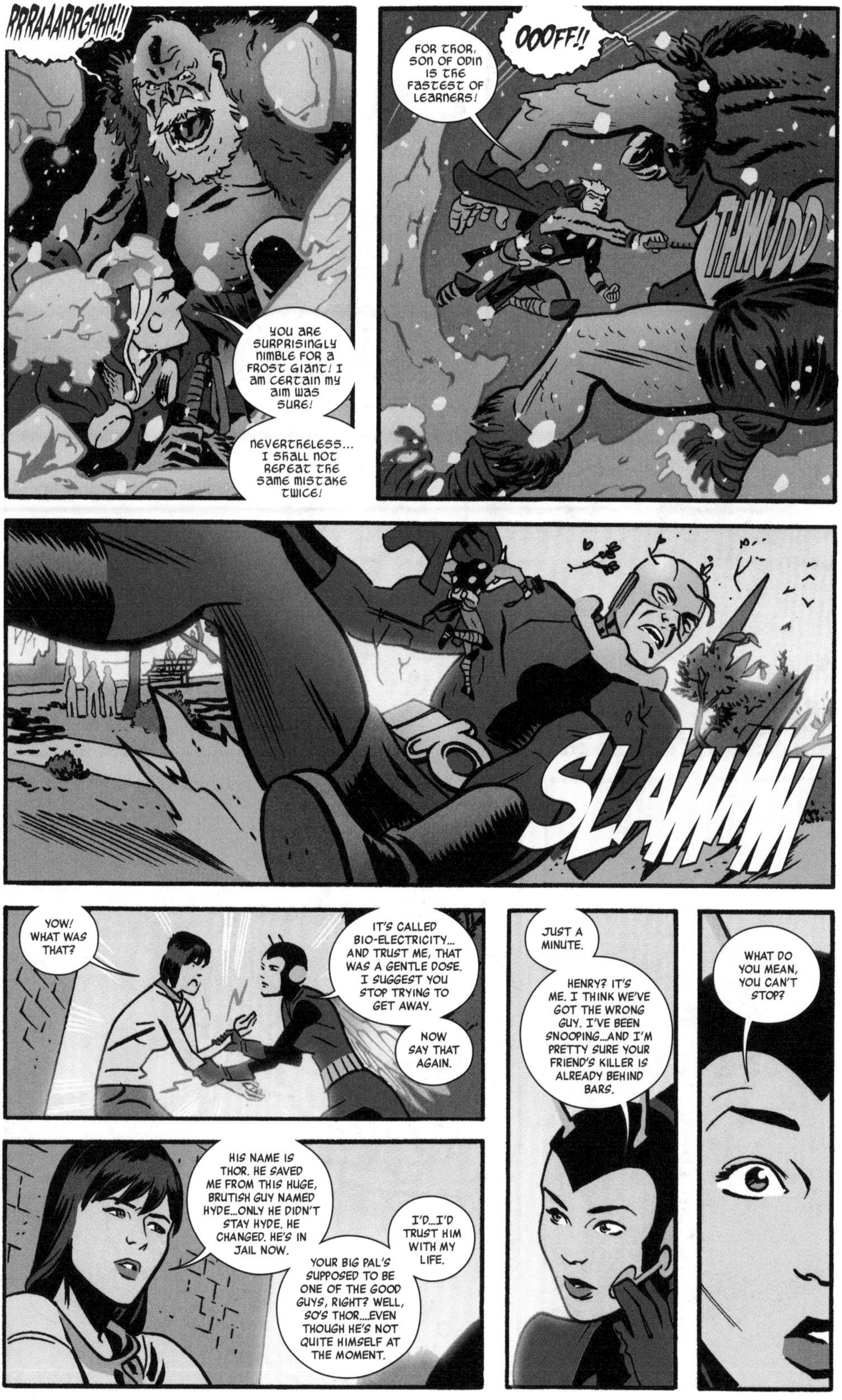
RRRAAARRGHHH!!
YOU ARE SURPRISINGLY NIMBLE FOR A FROST GIANT! I AM CERTAIN MY AIM WAS SURE!
NEVERTHELESS... I SHALL NOT REPEAT THE SAME MISTAKE TWICE!
OOOFF!!
FOR THOR, SON OF ODIN IS THE FASTEST OF LEARNERS!
THWUDD
SLAMMM
YOW! WHAT WAS THAT?
IT'S CALLED BIO-ELECTRICITY... AND TRUST ME, THAT WAS A GENTLE DOSE. I SUGGEST YOU STOP TRYING TO GET AWAY.
NOW SAY THAT AGAIN.
HIS NAME IS THOR. HE SAVED ME FROM THIS HUGE, BRUTISH GUY NAMED HYDE...ONLY HE DIDN'T STAY HYDE. HE CHANGED. HE'S IN JAIL NOW.
YOUR BIG PAL'S SUPPOSED TO BE ONE OF THE GOOD GUYS, RIGHT? WELL, SO'S THOR....EVEN THOUGH HE'S NOT QUITE HIMSELF AT THE MOMENT.
I'D...I'D TRUST HIM WITH MY LIFE.
JUST A MINUTE.
HENRY? IT'S ME. I THINK WE'VE GOT THE WRONG GUY. I'VE BEEN SNOOPING...AND I'M PRETTY SURE YOUR FRIEND'S KILLER IS ALREADY BEHIND BARS.
WHAT DO YOU MEAN, YOU CAN'T STOP?

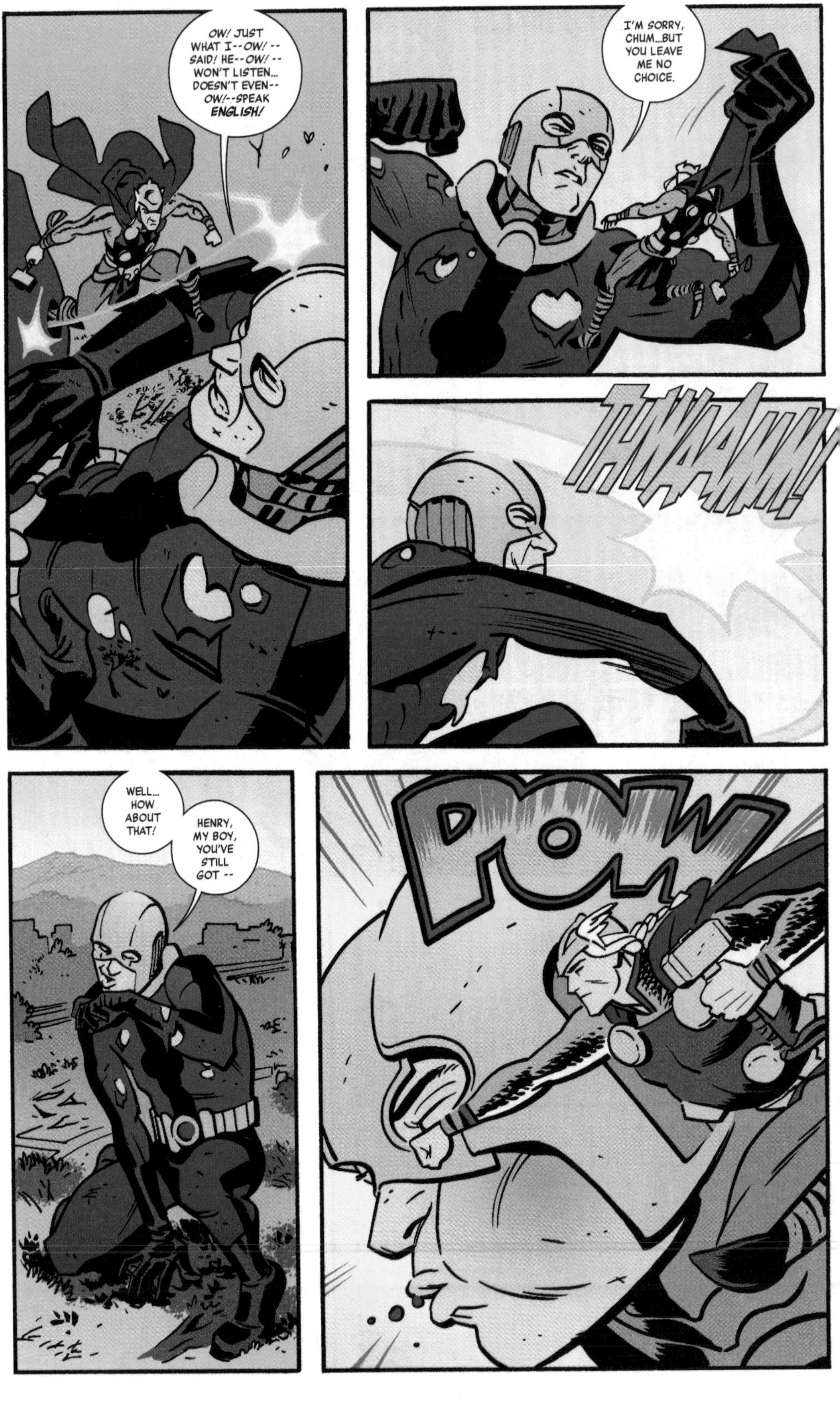
OW! JUST WHAT I--OW! --SAID! HE--OW! --WON'T LISTEN... DOESN'T EVEN--OW!--SPEAK ENGLISH!
I'M SORRY, CHUM...BUT YOU LEAVE ME NO CHOICE.
THWAAMM!
WELL... HOW ABOUT THAT!
HENRY, MY BOY, YOU'VE STILL GOT --
POW

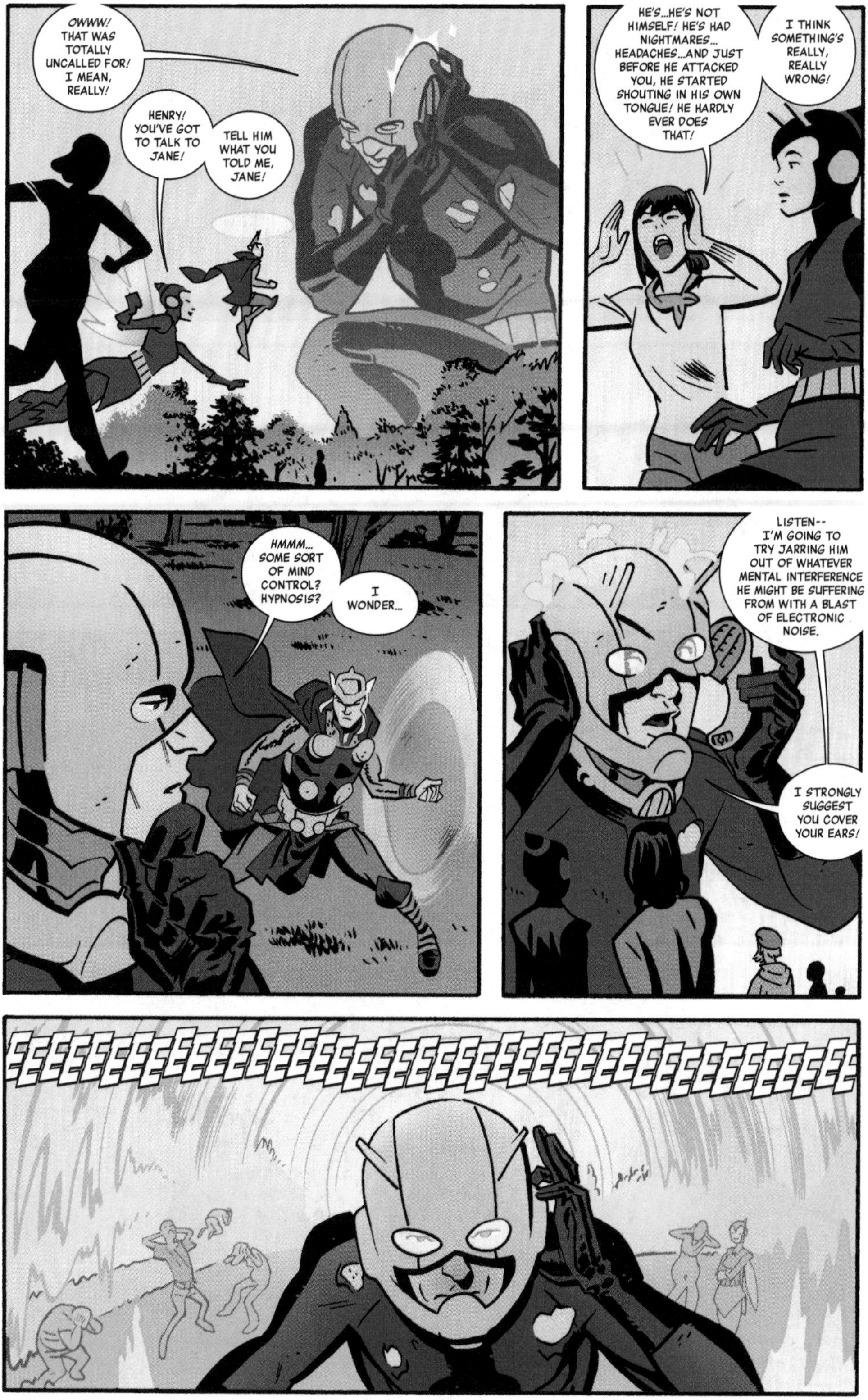
OWWW! THAT WAS TOTALLY UNCALLED FOR! I MEAN, REALLY!
HENRY! YOU'VE GOT TO TALK TO JANE!
TELL HIM WHAT YOU TOLD ME, JANE!
HE'S...HE'S NOT HIMSELF! HE'S HAD NIGHTMARES... HEADACHES...AND JUST BEFORE HE ATTACKED YOU, HE STARTED SHOUTING IN HIS OWN TONGUE! HE HARDLY EVER DOES THAT!
I THINK SOMETHING'S REALLY, REALLY WRONG!
HMMM... SOME SORT OF MIND CONTROL? HYPNOSIS?
I WONDER...
LISTEN-- I'M GOING TO TRY JARRING HIM OUT OF WHATEVER MENTAL INTERFERENCE HE MIGHT BE SUFFERING FROM WITH A BLAST OF ELECTRONIC NOISE.
I STRONGLY SUGGEST YOU COVER YOUR EARS!
EEEEEEEEEEEEEEEEEEEEEEEEEEEEEEEEEEEEEEEEEEE

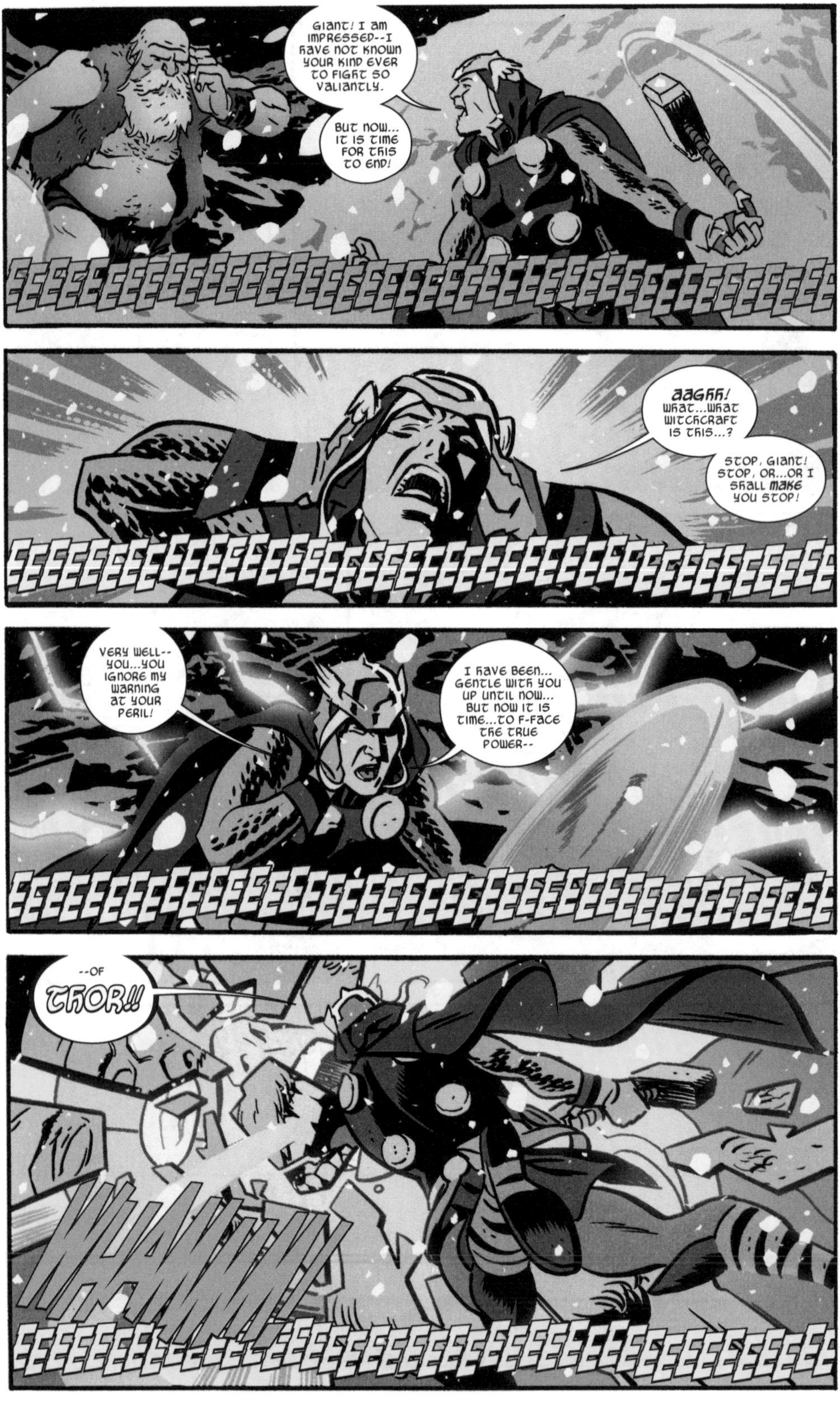
GIANT! I AM IMPRESSED--I HAVE NOT KNOWN YOUR KIND EVER TO FIGHT SO VALIANTLY.
BUT NOW... IT IS TIME FOR THIS TO END!
EEEEEEEEEEEEEEEEEEEEEEEEEEEEE
AAGHH! WHAT...WHAT WITCHCRAFT IS THIS...?
STOP, GIANT! STOP, OR...OR I SHALL MAKE YOU STOP!
EEEEEEEEEEEEEEEEEEEEEEEEEEEEE
VERY WELL--YOU...YOU IGNORE MY WARNING AT YOUR PERIL!
I HAVE BEEN... GENTLE WITH YOU UP UNTIL NOW... BUT NOW IT IS TIME...TO F-FACE THE TRUE POWER--
EEEEEEEEEEEEEEEEEEEEEEEEEEEEE
--OF THOR!!
WHAMMM!
EEEEEEEEEEEEEEEEEEEEEEEEEEEEE

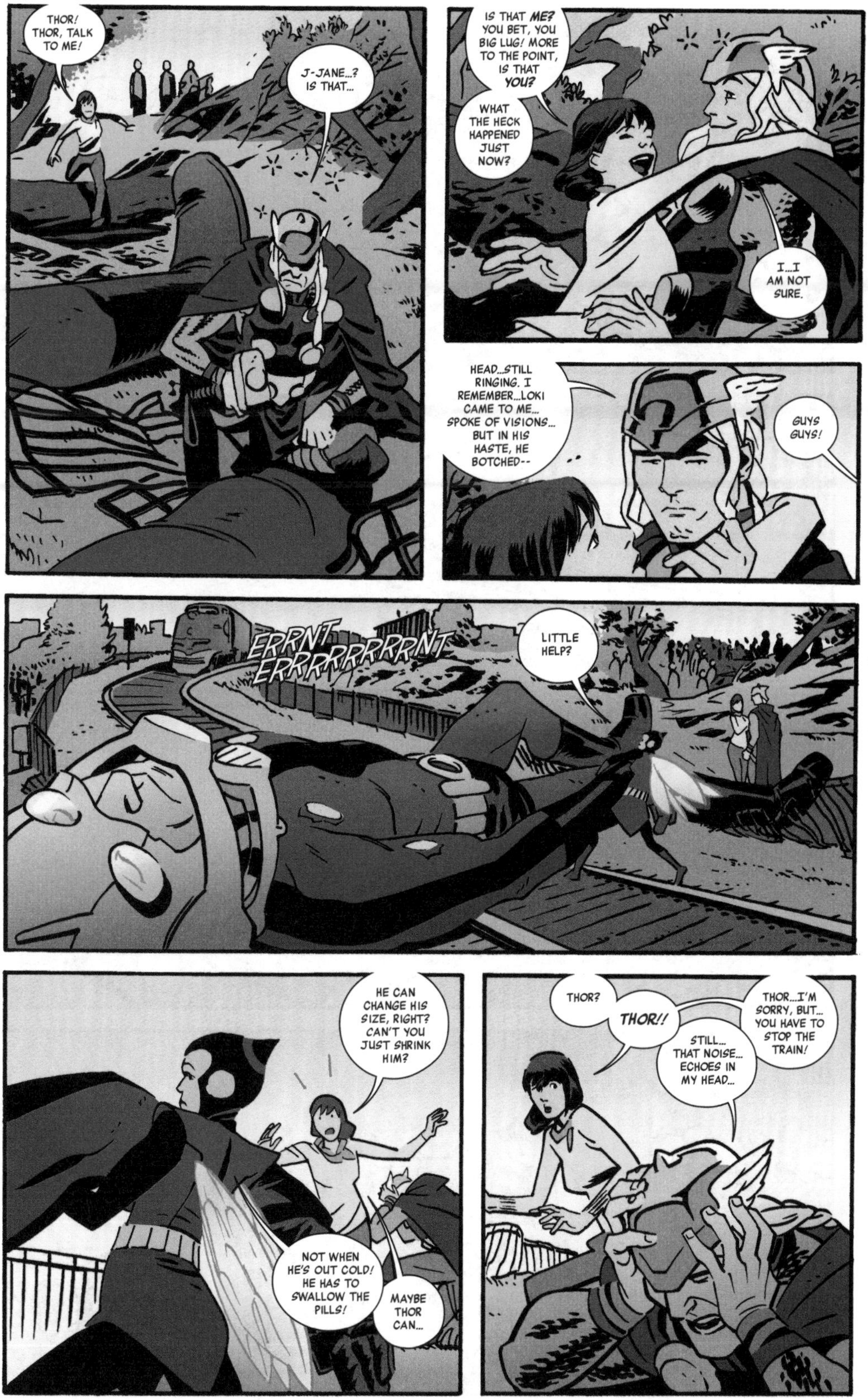
THOR! THOR, TALK TO ME!
J-JANE...? IS THAT...
IS THAT ME? YOU BET, YOU BIG LUG! MORE TO THE POINT, IS THAT YOU?
WHAT THE HECK HAPPENED JUST NOW?
I...I AM NOT SURE.
HEAD...STILL RINGING. I REMEMBER...LOKI CAME TO ME... SPOKE OF VISIONS... BUT IN HIS HASTE, HE BOTCHED--
GUYS GUYS!
ERRNT ERRRRRRRRNT
LITTLE HELP?
HE CAN CHANGE HIS SIZE, RIGHT? CAN'T YOU JUST SHRINK HIM?
NOT WHEN HE'S OUT COLD! HE HAS TO SWALLOW THE PILLS!
MAYBE THOR CAN...
THOR?
THOR!!
THOR...I'M SORRY, BUT... YOU HAVE TO STOP THE TRAIN!
STILL... THAT NOISE... ECHOES IN MY HEAD...

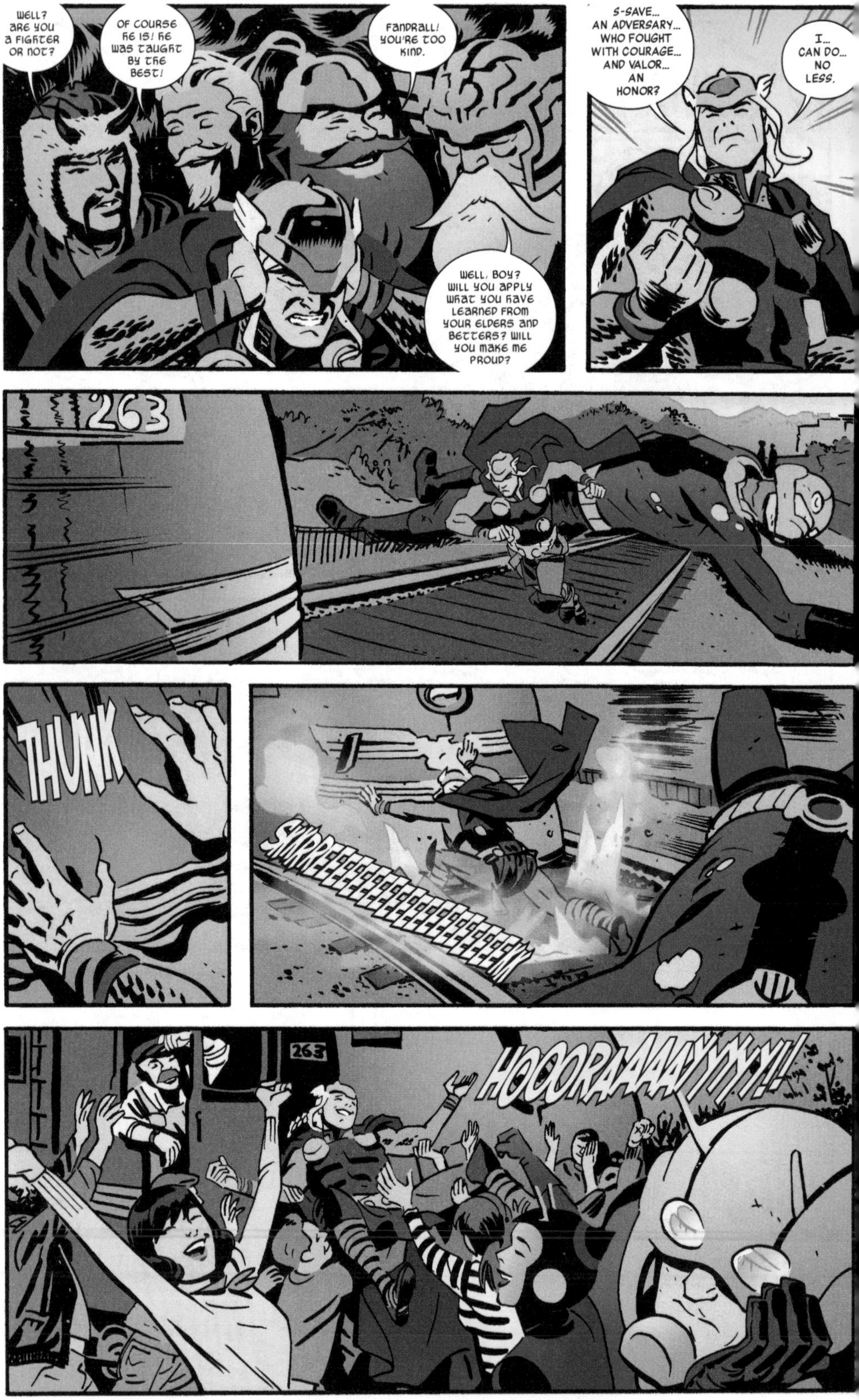

WELL? ARE YOU A FIGHTER OR NOT?
OF COURSE HE IS! HE WAS TAUGHT BY THE BEST!
FANDRALL! YOU'RE TOO KIND.
WELL, BOY? WILL YOU APPLY WHAT YOU HAVE LEARNED FROM YOUR ELDERS AND BETTERS? WILL YOU MAKE ME PROUD?
S-SAVE... AN ADVERSARY... WHO FOUGHT WITH COURAGE... AND VALOR... AN HONOR?
I... CAN DO... NO LESS.
263
THUNK
SKREEEEEEEEEEEEEEEEEEEEEEEK
263
HOOORAAAAYYYY!!

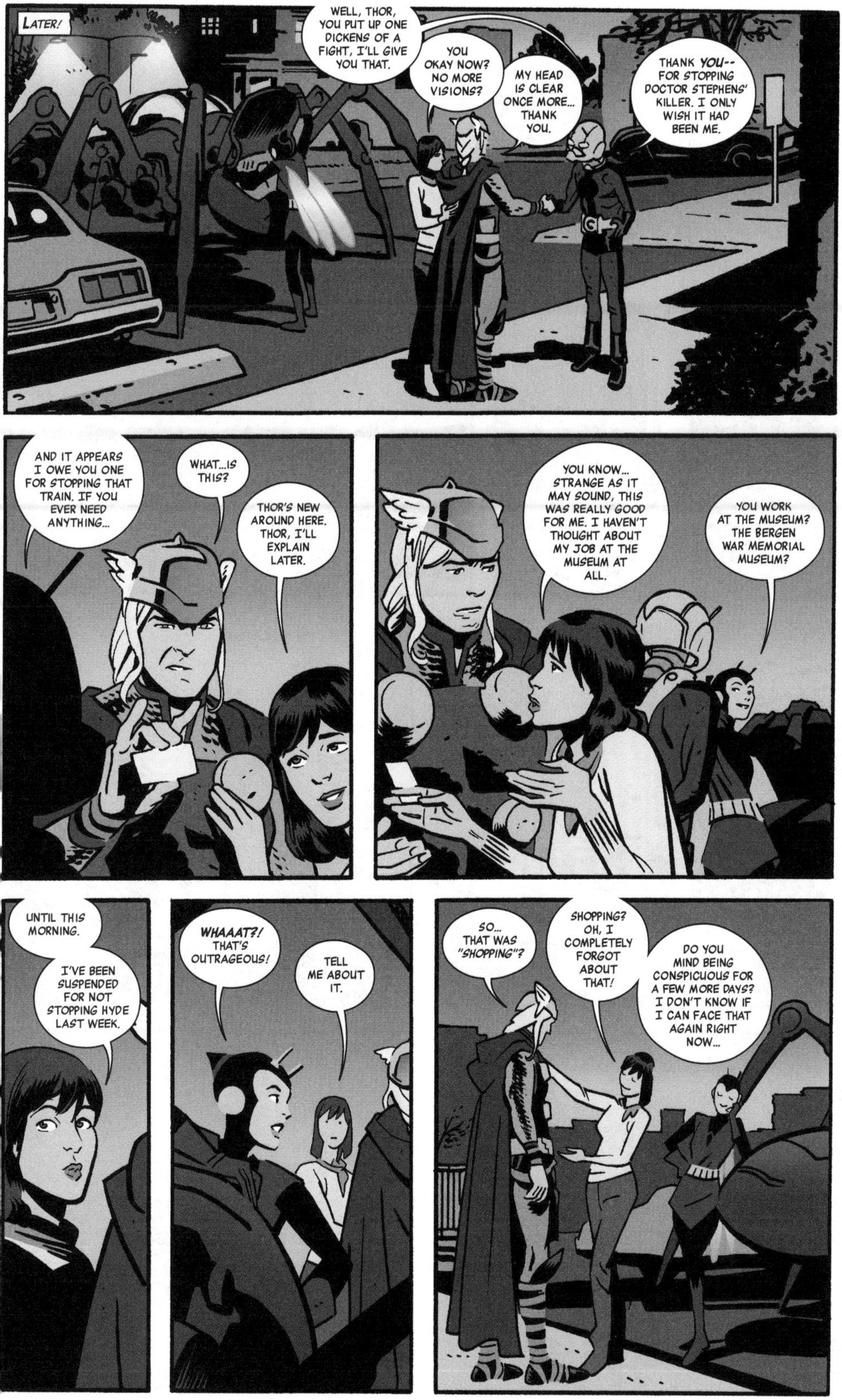

LATER!
WELL, THOR, YOU PUT UP ONE DICKENS OF A FIGHT, I'LL GIVE YOU THAT.
YOU OKAY NOW? NO MORE VISIONS?
MY HEAD IS CLEAR ONCE MORE... THANK YOU.
THANK YOU-- FOR STOPPING DOCTOR STEPHENS' KILLER. I ONLY WISH IT HAD BEEN ME.
AND IT APPEARS I OWE YOU ONE FOR STOPPING THAT TRAIN. IF YOU EVER NEED ANYTHING...
WHAT...IS THIS?
THOR'S NEW AROUND HERE. THOR, I'LL EXPLAIN LATER.
YOU KNOW... STRANGE AS IT MAY SOUND, THIS WAS REALLY GOOD FOR ME. I HAVEN'T THOUGHT ABOUT MY JOB AT THE MUSEUM AT ALL.
YOU WORK AT THE MUSEUM? THE BERGEN WAR MEMORIAL MUSEUM?
UNTIL THIS MORNING.
I'VE BEEN SUSPENDED FOR NOT STOPPING HYDE LAST WEEK.
WHAAAT?! THAT'S OUTRAGEOUS!
TELL ME ABOUT IT.
SO... THAT WAS "SHOPPING"?
SHOPPING? OH, I COMPLETELY FORGOT ABOUT THAT!
DO YOU MIND BEING CONSPICUOUS FOR A FEW MORE DAYS? I DON'T KNOW IF I CAN FACE THAT AGAIN RIGHT NOW...

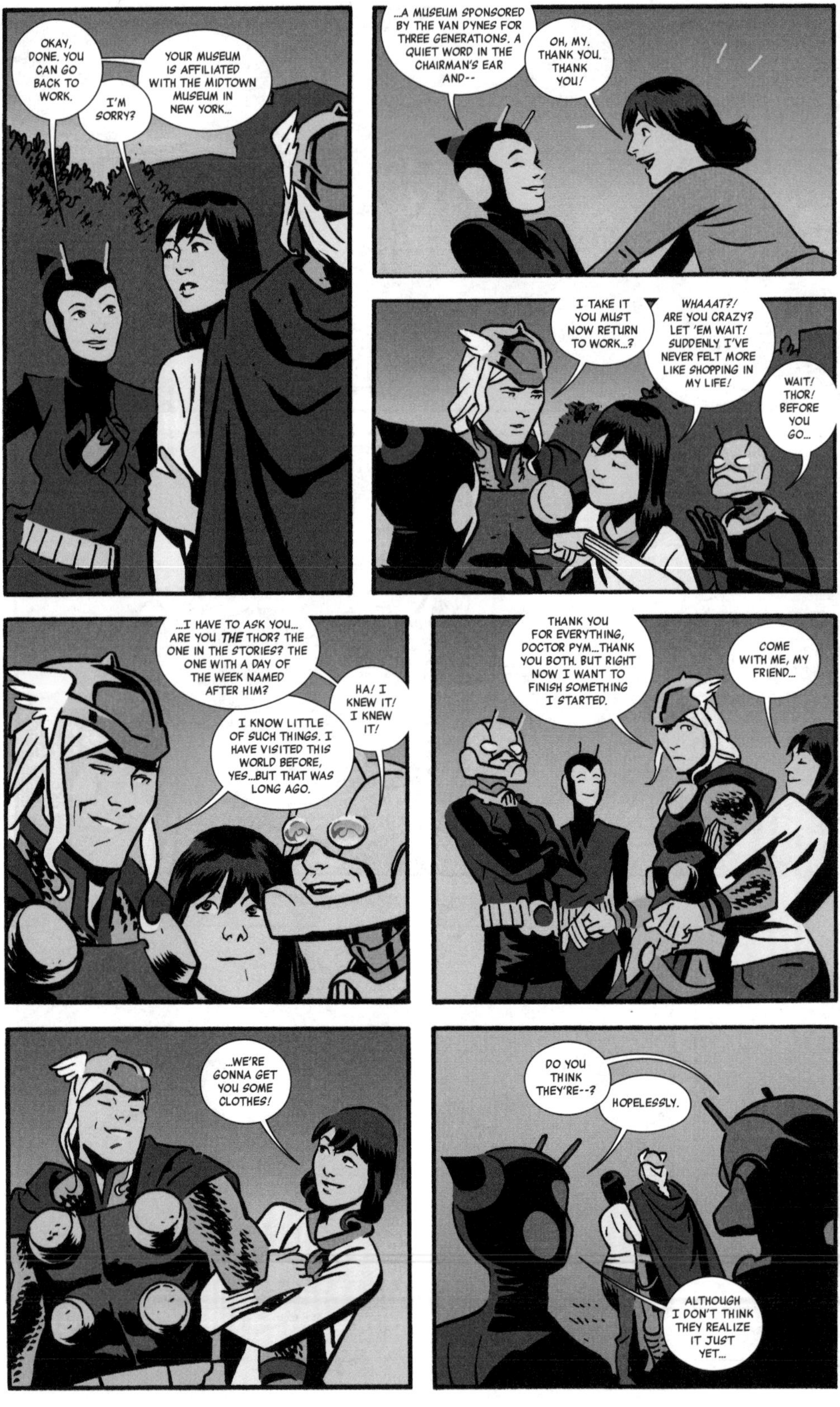
OKAY, DONE. YOU CAN GO BACK TO WORK.
YOUR MUSEUM IS AFFILIATED WITH THE MIDTOWN MUSEUM IN NEW YORK...
I'M SORRY?
...A MUSEUM SPONSORED BY THE VAN DYNES FOR THREE GENERATIONS. A QUIET WORD IN THE CHAIRMAN'S EAR AND--
OH, MY. THANK YOU. THANK YOU!
I TAKE IT YOU MUST NOW RETURN TO WORK...?
WHAAAT?! ARE YOU CRAZY? LET 'EM WAIT! SUDDENLY I'VE NEVER FELT MORE LIKE SHOPPING IN MY LIFE!
WAIT! THOR! BEFORE YOU GO...
...I HAVE TO ASK YOU... ARE YOU THE THOR? THE ONE IN THE STORIES? THE ONE WITH A DAY OF THE WEEK NAMED AFTER HIM?
I KNOW LITTLE OF SUCH THINGS. I HAVE VISITED THIS WORLD BEFORE, YES...BUT THAT WAS LONG AGO.
HA! I KNEW IT! I KNEW IT!
THANK YOU FOR EVERYTHING, DOCTOR PYM...THANK YOU BOTH. BUT RIGHT NOW I WANT TO FINISH SOMETHING I STARTED.
COME WITH ME, MY FRIEND...
...WE'RE GONNA GET YOU SOME CLOTHES!
DO YOU THINK THEY'RE--?
HOPELESSLY.
ALTHOUGH I DON'T THINK THEY REALIZE IT JUST YET...

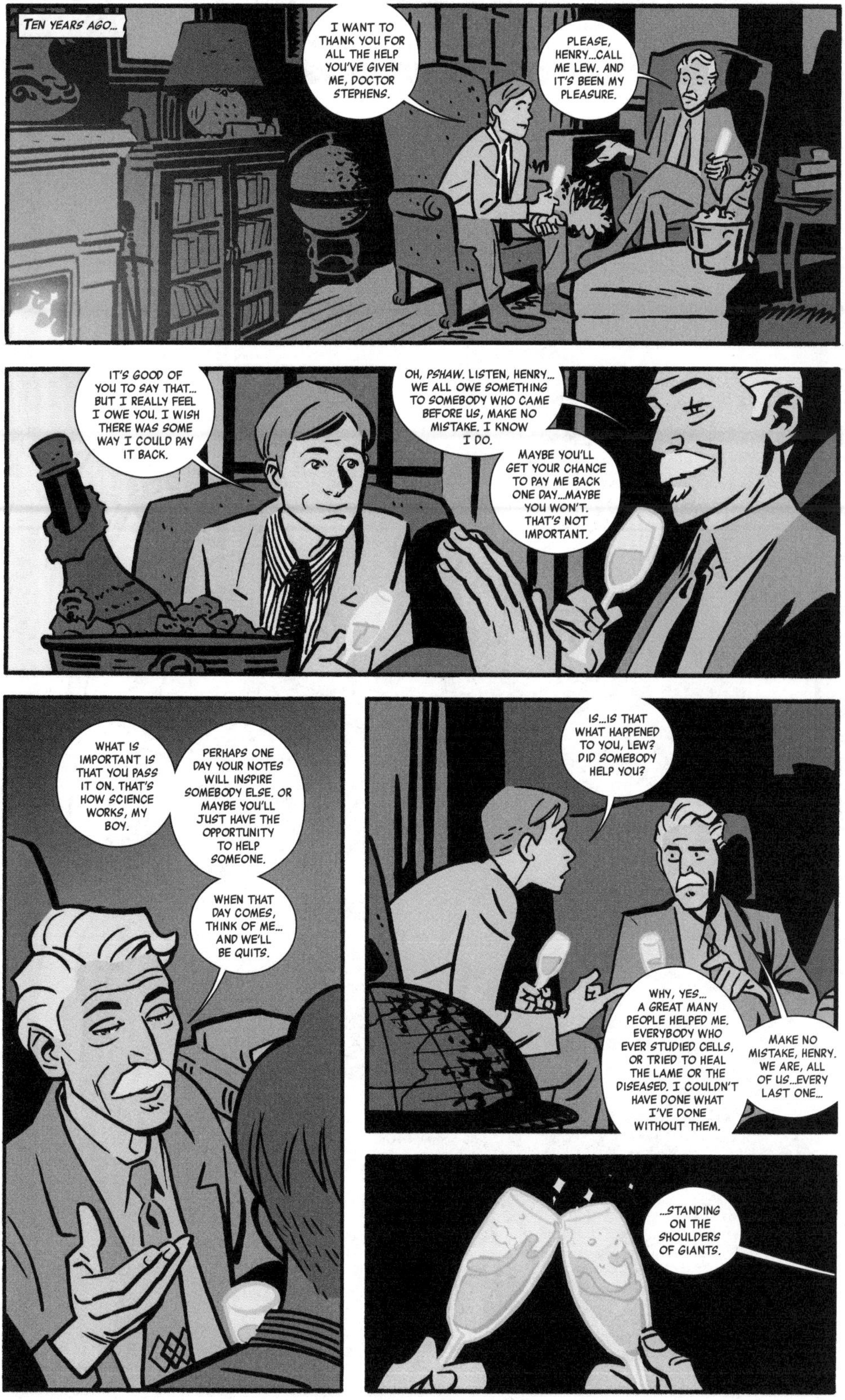

TEN YEARS AGO...
I WANT TO THANK YOU FOR ALL THE HELP YOU'VE GIVEN ME, DOCTOR STEPHENS.
PLEASE, HENRY...CALL ME LEW. AND IT'S BEEN MY PLEASURE.
IT'S GOOD OF YOU TO SAY THAT... BUT I REALLY FEEL I OWE YOU. I WISH THERE WAS SOME WAY I COULD PAY IT BACK.
OH, PSHAW. LISTEN, HENRY... WE ALL OWE SOMETHING TO SOMEBODY WHO CAME BEFORE US, MAKE NO MISTAKE. I KNOW I DO.
MAYBE YOU'LL GET YOUR CHANCE TO PAY ME BACK ONE DAY...MAYBE YOU WON'T. THAT'S NOT IMPORTANT.
WHAT IS IMPORTANT IS THAT YOU PASS IT ON. THAT'S HOW SCIENCE WORKS, MY BOY.
PERHAPS ONE DAY YOUR NOTES WILL INSPIRE SOMEBODY ELSE. OR MAYBE YOU'LL JUST HAVE THE OPPORTUNITY TO HELP SOMEONE.
WHEN THAT DAY COMES, THINK OF ME... AND WE'LL BE QUITS.
IS...IS THAT WHAT HAPPENED TO YOU, LEW? DID SOMEBODY HELP YOU?
WHY, YES... A GREAT MANY PEOPLE HELPED ME. EVERYBODY WHO EVER STUDIED CELLS, OR TRIED TO HEAL THE LAME OR THE DISEASED. I COULDN'T HAVE DONE WHAT I'VE DONE WITHOUT THEM.
MAKE NO MISTAKE, HENRY. WE ARE, ALL OF US...EVERY LAST ONE...
...STANDING ON THE SHOULDERS OF GIANTS.

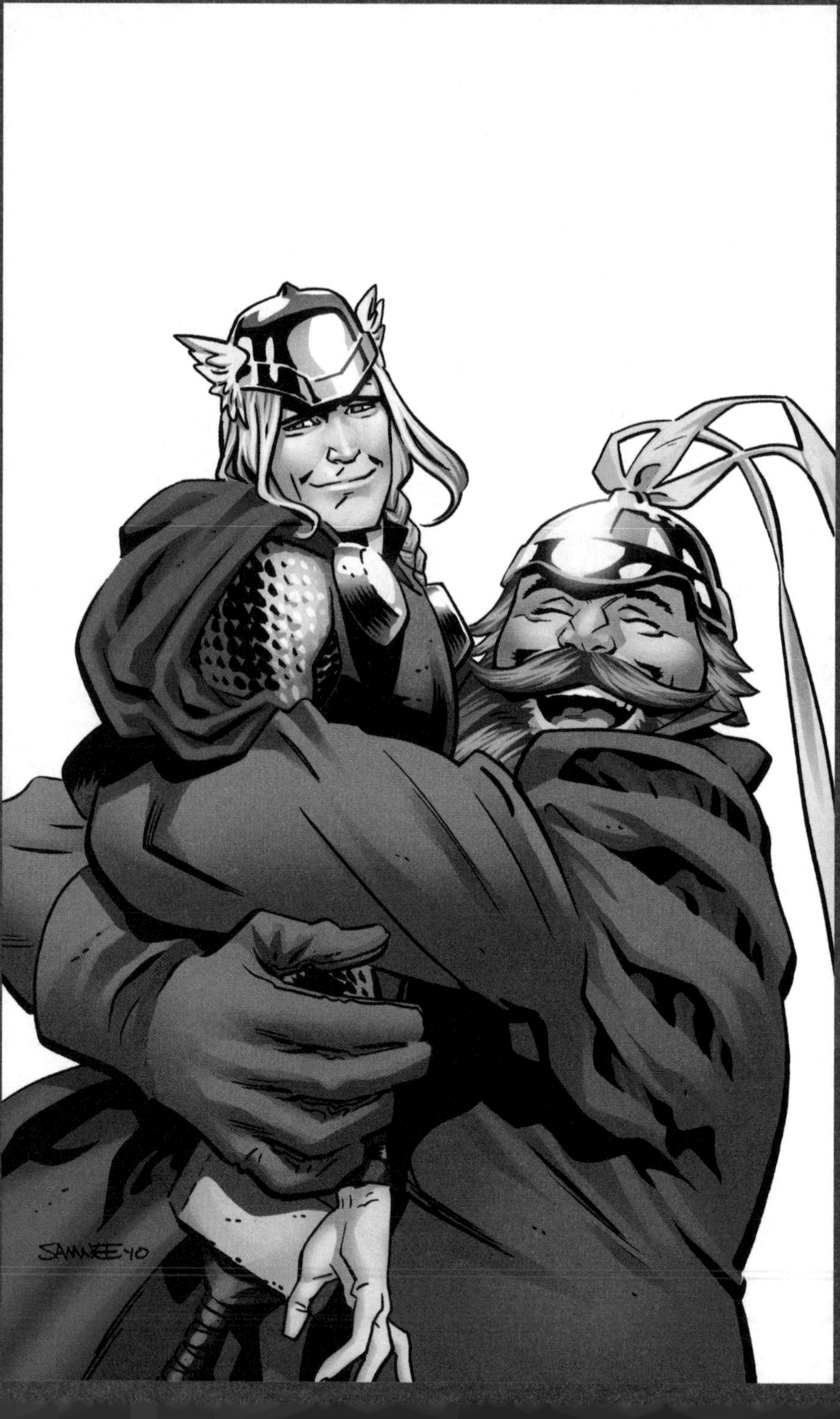
SAMNEE '10

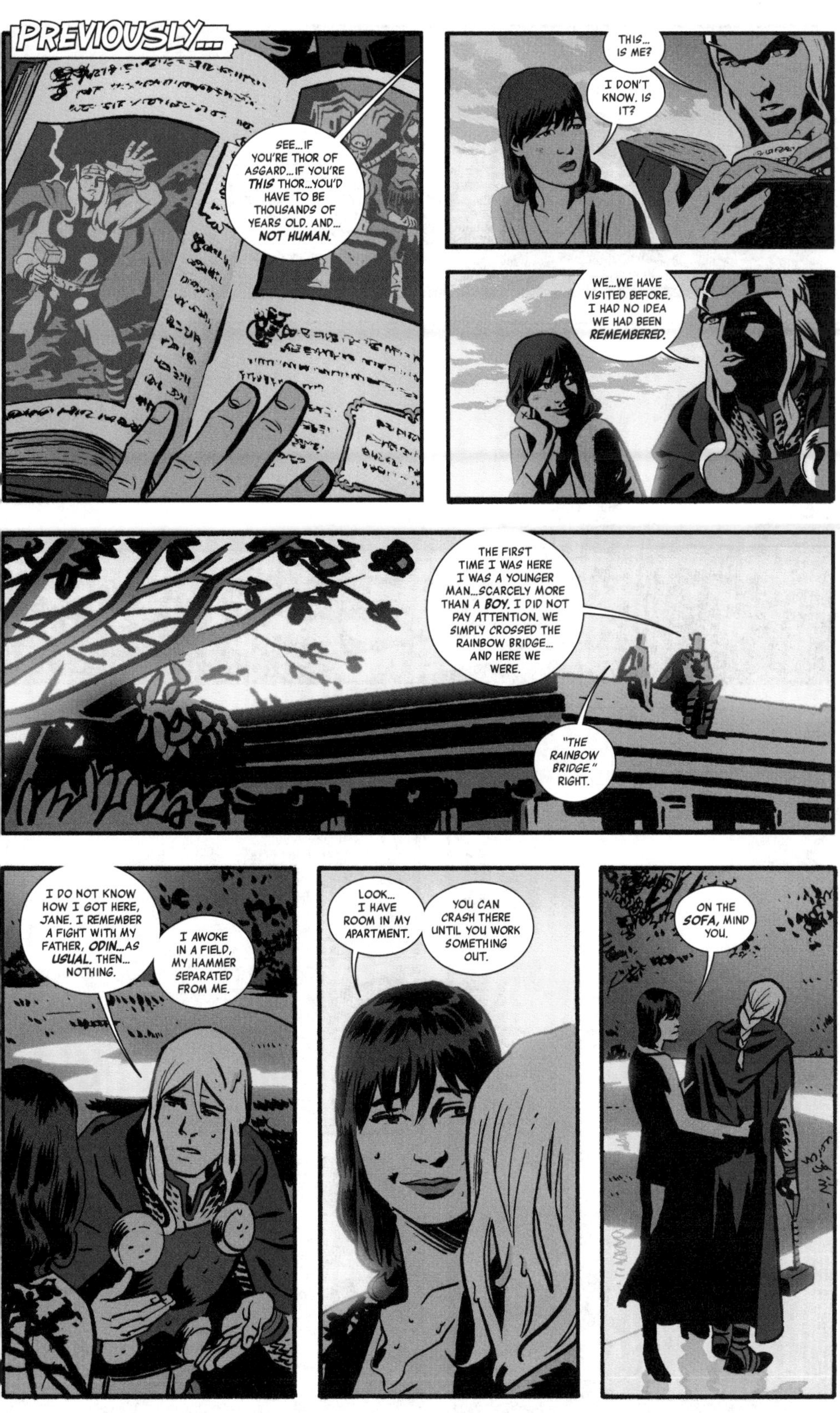
PREVIOUSLY...
SEE...IF YOU'RE THOR OF ASGARD...IF YOU'RE THIS THOR...YOU'D HAVE TO BE THOUSANDS OF YEARS OLD. AND... NOT HUMAN.
THIS... IS ME?
I DON'T KNOW. IS IT?
WE...WE HAVE VISITED BEFORE. I HAD NO IDEA WE HAD BEEN REMEMBERED.
THE FIRST TIME I WAS HERE I WAS A YOUNGER MAN...SCARCELY MORE THAN A BOY. I DID NOT PAY ATTENTION. WE SIMPLY CROSSED THE RAINBOW BRIDGE... AND HERE WE WERE.
"THE RAINBOW BRIDGE." RIGHT.
I DO NOT KNOW HOW I GOT HERE, JANE. I REMEMBER A FIGHT WITH MY FATHER, ODIN...AS USUAL. THEN... NOTHING.
I AWOKE IN A FIELD, MY HAMMER SEPARATED FROM ME.
LOOK... I HAVE ROOM IN MY APARTMENT.
YOU CAN CRASH THERE UNTIL YOU WORK SOMETHING OUT.
ON THE SOFA, MIND YOU.

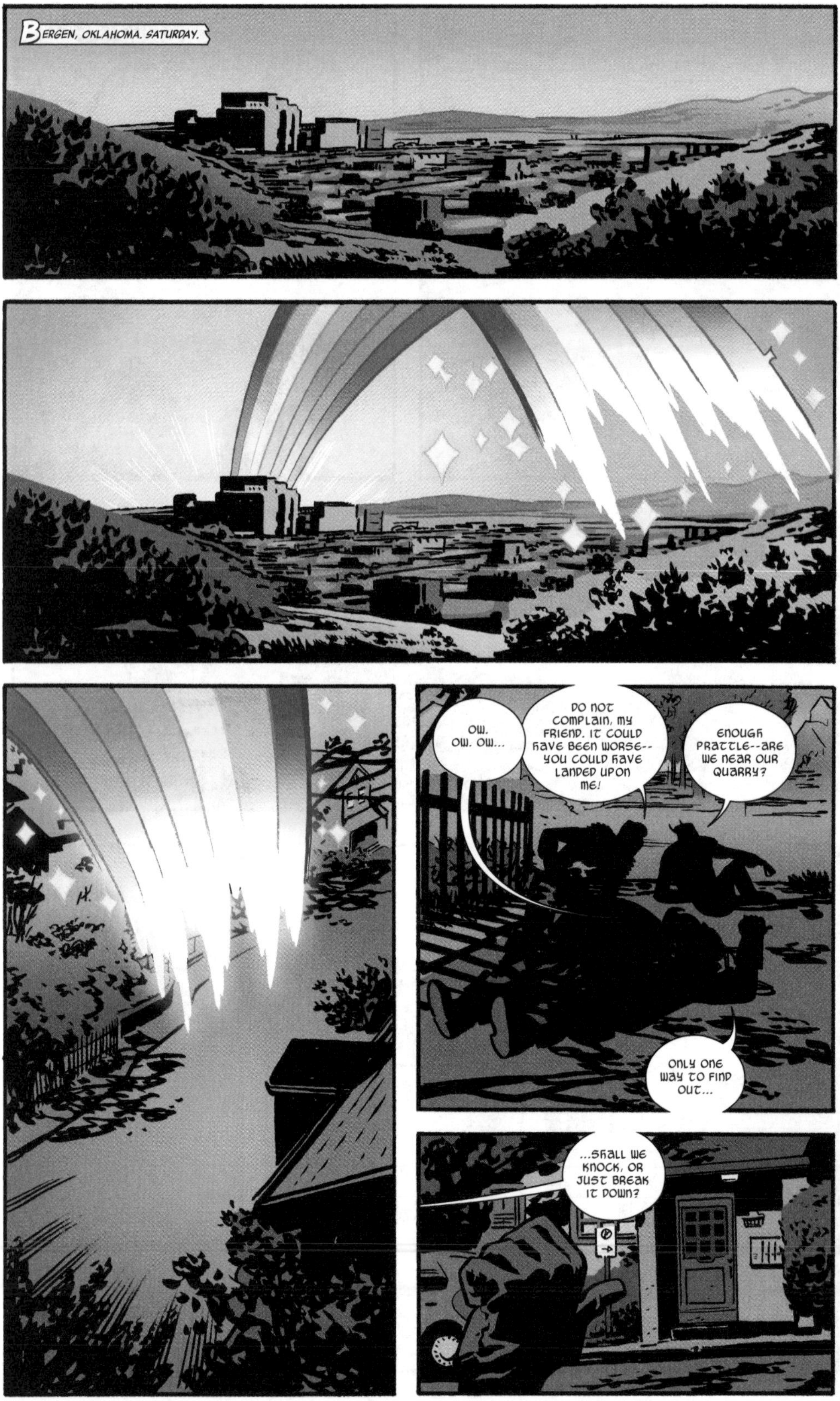
BERGEN, OKLAHOMA. SATURDAY.
OW. OW. OW...
DO NOT COMPLAIN, MY FRIEND. IT COULD HAVE BEEN WORSE-- YOU COULD HAVE LANDED UPON ME!
ENOUGH PRATTLE--ARE WE NEAR OUR QUARRY?
ONLY ONE WAY TO FIND OUT...
...SHALL WE KNOCK, OR JUST BREAK IT DOWN?

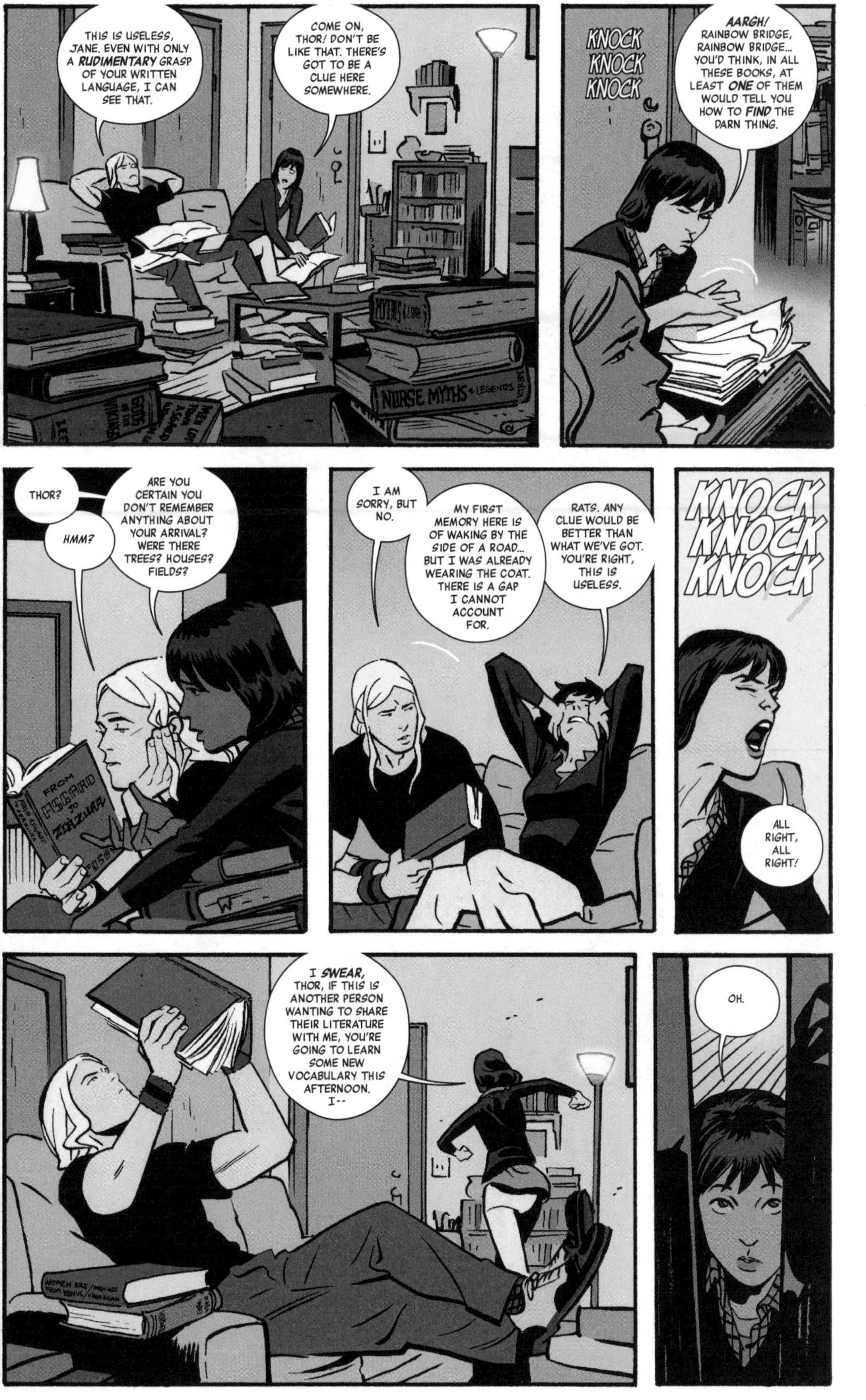

THIS IS USELESS, JANE. EVEN WITH ONLY A **RUDIMENTARY** GRASP OF YOUR WRITTEN LANGUAGE, I CAN SEE THAT.
COME ON, THOR! DON'T BE LIKE THAT. THERE'S GOT TO BE A CLUE HERE SOMEWHERE.
MYTHS & LORE
NORSE MYTHS & LEGENDS
GODS OF THE VIKINGS
KNOCK KNOCK KNOCK
AARGH! RAINBOW BRIDGE, RAINBOW BRIDGE... YOU'D THINK, IN ALL THESE BOOKS, AT LEAST ***ONE*** OF THEM WOULD TELL YOU HOW TO ***FIND*** THE DARN THING.
THOR?
HMM?
ARE YOU CERTAIN YOU DON'T REMEMBER ANYTHING ABOUT YOUR ARRIVAL? WERE THERE TREES? HOUSES? FIELDS?
FROM ASGARD TO ZARZURA
I AM SORRY, BUT NO.
MY FIRST MEMORY HERE IS OF WAKING BY THE SIDE OF A ROAD... BUT I WAS ALREADY WEARING THE COAT. THERE IS A GAP I CANNOT ACCOUNT FOR.
RATS. ANY CLUE WOULD BE BETTER THAN WHAT WE'VE GOT. YOU'RE RIGHT, THIS IS USELESS.
KNOCK KNOCK KNOCK
ALL RIGHT, ALL RIGHT!
I ***SWEAR,*** THOR, IF THIS IS ANOTHER PERSON WANTING TO SHARE THEIR LITERATURE WITH ME, YOU'RE GOING TO LEARN SOME NEW VOCABULARY THIS AFTERNOON. I--
OH.

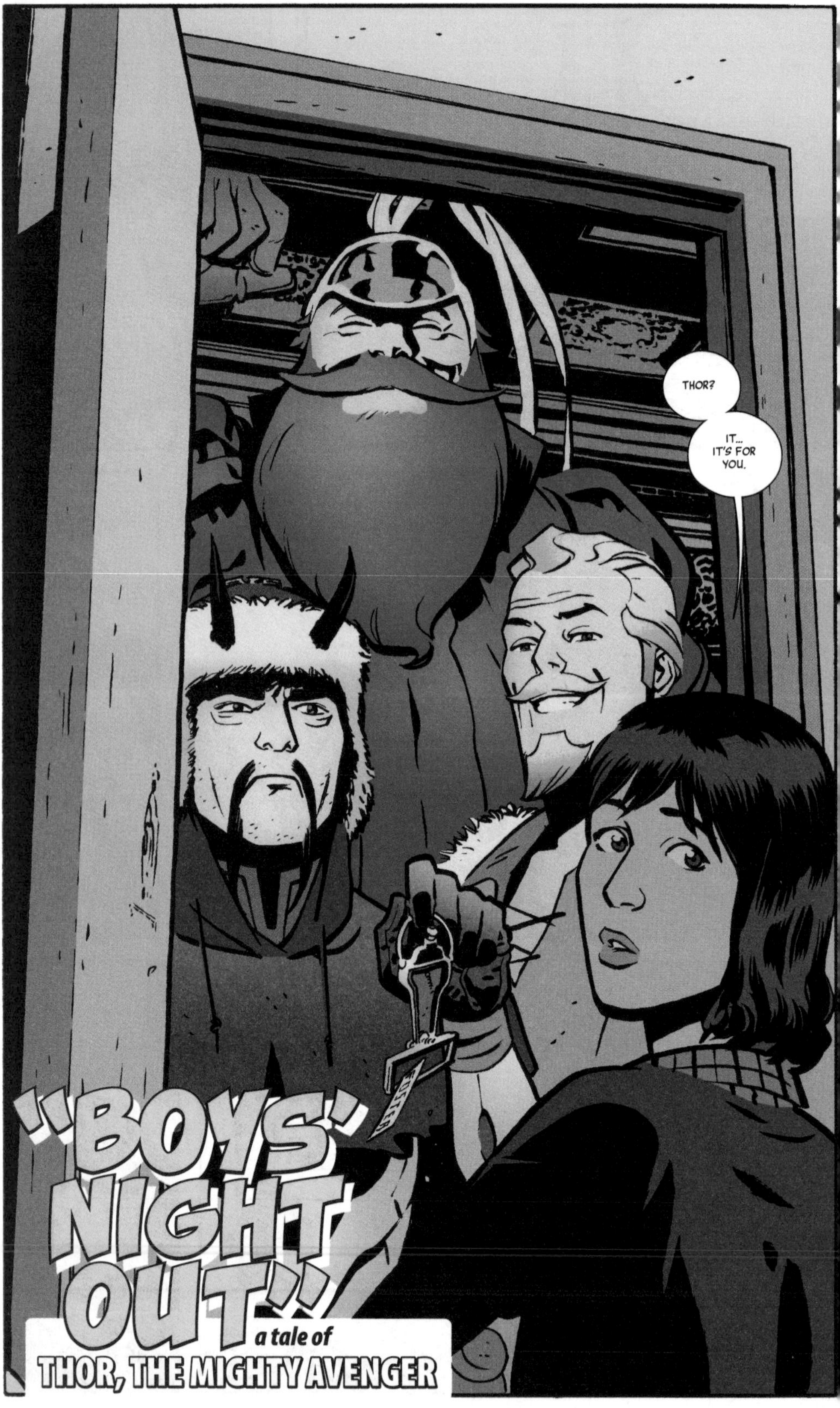
THOR?
IT... IT'S FOR YOU.
"BOYS" NIGHT OUT"
a tale of
THOR, THE MIGHTY AVENGER

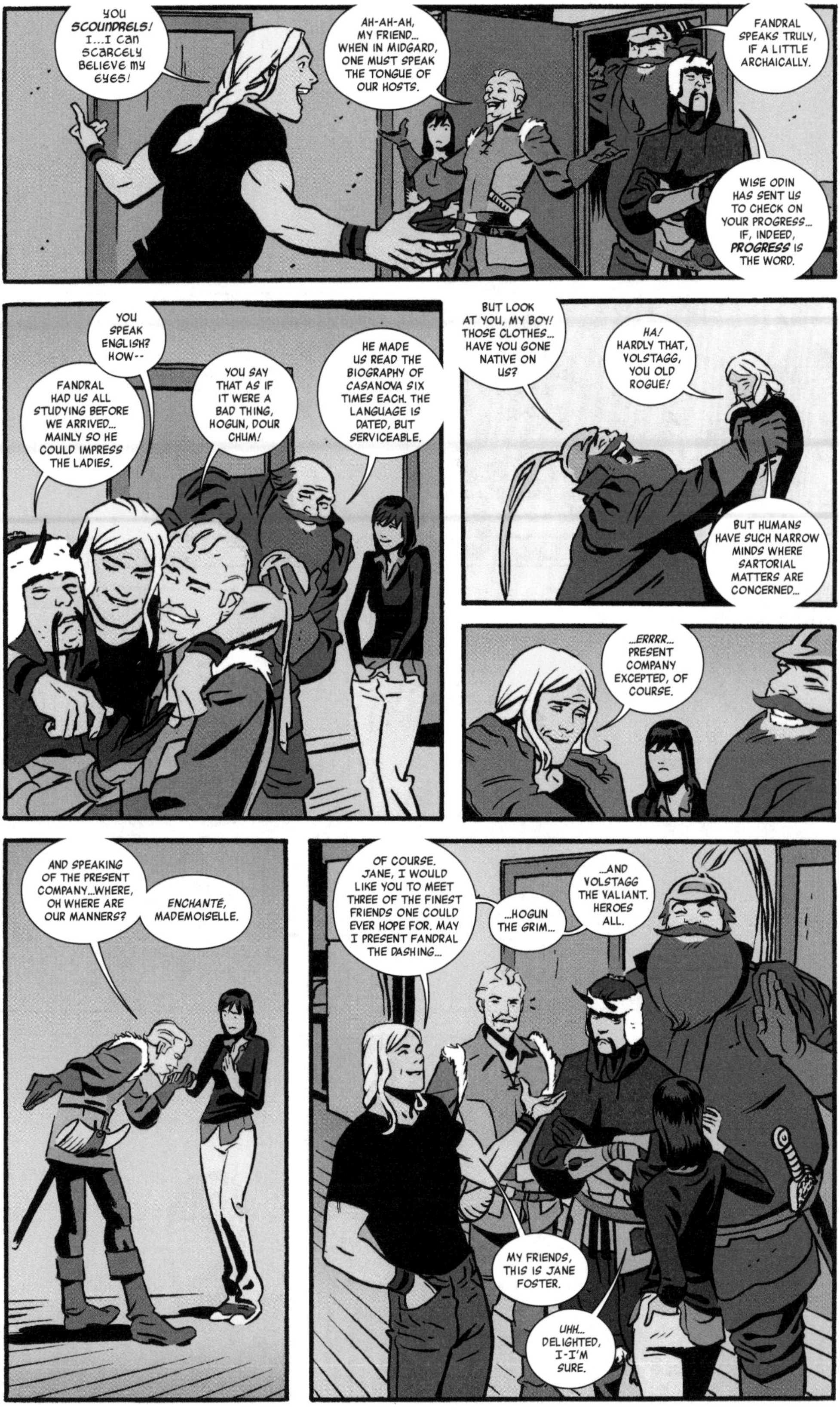
YOU SCOUNDRELS! I...I CAN SCARCELY BELIEVE MY EYES!
AH-AH-AH, MY FRIEND... WHEN IN MIDGARD, ONE MUST SPEAK THE TONGUE OF OUR HOSTS.
FANDRAL SPEAKS TRULY, IF A LITTLE ARCHAICALLY.
WISE ODIN HAS SENT US TO CHECK ON YOUR PROGRESS... IF, INDEED, PROGRESS IS THE WORD.
YOU SPEAK ENGLISH? HOW--
FANDRAL HAD US ALL STUDYING BEFORE WE ARRIVED... MAINLY SO HE COULD IMPRESS THE LADIES.
YOU SAY THAT AS IF IT WERE A BAD THING, HOGUN, DOUR CHUM!
HE MADE US READ THE BIOGRAPHY OF CASANOVA SIX TIMES EACH. THE LANGUAGE IS DATED, BUT SERVICEABLE.
BUT LOOK AT YOU, MY BOY! THOSE CLOTHES... HAVE YOU GONE NATIVE ON US?
HA! HARDLY THAT, VOLSTAGG, YOU OLD ROGUE!
BUT HUMANS HAVE SUCH NARROW MINDS WHERE SARTORIAL MATTERS ARE CONCERNED...
...ERRRR... PRESENT COMPANY EXCEPTED, OF COURSE.
AND SPEAKING OF THE PRESENT COMPANY...WHERE, OH WHERE ARE OUR MANNERS?
ENCHANTÉ, MADEMOISELLE.
OF COURSE. JANE, I WOULD LIKE YOU TO MEET THREE OF THE FINEST FRIENDS ONE COULD EVER HOPE FOR. MAY I PRESENT FANDRAL THE DASHING...
...HOGUN THE GRIM...
...AND VOLSTAGG THE VALIANT. HEROES ALL.
MY FRIENDS, THIS IS JANE FOSTER.
UHH... DELIGHTED, I-I'M SURE.

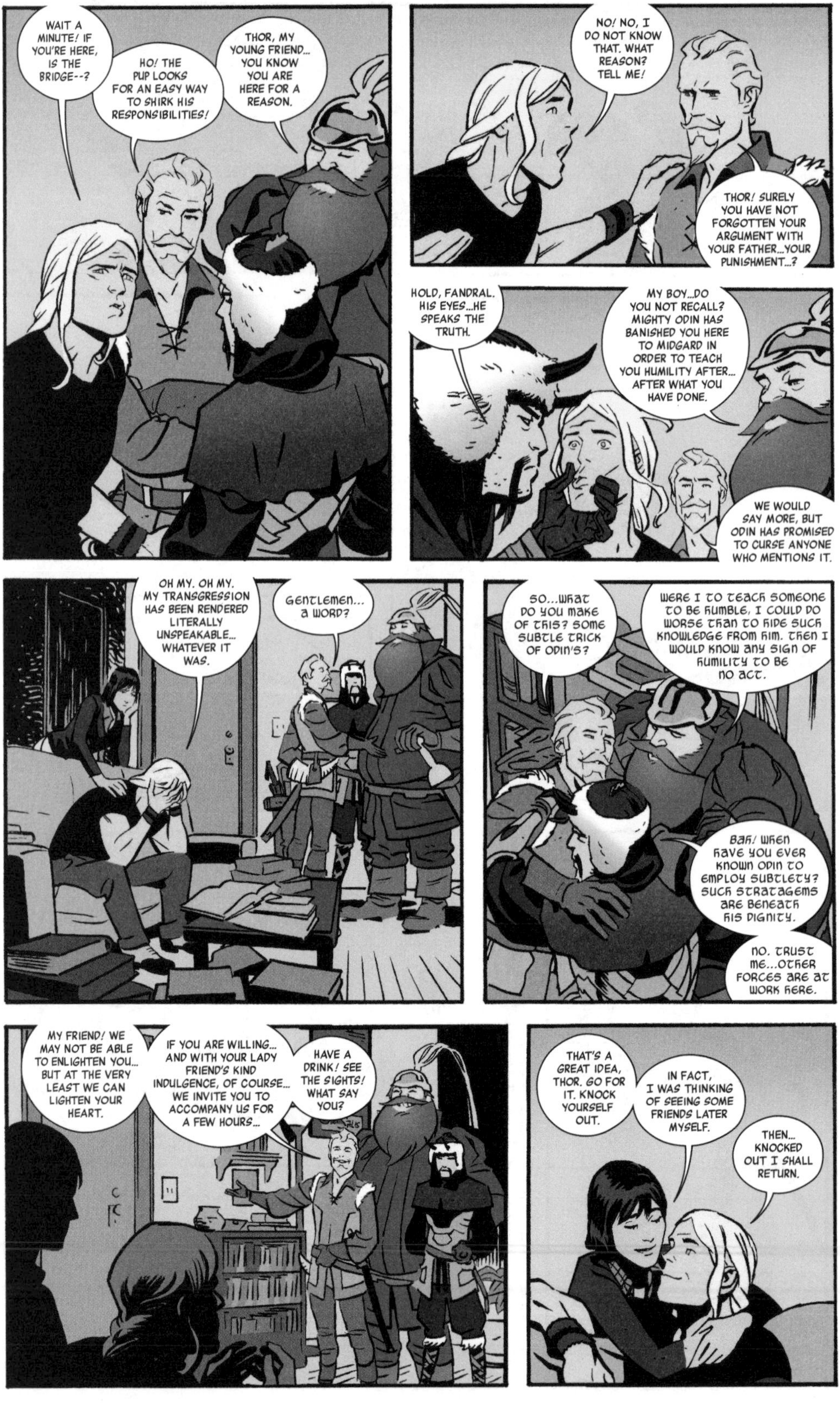
WAIT A MINUTE! IF YOU'RE HERE, IS THE BRIDGE--?
HO! THE PUP LOOKS FOR AN EASY WAY TO SHIRK HIS RESPONSIBILITIES!
THOR, MY YOUNG FRIEND... YOU KNOW YOU ARE HERE FOR A REASON.
NO! NO, I DO NOT KNOW THAT. WHAT REASON? TELL ME!
THOR! SURELY YOU HAVE NOT FORGOTTEN YOUR ARGUMENT WITH YOUR FATHER...YOUR PUNISHMENT...?
HOLD, FANDRAL. HIS EYES...HE SPEAKS THE TRUTH.
MY BOY...DO YOU NOT RECALL? MIGHTY ODIN HAS BANISHED YOU HERE TO MIDGARD IN ORDER TO TEACH YOU HUMILITY AFTER... AFTER WHAT YOU HAVE DONE.
WE WOULD SAY MORE, BUT ODIN HAS PROMISED TO CURSE ANYONE WHO MENTIONS IT.
OH MY. OH MY. MY TRANSGRESSION HAS BEEN RENDERED LITERALLY UNSPEAKABLE... WHATEVER IT WAS.
GENTLEMEN... A WORD?
SO...WHAT DO YOU MAKE OF THIS? SOME SUBTLE TRICK OF ODIN'S?
WERE I TO TEACH SOMEONE TO BE HUMBLE, I COULD DO WORSE THAN TO HIDE SUCH KNOWLEDGE FROM HIM. THEN I WOULD KNOW ANY SIGN OF HUMILITY TO BE NO ACT.
BAH! WHEN HAVE YOU EVER KNOWN ODIN TO EMPLOY SUBTLETY? SUCH STRATAGEMS ARE BENEATH HIS DIGNITY.
NO. TRUST ME...OTHER FORCES ARE AT WORK HERE.
MY FRIEND! WE MAY NOT BE ABLE TO ENLIGHTEN YOU... BUT AT THE VERY LEAST WE CAN LIGHTEN YOUR HEART.
IF YOU ARE WILLING... AND WITH YOUR LADY FRIEND'S KIND INDULGENCE, OF COURSE... WE INVITE YOU TO ACCOMPANY US FOR A FEW HOURS...
HAVE A DRINK! SEE THE SIGHTS! WHAT SAY YOU?
THAT'S A GREAT IDEA, THOR. GO FOR IT. KNOCK YOURSELF OUT.
IN FACT, I WAS THINKING OF SEEING SOME FRIENDS LATER MYSELF.
THEN... KNOCKED OUT I SHALL RETURN.

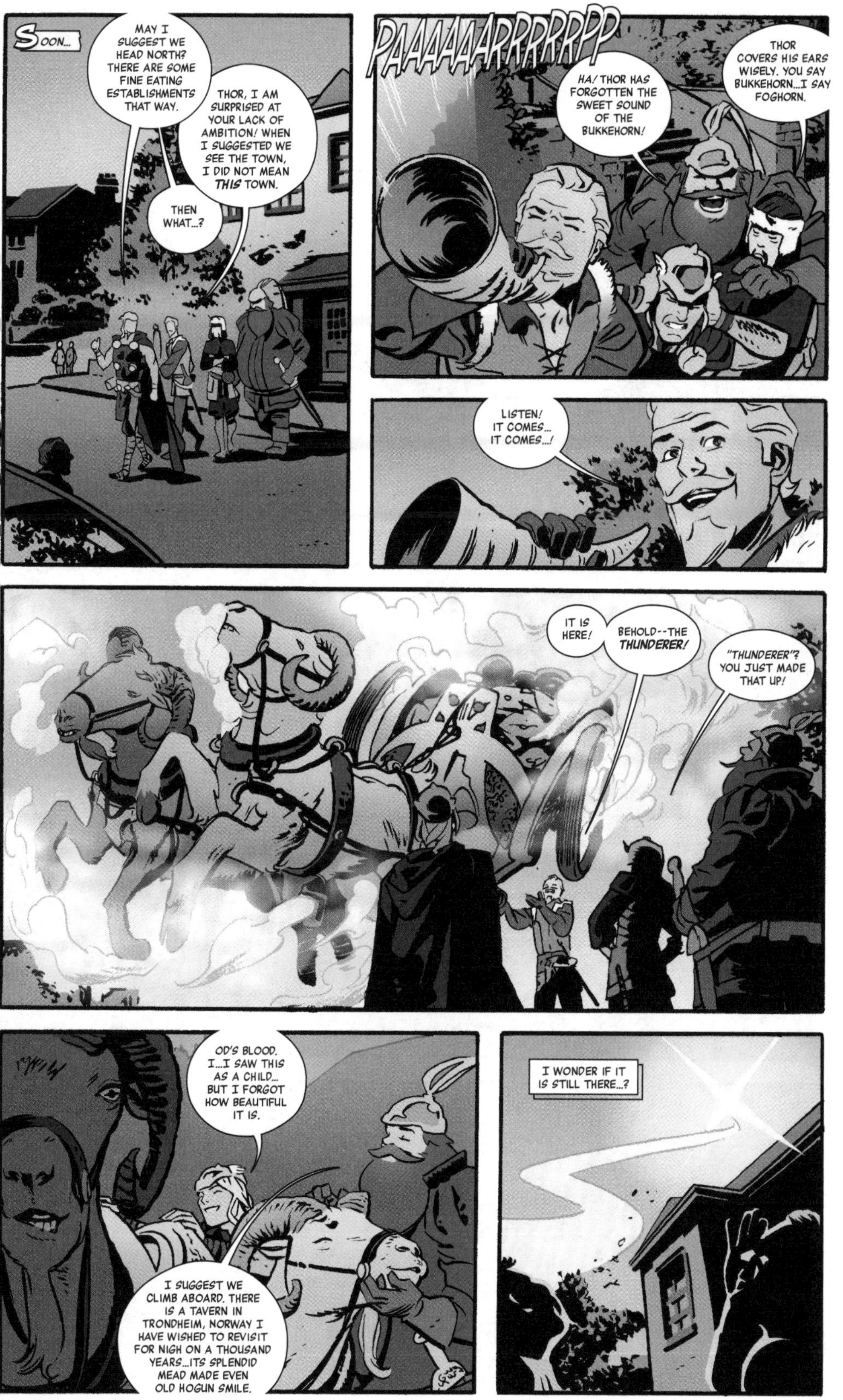
SOON...
MAY I SUGGEST WE HEAD NORTH? THERE ARE SOME FINE EATING ESTABLISHMENTS THAT WAY.
THOR, I AM SURPRISED AT YOUR LACK OF AMBITION! WHEN I SUGGESTED WE SEE THE TOWN, I DID NOT MEAN THIS TOWN.
THEN WHAT...?
PAAAAAARRRRRPP
HA! THOR HAS FORGOTTEN THE SWEET SOUND OF THE BUKKEHORN!
THOR COVERS HIS EARS WISELY. YOU SAY BUKKEHORN...I SAY FOGHORN.
LISTEN! IT COMES... IT COMES...!
IT IS HERE!
BEHOLD--THE THUNDERER!
"THUNDERER"? YOU JUST MADE THAT UP!
OD'S BLOOD. I...I SAW THIS AS A CHILD... BUT I FORGOT HOW BEAUTIFUL IT IS.
I SUGGEST WE CLIMB ABOARD. THERE IS A TAVERN IN TRONDHEIM, NORWAY I HAVE WISHED TO REVISIT FOR NIGH ON A THOUSAND YEARS...ITS SPLENDID MEAD MADE EVEN OLD HOGUN SMILE.
I WONDER IF IT IS STILL THERE...?

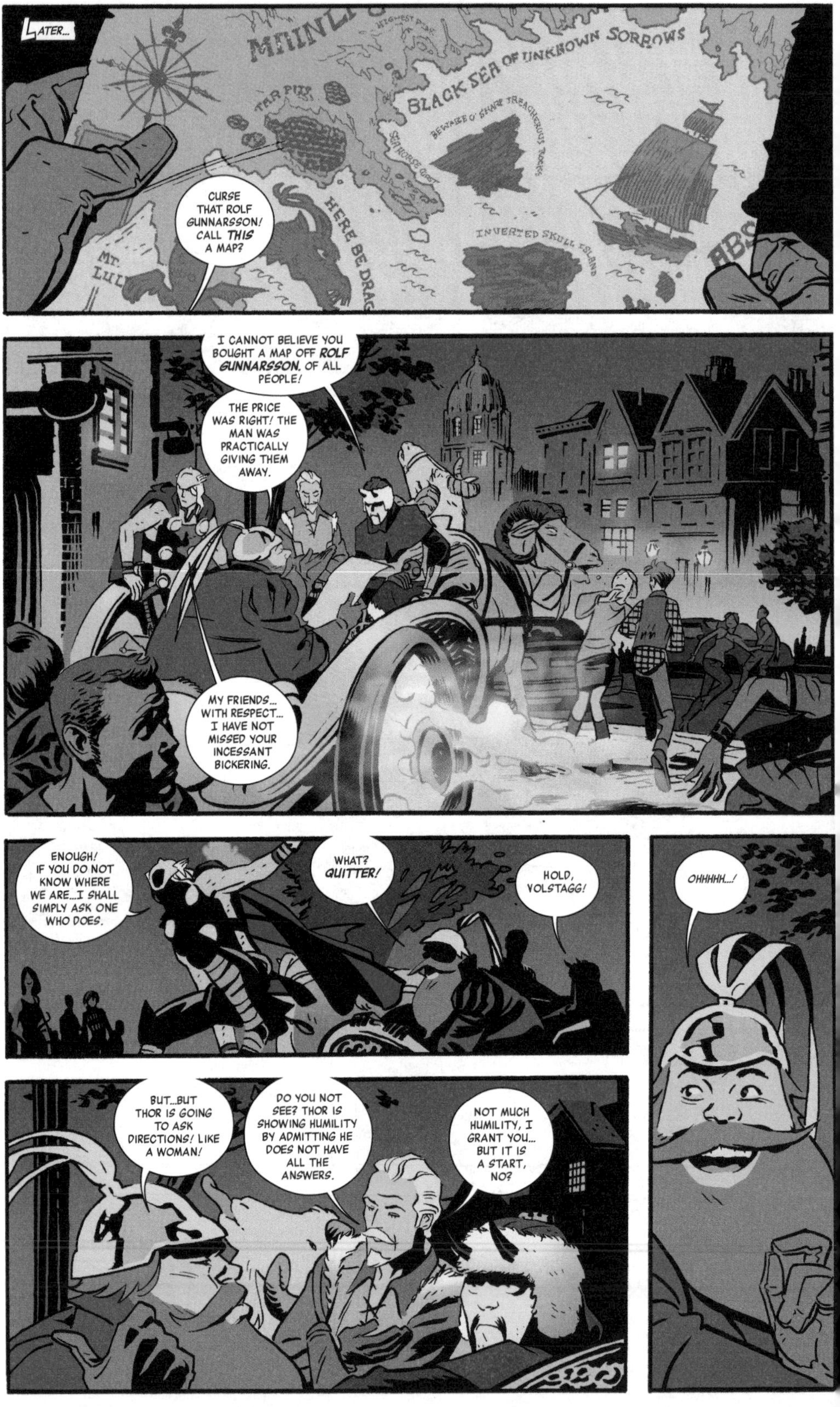
LATER...
HIGHEST PEAK
BLACK SEA OF UNKNOWN SORROWS
TAR PITS
BEWARE O' SHARP TREACHEROUS ROCKS
SEA HORSE COAST
HERE BE DRAG
INVERTED SKULL ISLAND
MT. LUL
CURSE THAT ROLF GUNNARSSON! CALL THIS A MAP?
I CANNOT BELIEVE YOU BOUGHT A MAP OFF ROLF GUNNARSSON, OF ALL PEOPLE!
THE PRICE WAS RIGHT! THE MAN WAS PRACTICALLY GIVING THEM AWAY.
MY FRIENDS... WITH RESPECT... I HAVE NOT MISSED YOUR INCESSANT BICKERING.
ENOUGH! IF YOU DO NOT KNOW WHERE WE ARE...I SHALL SIMPLY ASK ONE WHO DOES.
WHAT? QUITTER!
HOLD, VOLSTAGG!
OHHHHH...!
BUT...BUT THOR IS GOING TO ASK DIRECTIONS! LIKE A WOMAN!
DO YOU NOT SEE? THOR IS SHOWING HUMILITY BY ADMITTING HE DOES NOT HAVE ALL THE ANSWERS.
NOT MUCH HUMILITY, I GRANT YOU... BUT IT IS A START, NO?

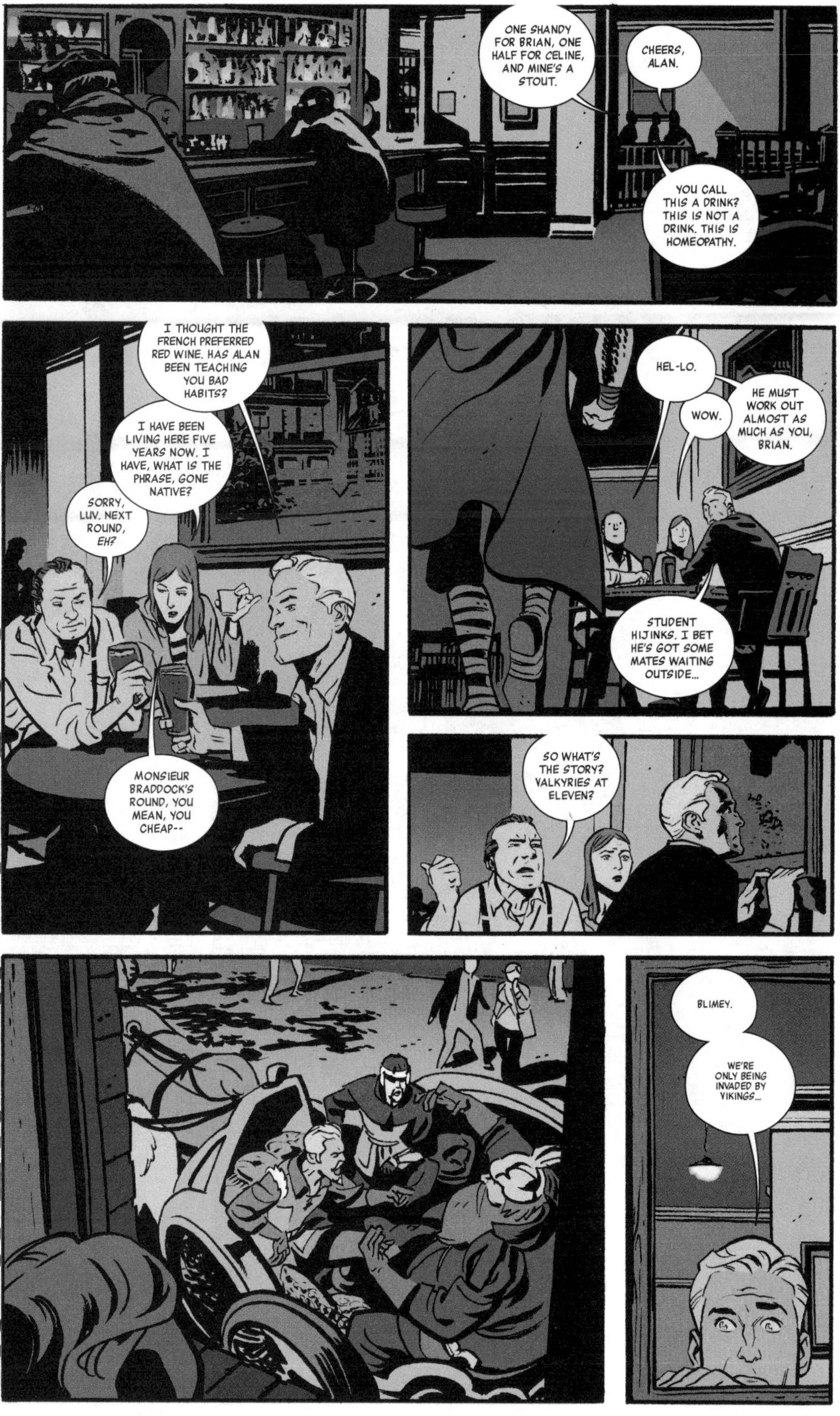
ONE SHANDY FOR BRIAN, ONE HALF FOR CELINE, AND MINE'S A STOUT.
CHEERS, ALAN.
YOU CALL THIS A DRINK? THIS IS NOT A DRINK. THIS IS HOMEOPATHY.
I THOUGHT THE FRENCH PREFERRED RED WINE. HAS ALAN BEEN TEACHING YOU BAD HABITS?
I HAVE BEEN LIVING HERE FIVE YEARS NOW. I HAVE, WHAT IS THE PHRASE, GONE NATIVE?
SORRY, LUV. NEXT ROUND, EH?
MONSIEUR BRADDOCK'S ROUND, YOU MEAN, YOU CHEAP--
HEL-LO.
WOW.
HE MUST WORK OUT ALMOST AS MUCH AS YOU, BRIAN.
STUDENT HIJINKS. I BET HE'S GOT SOME MATES WAITING OUTSIDE...
SO WHAT'S THE STORY? VALKYRIES AT ELEVEN?
BLIMEY.
WE'RE ONLY BEING INVADED BY VIKINGS...

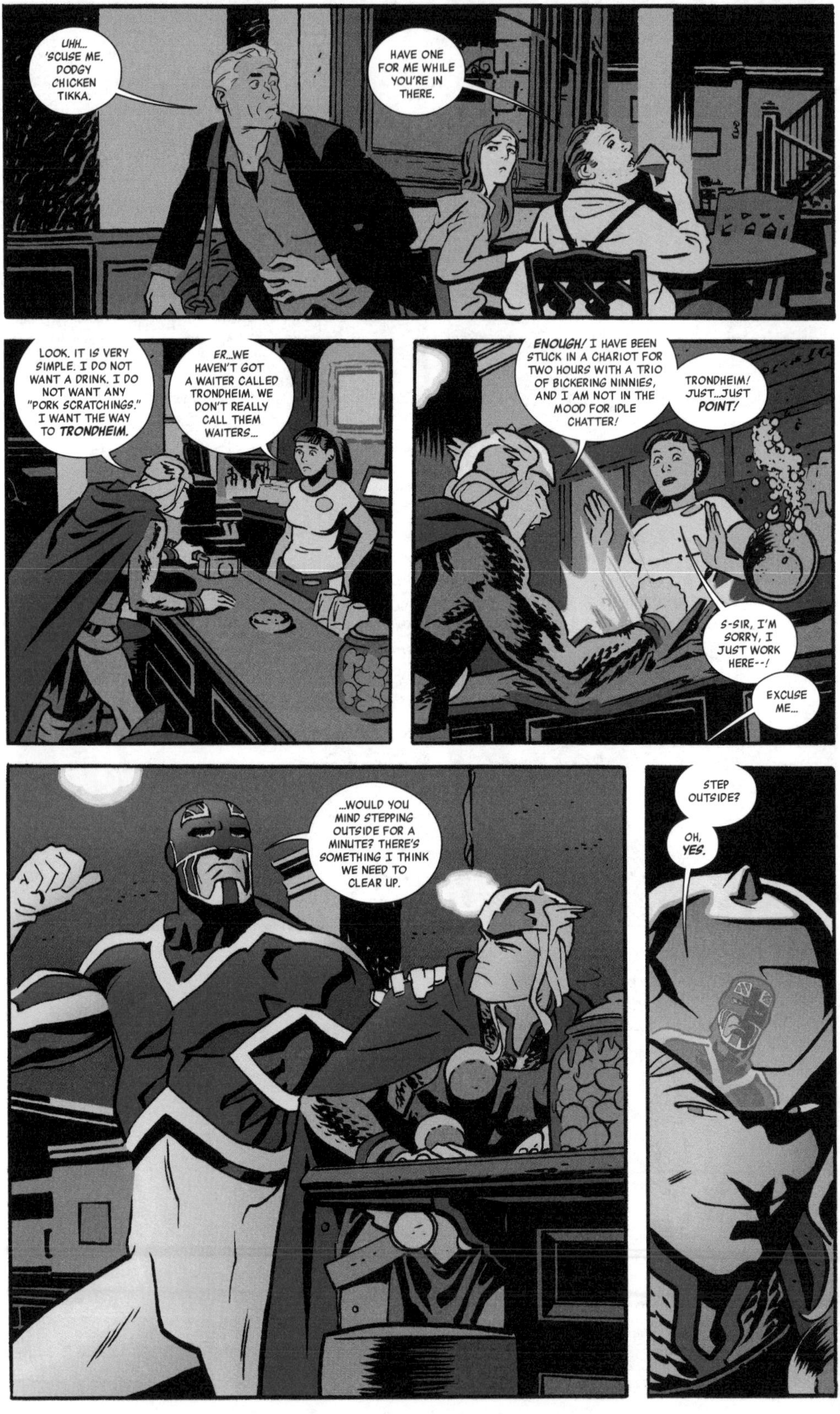

UHH... 'SCUSE ME. DODGY CHICKEN TIKKA.
HAVE ONE FOR ME WHILE YOU'RE IN THERE.
LOOK. IT IS VERY SIMPLE. I DO NOT WANT A DRINK. I DO NOT WANT ANY "PORK SCRATCHINGS." I WANT THE WAY TO TRONDHEIM.
ER...WE HAVEN'T GOT A WAITER CALLED TRONDHEIM. WE DON'T REALLY CALL THEM WAITERS...
ENOUGH! I HAVE BEEN STUCK IN A CHARIOT FOR TWO HOURS WITH A TRIO OF BICKERING NINNIES, AND I AM NOT IN THE MOOD FOR IDLE CHATTER!
TRONDHEIM! JUST...JUST POINT!
S-SIR, I'M SORRY, I JUST WORK HERE--!
EXCUSE ME...
...WOULD YOU MIND STEPPING OUTSIDE FOR A MINUTE? THERE'S SOMETHING I THINK WE NEED TO CLEAR UP.
STEP OUTSIDE?
OH, YES.

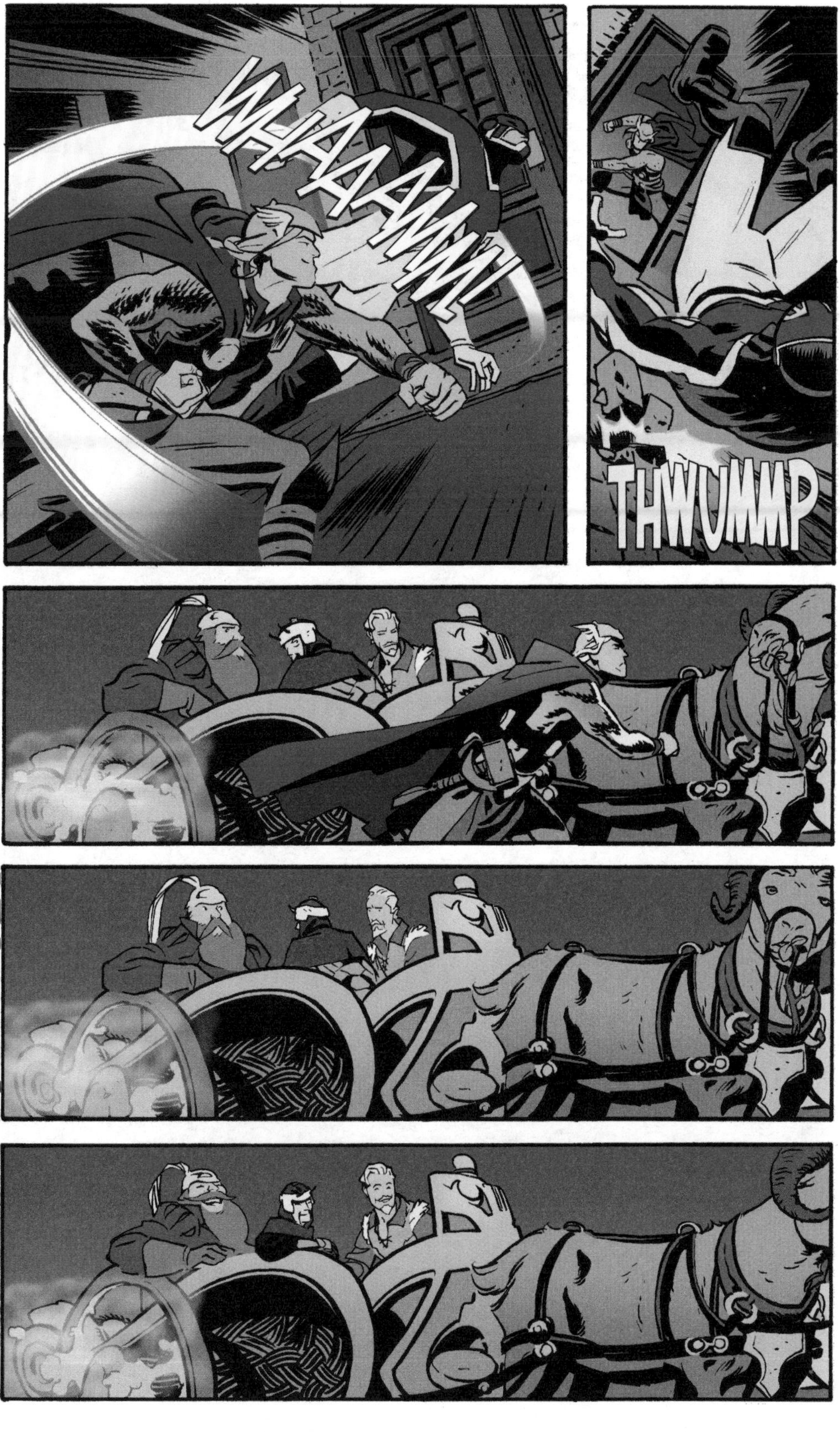
WHAAAMM!
THWUMMP

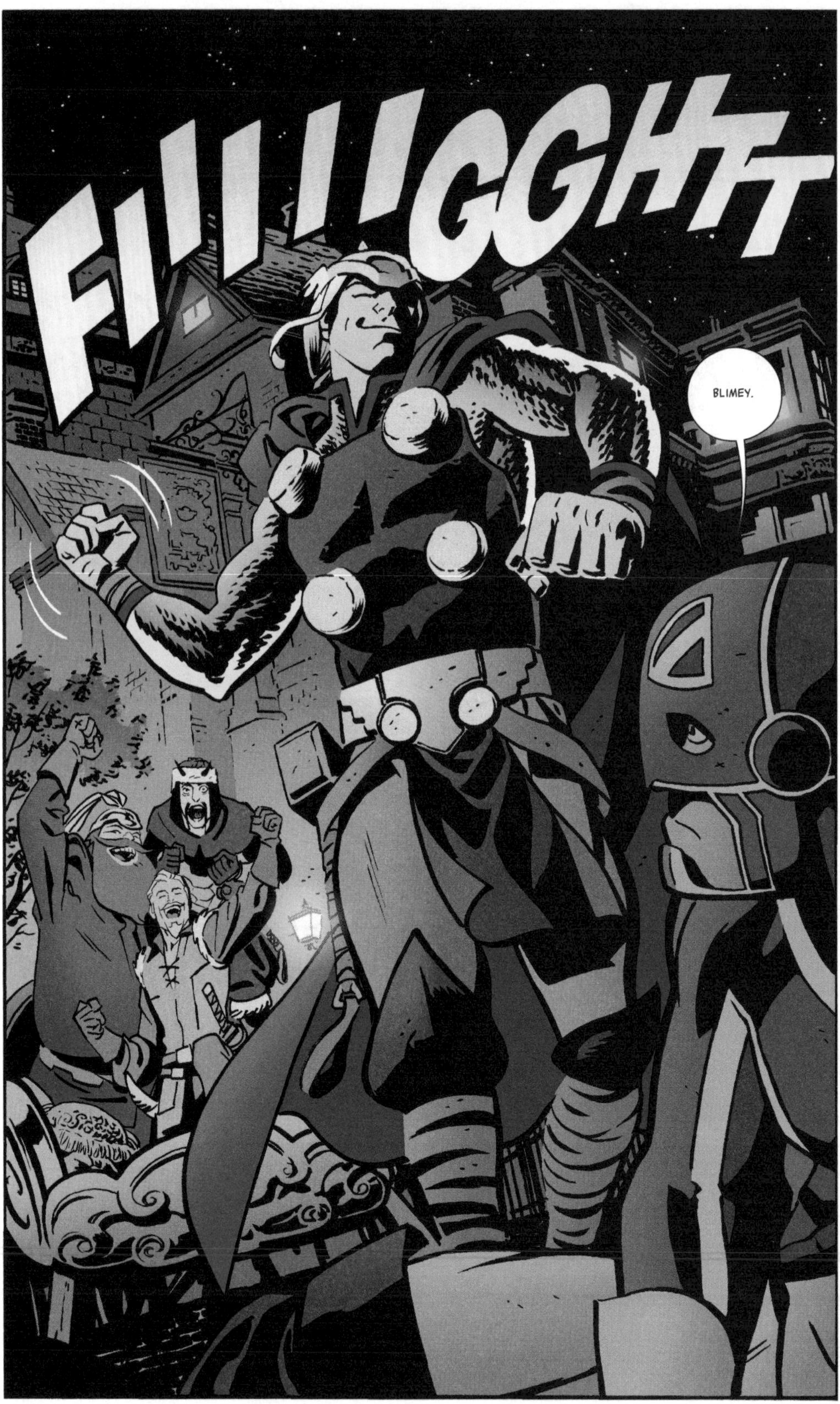
FIIIIIGGHTT
BLIMEY.

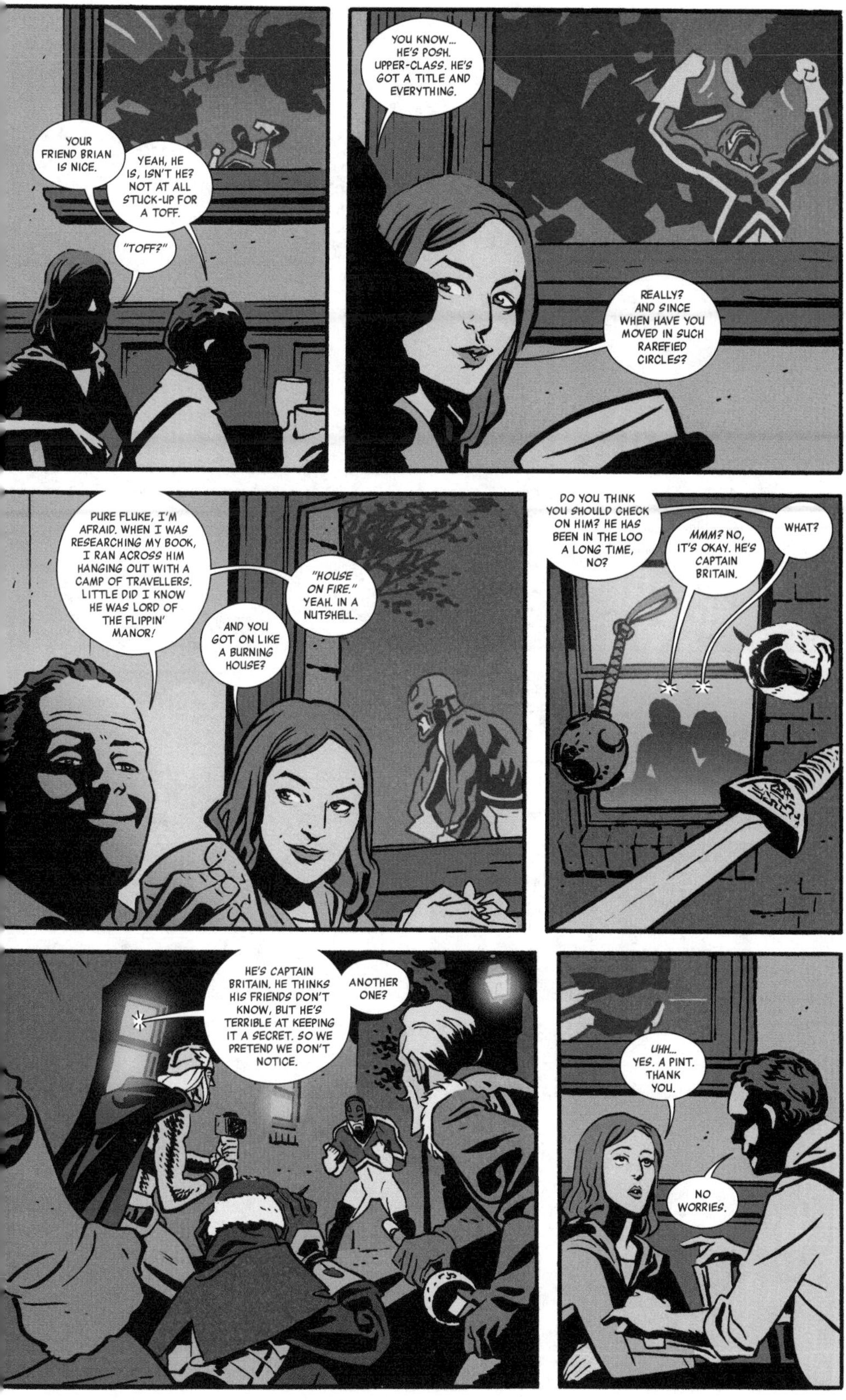
YOUR FRIEND BRIAN IS NICE.
YEAH, HE IS, ISN'T HE? NOT AT ALL STUCK-UP FOR A TOFF.
"TOFF?"
YOU KNOW... HE'S POSH. UPPER-CLASS. HE'S GOT A TITLE AND EVERYTHING.
REALLY? AND SINCE WHEN HAVE YOU MOVED IN SUCH RAREFIED CIRCLES?
PURE FLUKE, I'M AFRAID. WHEN I WAS RESEARCHING MY BOOK, I RAN ACROSS HIM HANGING OUT WITH A CAMP OF TRAVELLERS. LITTLE DID I KNOW HE WAS LORD OF THE FLIPPIN' MANOR!
AND YOU GOT ON LIKE A BURNING HOUSE?
"HOUSE ON FIRE." YEAH. IN A NUTSHELL.
DO YOU THINK YOU SHOULD CHECK ON HIM? HE HAS BEEN IN THE LOO A LONG TIME, NO?
MMM? NO, IT'S OKAY. HE'S CAPTAIN BRITAIN.
WHAT?
HE'S CAPTAIN BRITAIN. HE THINKS HIS FRIENDS DON'T KNOW, BUT HE'S TERRIBLE AT KEEPING IT A SECRET. SO WE PRETEND WE DON'T NOTICE.
ANOTHER ONE?
UHH... YES. A PINT. THANK YOU.
NO WORRIES.

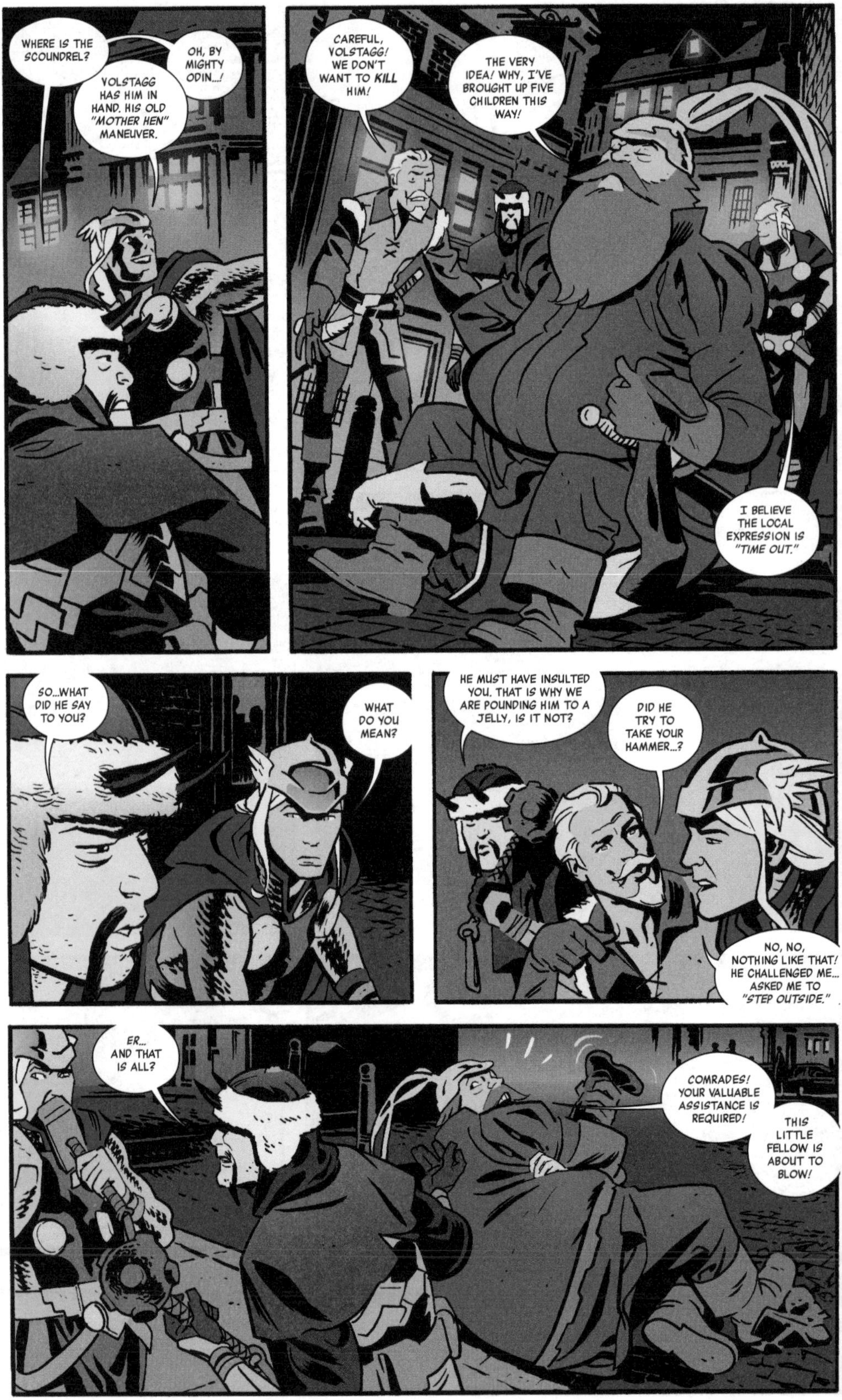
WHERE IS THE SCOUNDREL?
OH, BY MIGHTY ODIN...!
VOLSTAGG HAS HIM IN HAND. HIS OLD "MOTHER HEN" MANEUVER.
CAREFUL, VOLSTAGG! WE DON'T WANT TO KILL HIM!
THE VERY IDEA! WHY, I'VE BROUGHT UP FIVE CHILDREN THIS WAY!
I BELIEVE THE LOCAL EXPRESSION IS "TIME OUT."
SO...WHAT DID HE SAY TO YOU?
WHAT DO YOU MEAN?
HE MUST HAVE INSULTED YOU. THAT IS WHY WE ARE POUNDING HIM TO A JELLY, IS IT NOT?
DID HE TRY TO TAKE YOUR HAMMER...?
NO, NO, NOTHING LIKE THAT! HE CHALLENGED ME... ASKED ME TO "STEP OUTSIDE."
ER... AND THAT IS ALL?
COMRADES! YOUR VALUABLE ASSISTANCE IS REQUIRED!
THIS LITTLE FELLOW IS ABOUT TO BLOW!

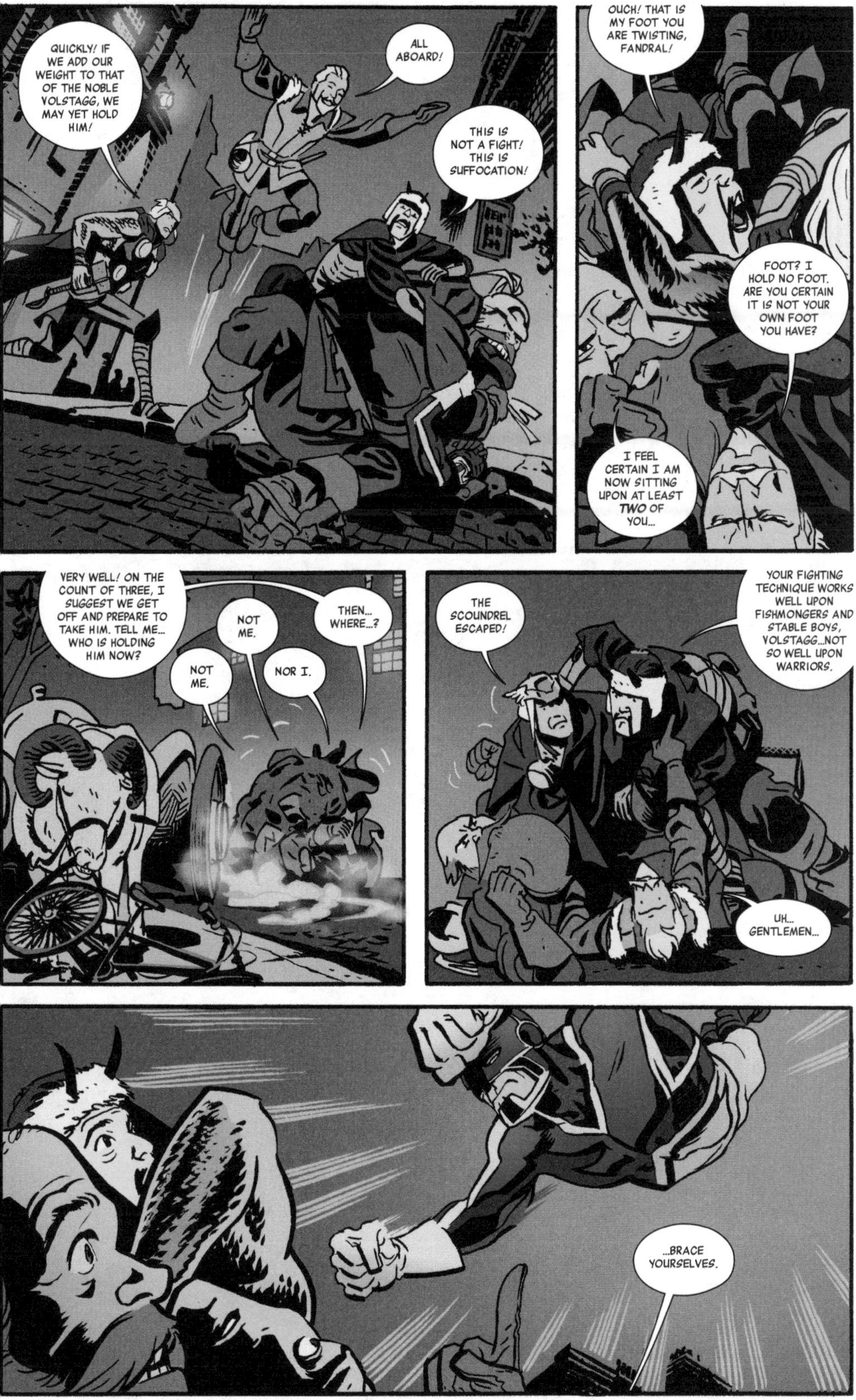
QUICKLY! IF WE ADD OUR WEIGHT TO THAT OF THE NOBLE VOLSTAGG, WE MAY YET HOLD HIM!
ALL ABOARD!
THIS IS NOT A FIGHT! THIS IS SUFFOCATION!
OUCH! THAT IS MY FOOT YOU ARE TWISTING, FANDRAL!
FOOT? I HOLD NO FOOT. ARE YOU CERTAIN IT IS NOT YOUR OWN FOOT YOU HAVE?
I FEEL CERTAIN I AM NOW SITTING UPON AT LEAST TWO OF YOU...
VERY WELL! ON THE COUNT OF THREE, I SUGGEST WE GET OFF AND PREPARE TO TAKE HIM. TELL ME... WHO IS HOLDING HIM NOW?
NOT ME.
NOT ME.
NOR I.
THEN... WHERE...?
THE SCOUNDREL ESCAPED!
YOUR FIGHTING TECHNIQUE WORKS WELL UPON FISHMONGERS AND STABLE BOYS, VOLSTAGG...NOT SO WELL UPON WARRIORS.
UH... GENTLEMEN...
...BRACE YOURSELVES.

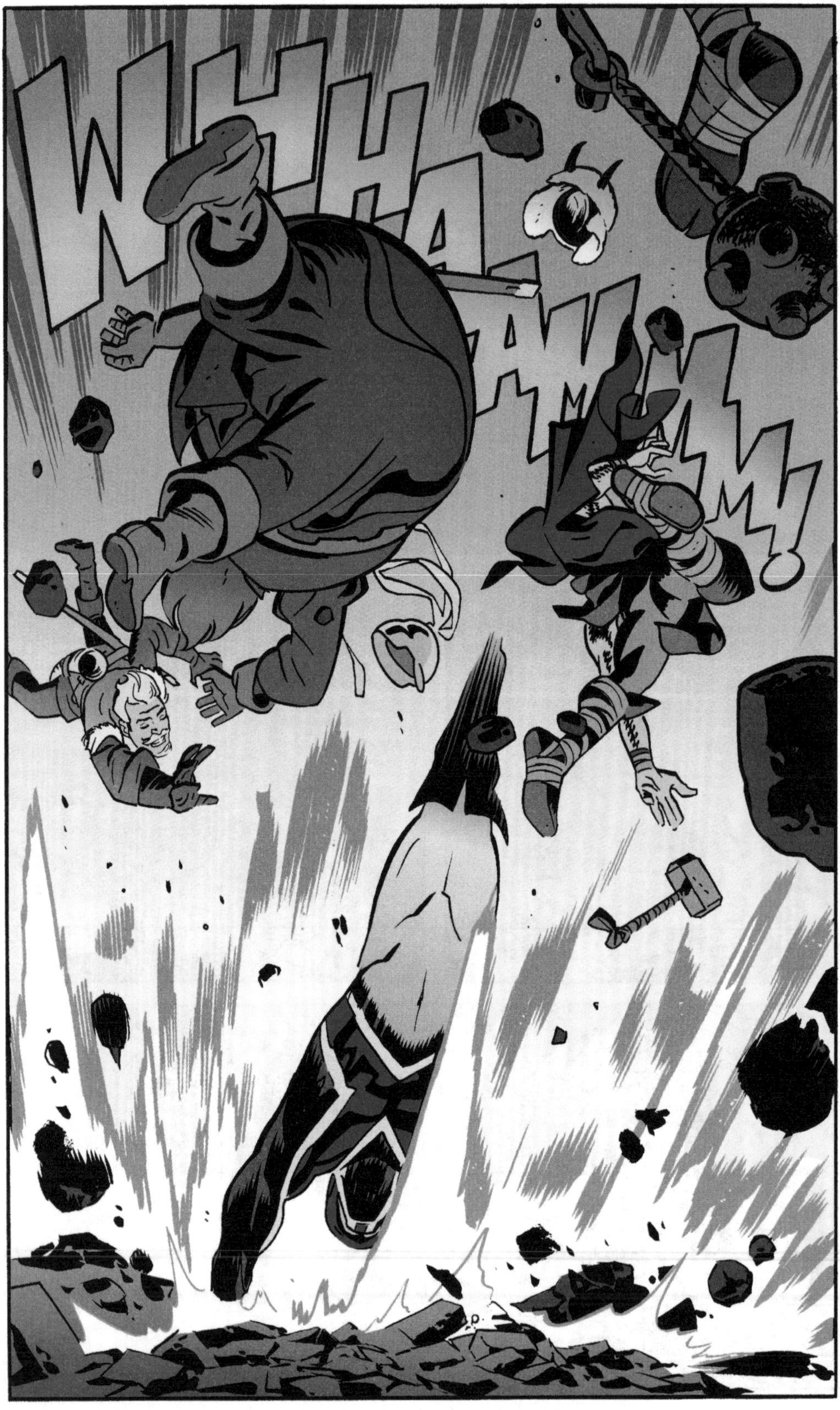
WHHAAMMM!

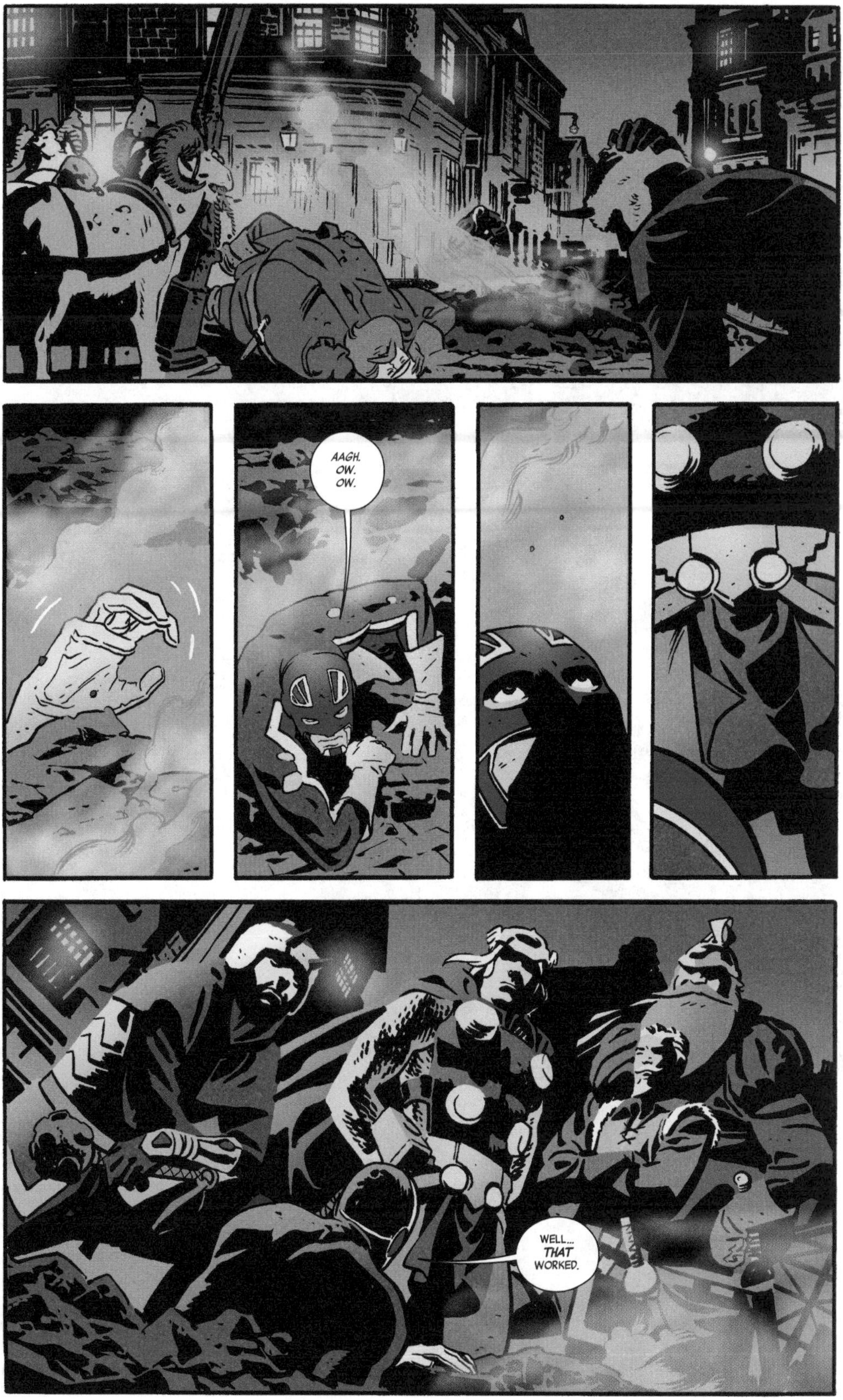
AAGH. OW. OW.
WELL... THAT WORKED.

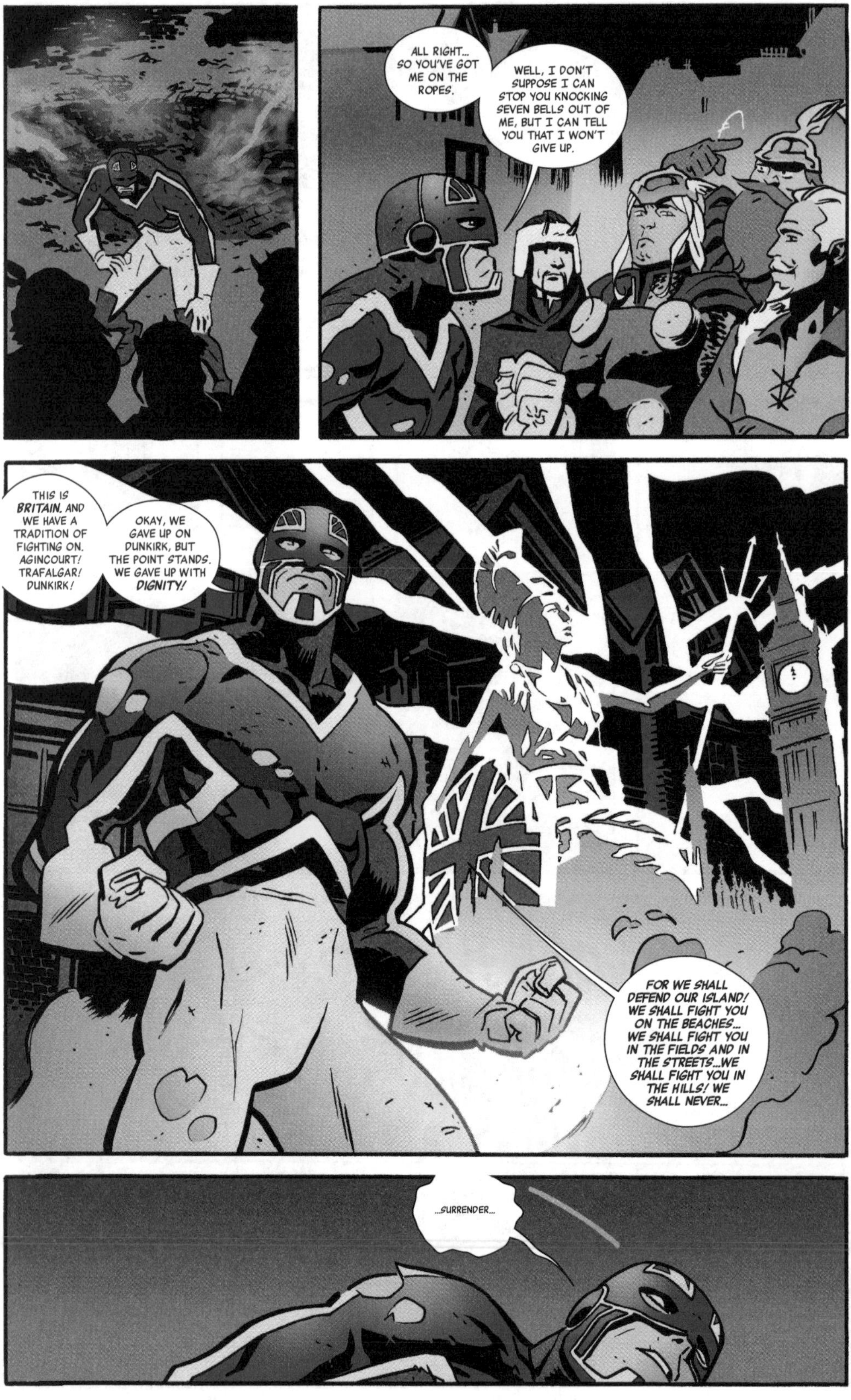
ALL RIGHT... SO YOU'VE GOT ME ON THE ROPES.
WELL, I DON'T SUPPOSE I CAN STOP YOU KNOCKING SEVEN BELLS OUT OF ME, BUT I CAN TELL YOU THAT I WON'T GIVE UP.
THIS IS BRITAIN. AND WE HAVE A TRADITION OF FIGHTING ON. AGINCOURT! TRAFALGAR! DUNKIRK!
OKAY, WE GAVE UP ON DUNKIRK, BUT THE POINT STANDS. WE GAVE UP WITH DIGNITY!
FOR WE SHALL DEFEND OUR ISLAND! WE SHALL FIGHT YOU ON THE BEACHES... WE SHALL FIGHT YOU IN THE FIELDS AND IN THE STREETS...WE SHALL FIGHT YOU IN THE HILLS! WE SHALL NEVER...
...SURRENDER...

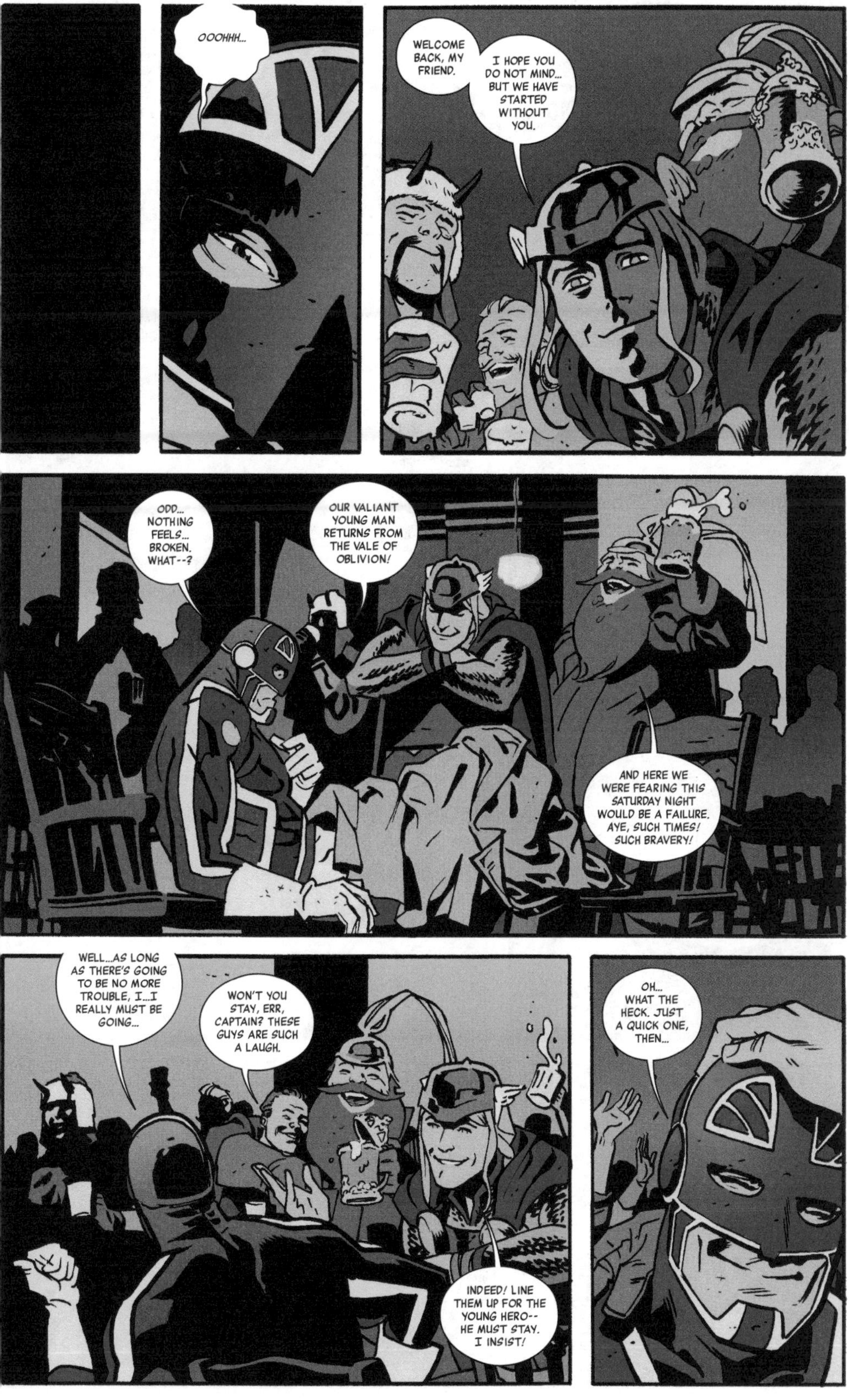
OOOHHH...
WELCOME BACK, MY FRIEND.
I HOPE YOU DO NOT MIND... BUT WE HAVE STARTED WITHOUT YOU.
ODD... NOTHING FEELS... BROKEN. WHAT--?
OUR VALIANT YOUNG MAN RETURNS FROM THE VALE OF OBLIVION!
AND HERE WE WERE FEARING THIS SATURDAY NIGHT WOULD BE A FAILURE. AYE, SUCH TIMES! SUCH BRAVERY!
WELL...AS LONG AS THERE'S GOING TO BE NO MORE TROUBLE, I...I REALLY MUST BE GOING...
WON'T YOU STAY, ERR, CAPTAIN? THESE GUYS ARE SUCH A LAUGH.
INDEED! LINE THEM UP FOR THE YOUNG HERO-- HE MUST STAY. I INSIST!
OH... WHAT THE HECK. JUST A QUICK ONE, THEN...

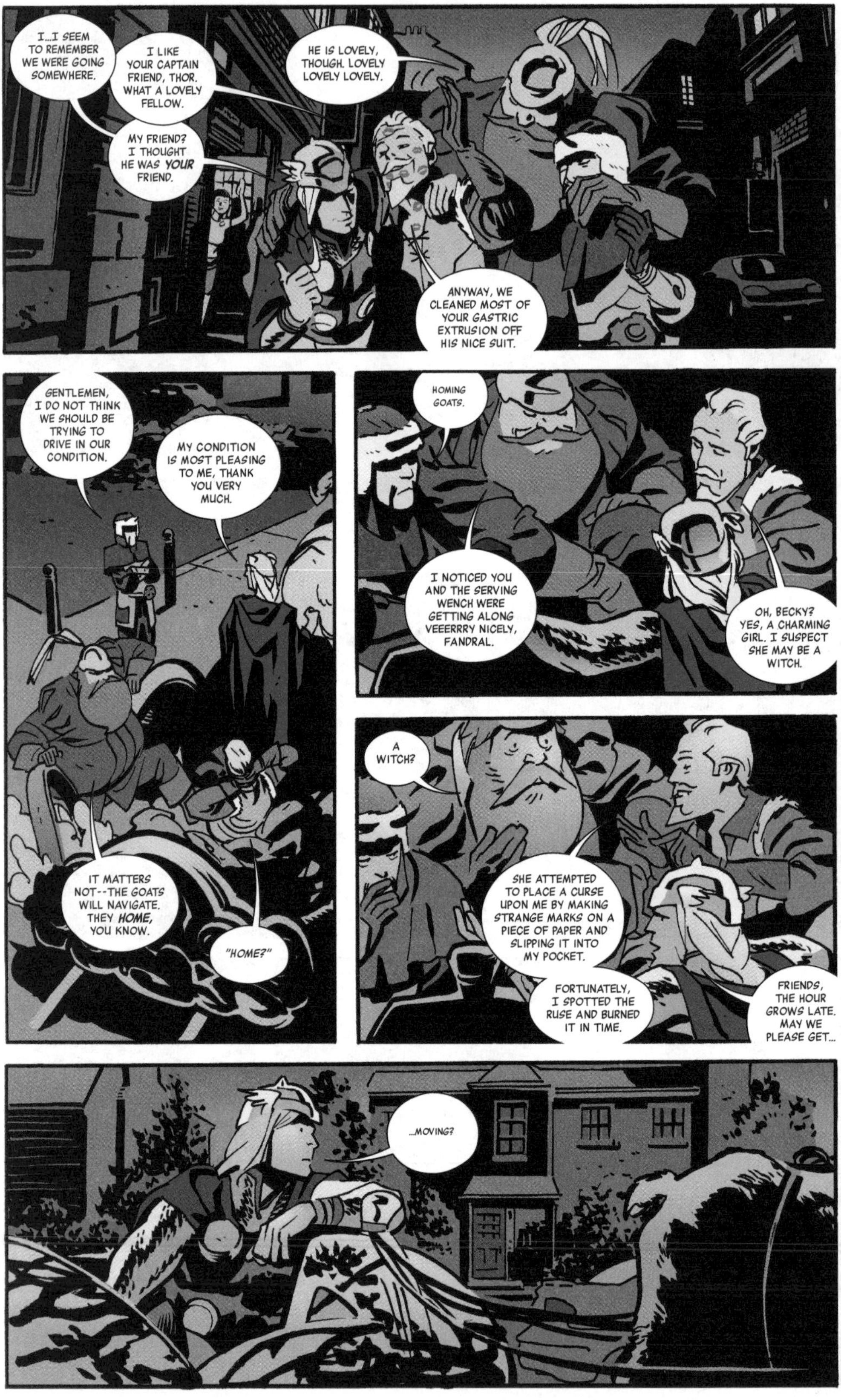
I...I SEEM TO REMEMBER WE WERE GOING SOMEWHERE.
I LIKE YOUR CAPTAIN FRIEND, THOR. WHAT A LOVELY FELLOW.
MY FRIEND? I THOUGHT HE WAS *YOUR* FRIEND.
HE IS LOVELY, THOUGH. LOVELY LOVELY LOVELY.
ANYWAY, WE CLEANED MOST OF YOUR GASTRIC EXTRUSION OFF HIS NICE SUIT.
GENTLEMEN, I DO NOT THINK WE SHOULD BE TRYING TO DRIVE IN OUR CONDITION.
MY CONDITION IS MOST PLEASING TO ME, THANK YOU VERY MUCH.
IT MATTERS NOT--THE GOATS WILL NAVIGATE. THEY *HOME,* YOU KNOW.
"HOME?"
HOMING GOATS.
I NOTICED YOU AND THE SERVING WENCH WERE GETTING ALONG VEEERRRY NICELY, FANDRAL.
OH, BECKY? YES, A CHARMING GIRL. I SUSPECT SHE MAY BE A WITCH.
A WITCH?
SHE ATTEMPTED TO PLACE A CURSE UPON ME BY MAKING STRANGE MARKS ON A PIECE OF PAPER AND SLIPPING IT INTO MY POCKET.
FORTUNATELY, I SPOTTED THE RUSE AND BURNED IT IN TIME.
FRIENDS, THE HOUR GROWS LATE. MAY WE PLEASE GET...
...MOVING?

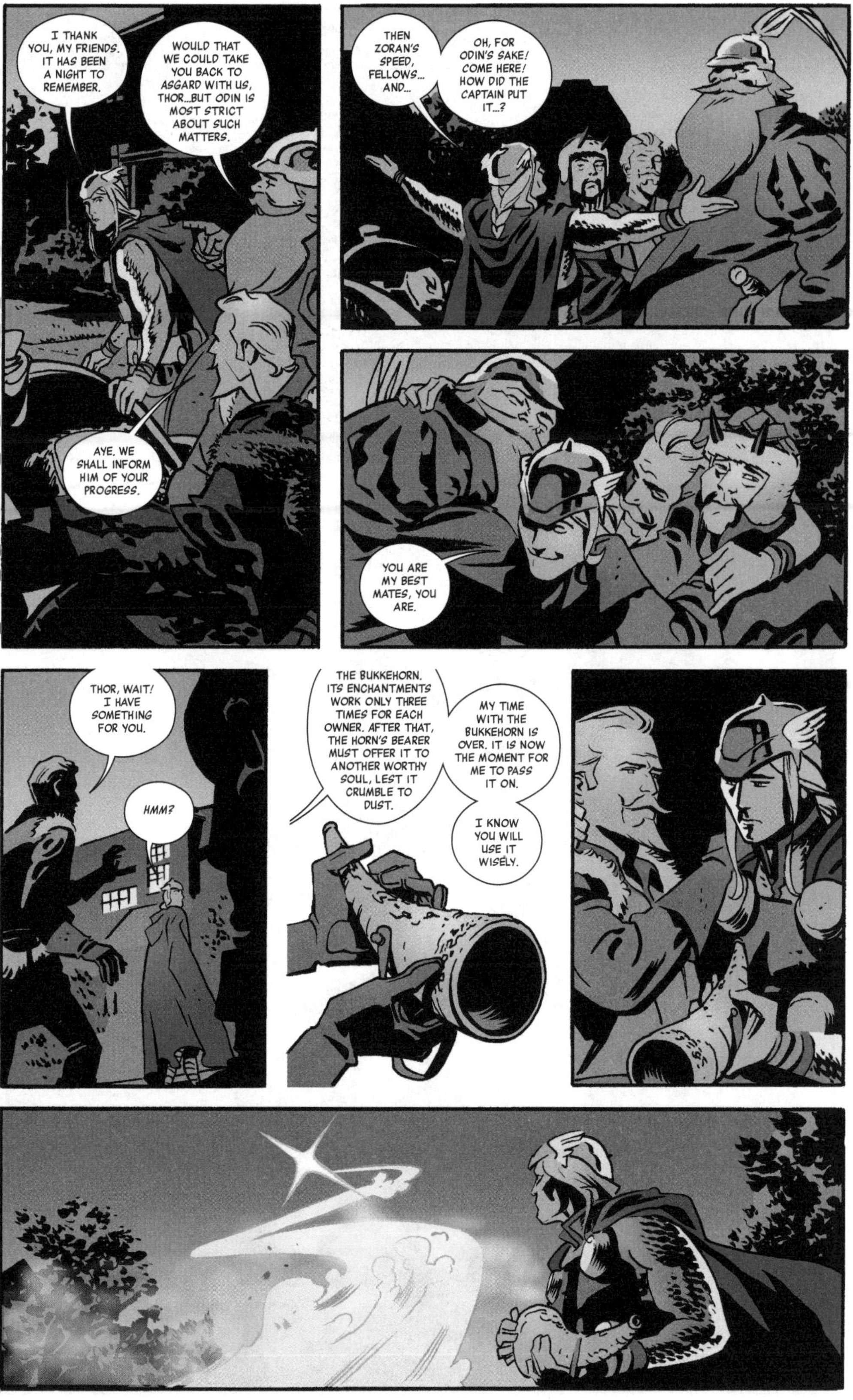
I THANK YOU, MY FRIENDS. IT HAS BEEN A NIGHT TO REMEMBER.
WOULD THAT WE COULD TAKE YOU BACK TO ASGARD WITH US, THOR...BUT ODIN IS MOST STRICT ABOUT SUCH MATTERS.
AYE. WE SHALL INFORM HIM OF YOUR PROGRESS.
THEN ZORAN'S SPEED, FELLOWS... AND...
OH, FOR ODIN'S SAKE! COME HERE! HOW DID THE CAPTAIN PUT IT...?
YOU ARE MY BEST MATES, YOU ARE.
THOR, WAIT! I HAVE SOMETHING FOR YOU.
HMM?
THE BUKKEHORN. ITS ENCHANTMENTS WORK ONLY THREE TIMES FOR EACH OWNER. AFTER THAT, THE HORN'S BEARER MUST OFFER IT TO ANOTHER WORTHY SOUL, LEST IT CRUMBLE TO DUST.
MY TIME WITH THE BUKKEHORN IS OVER. IT IS NOW THE MOMENT FOR ME TO PASS IT ON.
I KNOW YOU WILL USE IT WISELY.

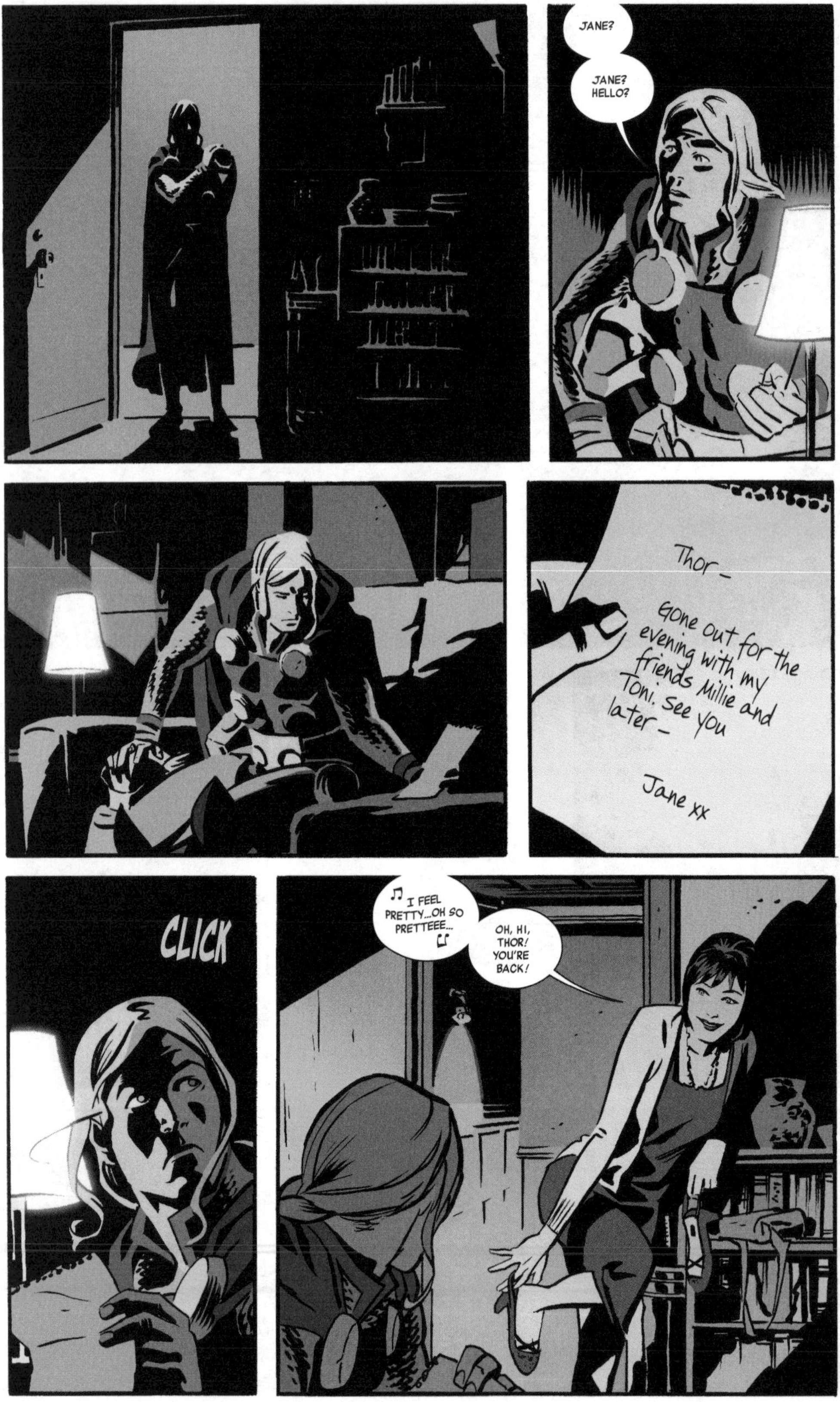
JANE?
JANE? HELLO?
Thor–
Gone out for the evening with my friends Millie and Toni. See you later–
Jane xx
CLICK
♫ I FEEL PRETTY...OH SO PRETTEEE... ♫
OH, HI, THOR! YOU'RE BACK!

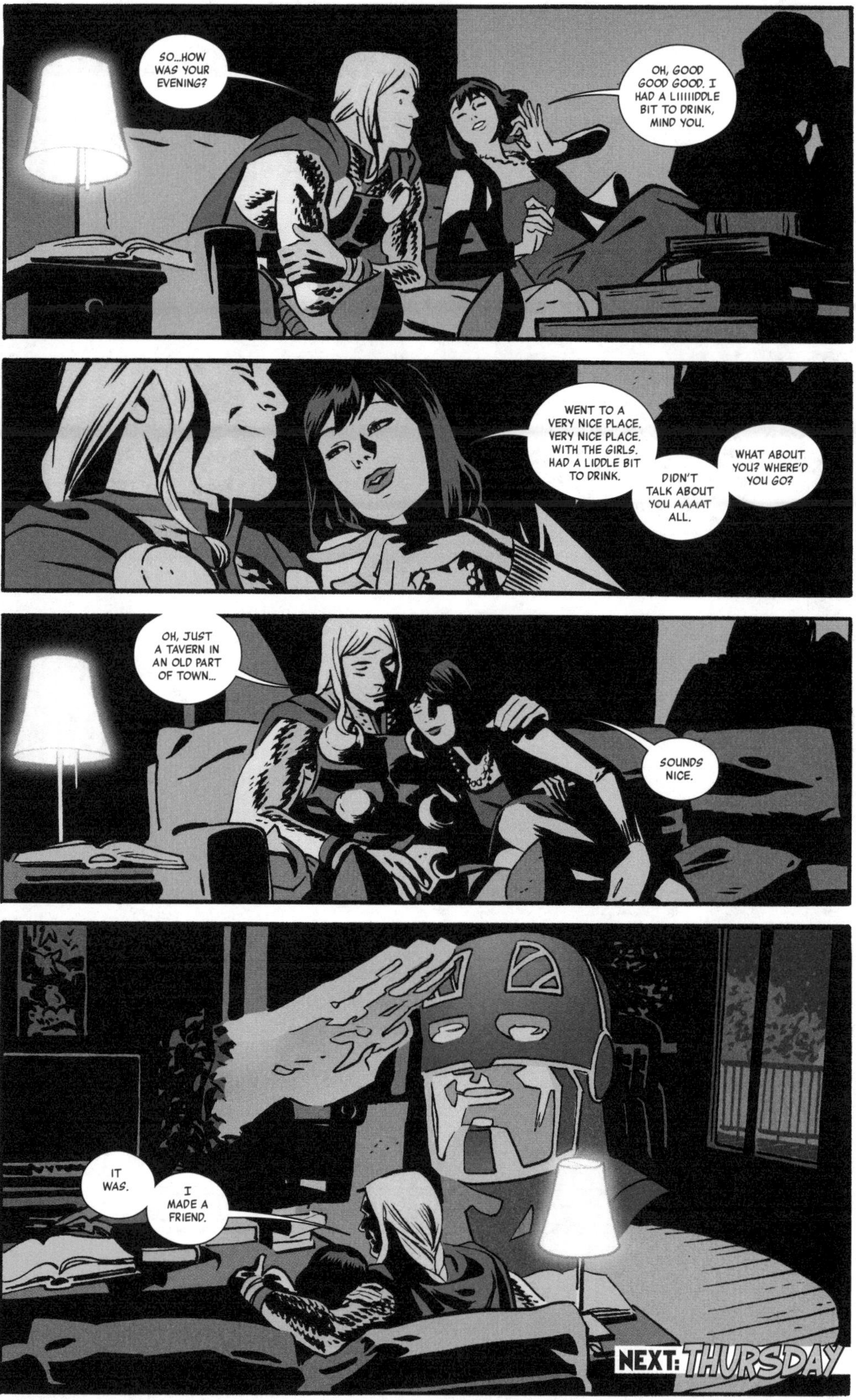
SO...HOW WAS YOUR EVENING?
OH, GOOD GOOD GOOD. I HAD A LIIIIIDDLE BIT TO DRINK, MIND YOU.
WENT TO A VERY NICE PLACE. VERY NICE PLACE. WITH THE GIRLS. HAD A LIDDLE BIT TO DRINK.
DIDN'T TALK ABOUT YOU AAAAT ALL.
WHAT ABOUT YOU? WHERE'D YOU GO?
OH, JUST A TAVERN IN AN OLD PART OF TOWN...
SOUNDS NICE.
IT WAS.
I MADE A FRIEND.
NEXT: THURSDAY

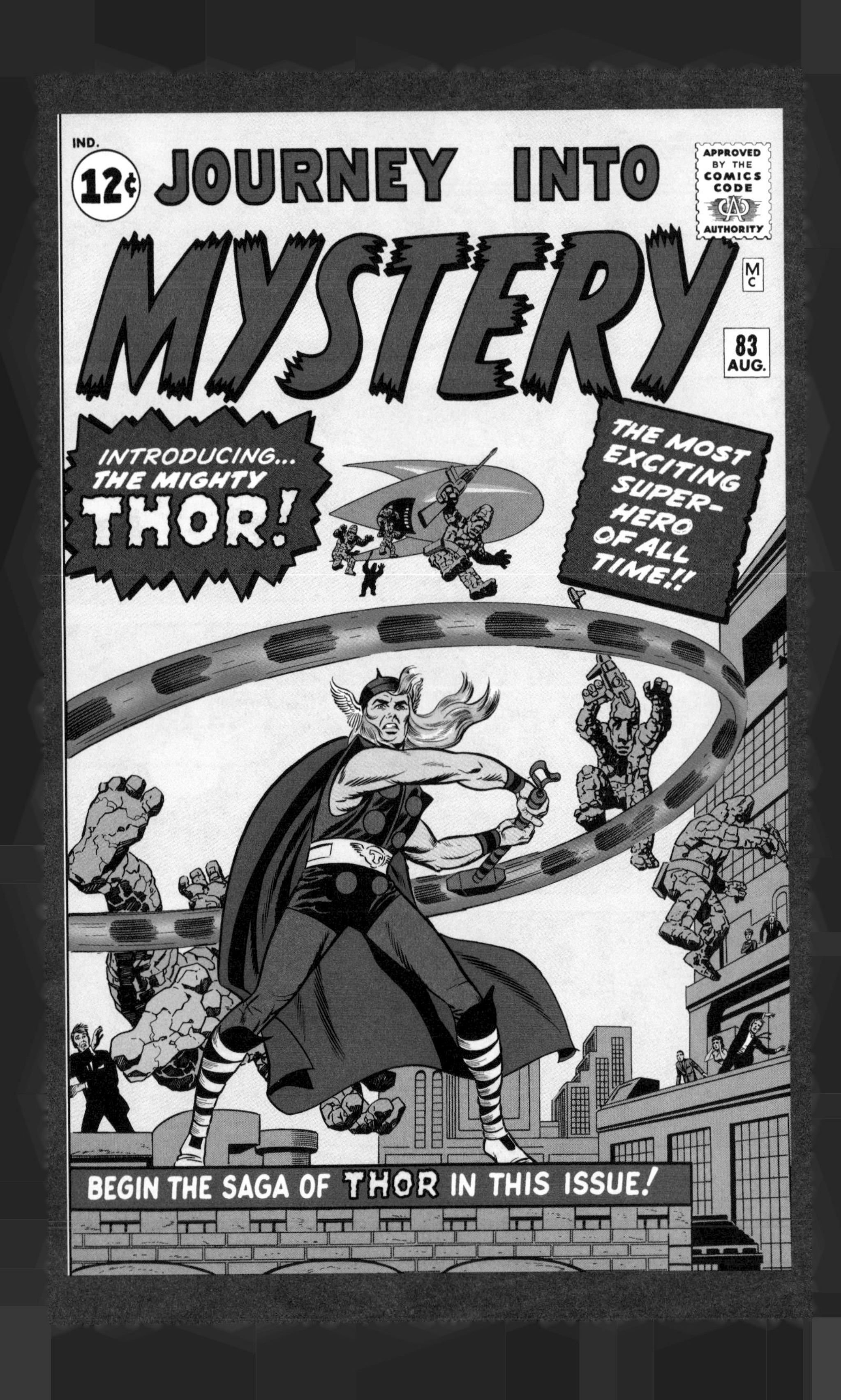

IND.
12¢
JOURNEY INTO
APPROVED BY THE COMICS CODE AUTHORITY
MYSTERY
MC
83
AUG.
INTRODUCING... THE MIGHTY THOR!
THE MOST EXCITING SUPER-HERO OF ALL TIME!!
BEGIN THE SAGA OF THOR IN THIS ISSUE!

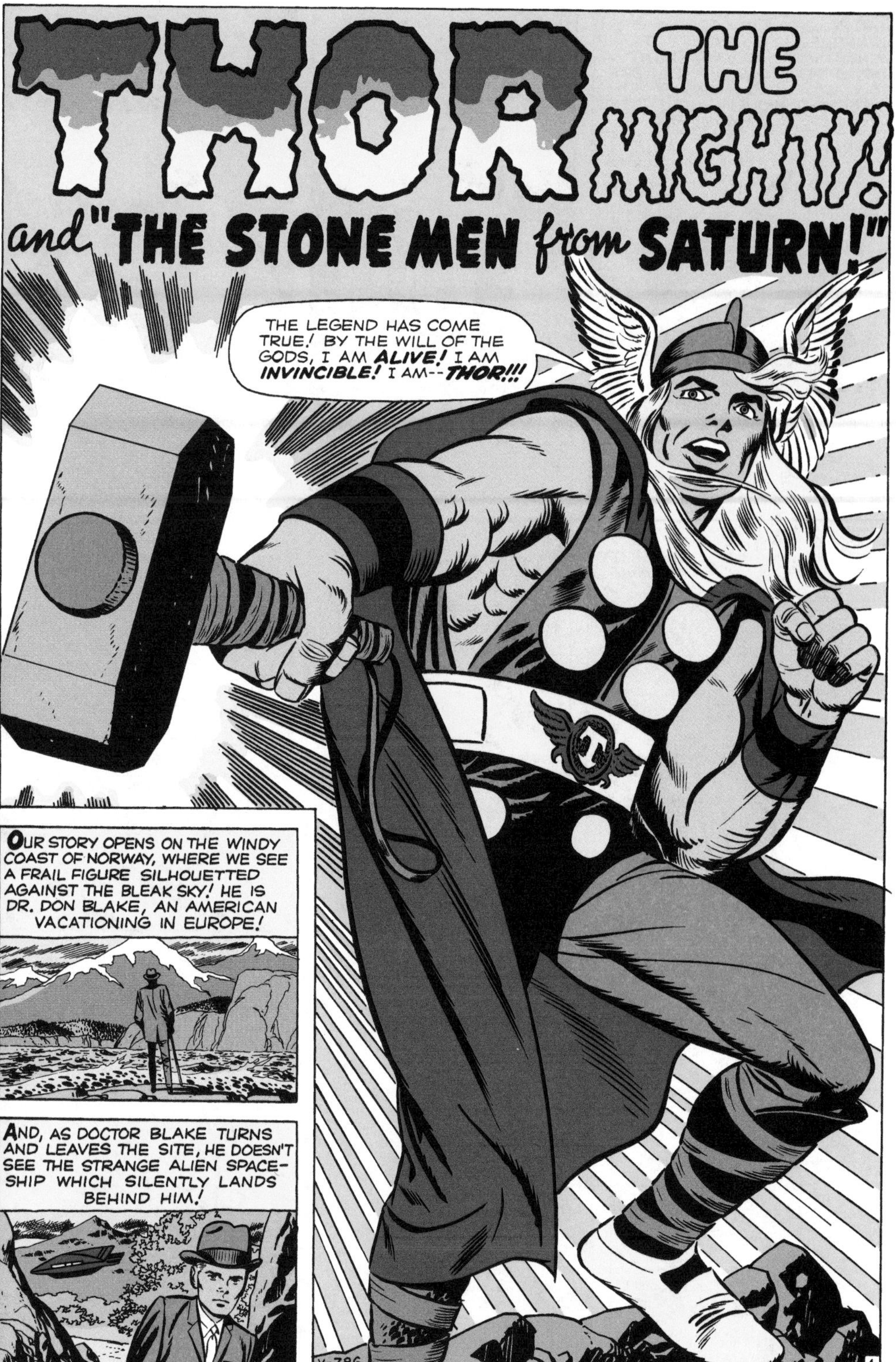
THOR THE MIGHTY!
and "THE STONE MEN from SATURN!"
THE LEGEND HAS COME TRUE! BY THE WILL OF THE GODS, I AM ALIVE! I AM INVINCIBLE! I AM--THOR!!!
OUR STORY OPENS ON THE WINDY COAST OF NORWAY, WHERE WE SEE A FRAIL FIGURE SILHOUETTED AGAINST THE BLEAK SKY! HE IS DR. DON BLAKE, AN AMERICAN VACATIONING IN EUROPE!
AND, AS DOCTOR BLAKE TURNS AND LEAVES THE SITE, HE DOESN'T SEE THE STRANGE ALIEN SPACE-SHIP WHICH SILENTLY LANDS BEHIND HIM!
V-786
1

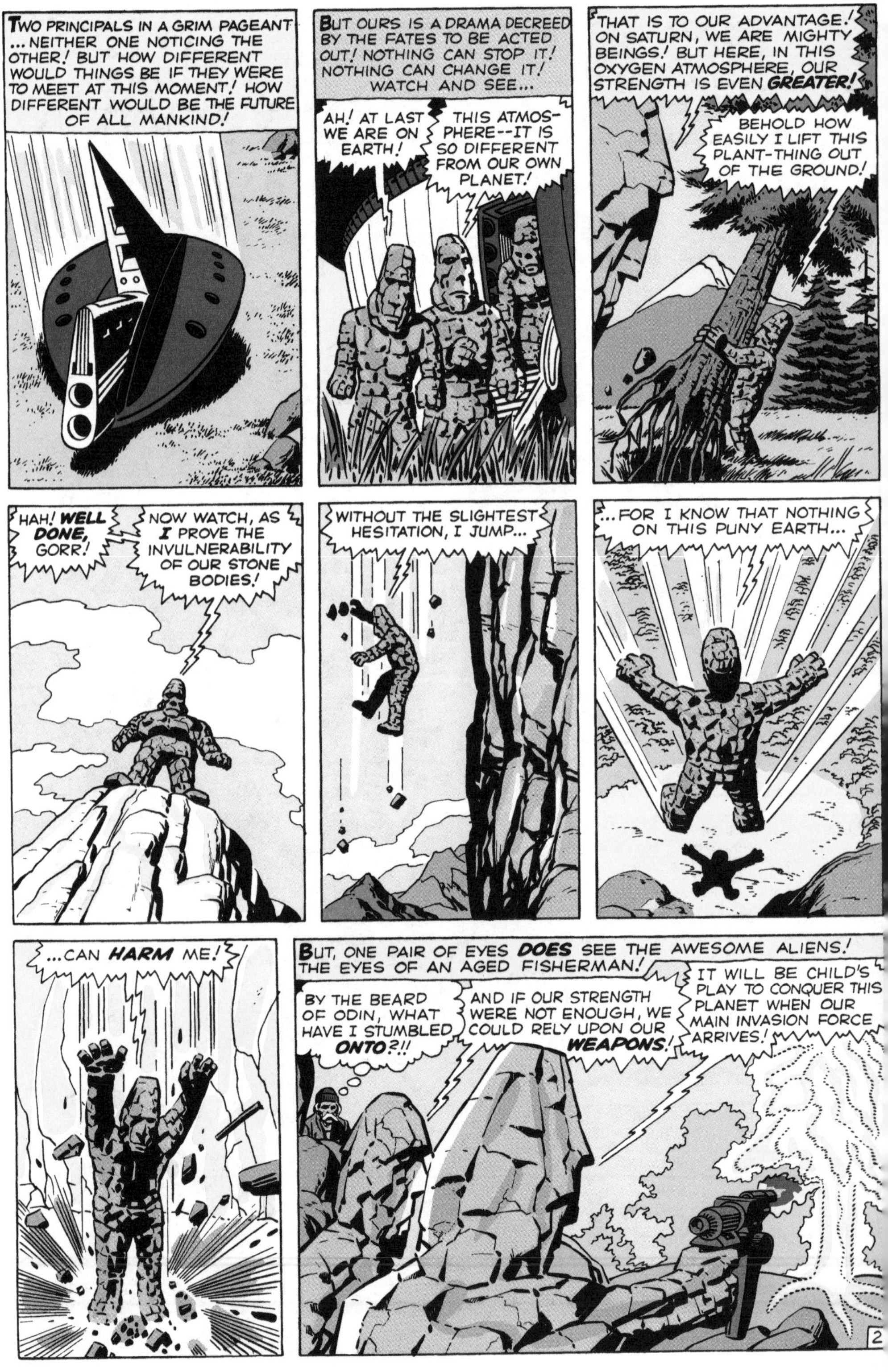
TWO PRINCIPALS IN A GRIM PAGEANT ...NEITHER ONE NOTICING THE OTHER! BUT HOW DIFFERENT WOULD THINGS BE IF THEY WERE TO MEET AT THIS MOMENT! HOW DIFFERENT WOULD BE THE FUTURE OF ALL MANKIND!
BUT OURS IS A DRAMA DECREED BY THE FATES TO BE ACTED OUT! NOTHING CAN STOP IT! NOTHING CAN CHANGE IT! WATCH AND SEE...
AH! AT LAST WE ARE ON EARTH!
THIS ATMOSPHERE--IT IS SO DIFFERENT FROM OUR OWN PLANET!
THAT IS TO OUR ADVANTAGE! ON SATURN, WE ARE MIGHTY BEINGS! BUT HERE, IN THIS OXYGEN ATMOSPHERE, OUR STRENGTH IS EVEN GREATER!
BEHOLD HOW EASILY I LIFT THIS PLANT-THING OUT OF THE GROUND!
HAH! WELL DONE, GORR!
NOW WATCH, AS I PROVE THE INVULNERABILITY OF OUR STONE BODIES!
WITHOUT THE SLIGHTEST HESITATION, I JUMP...
...FOR I KNOW THAT NOTHING ON THIS PUNY EARTH...
...CAN HARM ME!
BUT, ONE PAIR OF EYES DOES SEE THE AWESOME ALIENS! THE EYES OF AN AGED FISHERMAN!
BY THE BEARD OF ODIN, WHAT HAVE I STUMBLED ONTO?!!
AND IF OUR STRENGTH WERE NOT ENOUGH, WE COULD RELY UPON OUR WEAPONS!
IT WILL BE CHILD'S PLAY TO CONQUER THIS PLANET WHEN OUR MAIN INVASION FORCE ARRIVES!
2

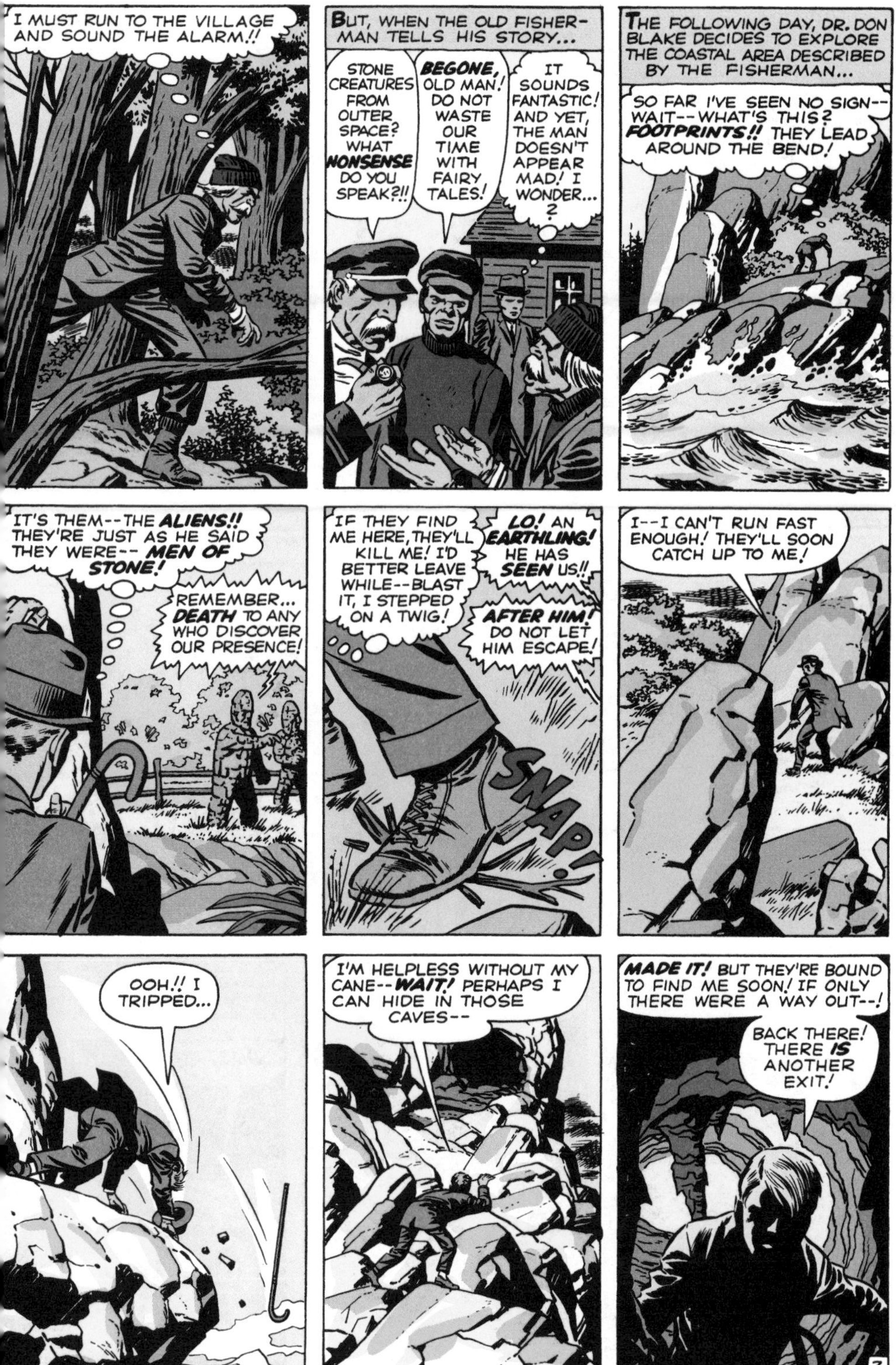
I MUST RUN TO THE VILLAGE AND SOUND THE ALARM!!
BUT, WHEN THE OLD FISHERMAN TELLS HIS STORY...
STONE CREATURES FROM OUTER SPACE? WHAT NONSENSE DO YOU SPEAK?!!
BEGONE, OLD MAN! DO NOT WASTE OUR TIME WITH FAIRY TALES!
IT SOUNDS FANTASTIC! AND YET, THE MAN DOESN'T APPEAR MAD! I WONDER...?
THE FOLLOWING DAY, DR. DON BLAKE DECIDES TO EXPLORE THE COASTAL AREA DESCRIBED BY THE FISHERMAN...
SO FAR I'VE SEEN NO SIGN--WAIT--WHAT'S THIS? FOOTPRINTS!! THEY LEAD AROUND THE BEND!
IT'S THEM--THE ALIENS!! THEY'RE JUST AS HE SAID THEY WERE--MEN OF STONE!
REMEMBER... DEATH TO ANY WHO DISCOVER OUR PRESENCE!
IF THEY FIND ME HERE, THEY'LL KILL ME! I'D BETTER LEAVE WHILE--BLAST IT, I STEPPED ON A TWIG!
LO! AN EARTHLING! HE HAS SEEN US!!
AFTER HIM! DO NOT LET HIM ESCAPE!
SNAP!
I--I CAN'T RUN FAST ENOUGH! THEY'LL SOON CATCH UP TO ME!
OOH!! I TRIPPED...
I'M HELPLESS WITHOUT MY CANE--WAIT! PERHAPS I CAN HIDE IN THOSE CAVES--
MADE IT! BUT THEY'RE BOUND TO FIND ME SOON! IF ONLY THERE WERE A WAY OUT--!
BACK THERE! THERE IS ANOTHER EXIT!
3

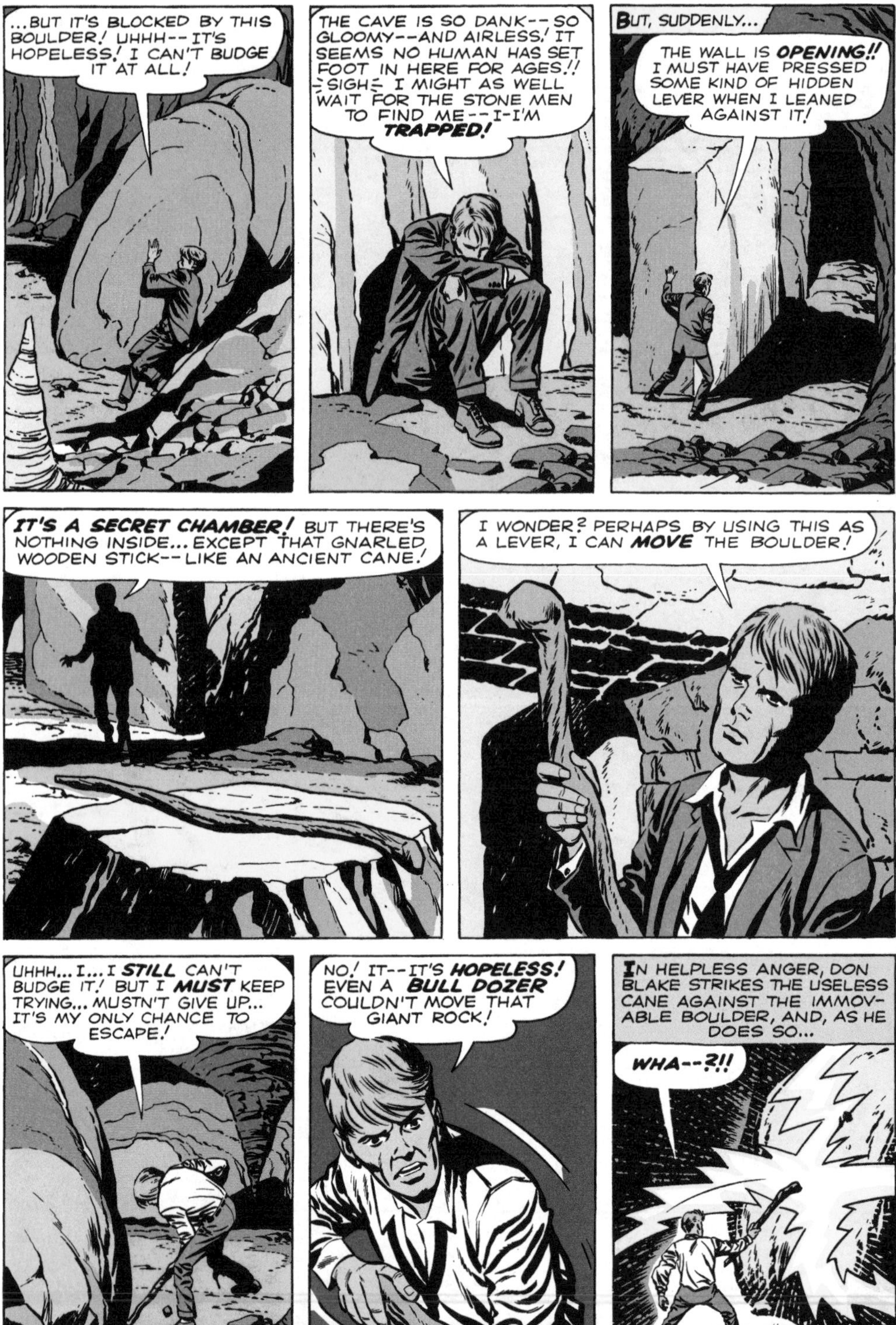
...BUT IT'S BLOCKED BY THIS BOULDER! UHHH--IT'S HOPELESS! I CAN'T BUDGE IT AT ALL!
THE CAVE IS SO DANK--SO GLOOMY--AND AIRLESS! IT SEEMS NO HUMAN HAS SET FOOT IN HERE FOR AGES!! SIGH I MIGHT AS WELL WAIT FOR THE STONE MEN TO FIND ME--I-I'M TRAPPED!
BUT, SUDDENLY...
THE WALL IS OPENING!! I MUST HAVE PRESSED SOME KIND OF HIDDEN LEVER WHEN I LEANED AGAINST IT!
IT'S A SECRET CHAMBER! BUT THERE'S NOTHING INSIDE... EXCEPT THAT GNARLED WOODEN STICK--LIKE AN ANCIENT CANE!
I WONDER? PERHAPS BY USING THIS AS A LEVER, I CAN MOVE THE BOULDER!
UHHH... I... I STILL CAN'T BUDGE IT! BUT I MUST KEEP TRYING... MUSTN'T GIVE UP... IT'S MY ONLY CHANCE TO ESCAPE!
NO! IT--IT'S HOPELESS! EVEN A BULL DOZER COULDN'T MOVE THAT GIANT ROCK!
IN HELPLESS ANGER, DON BLAKE STRIKES THE USELESS CANE AGAINST THE IMMOVABLE BOULDER, AND, AS HE DOES SO...
WHA--?!!
4

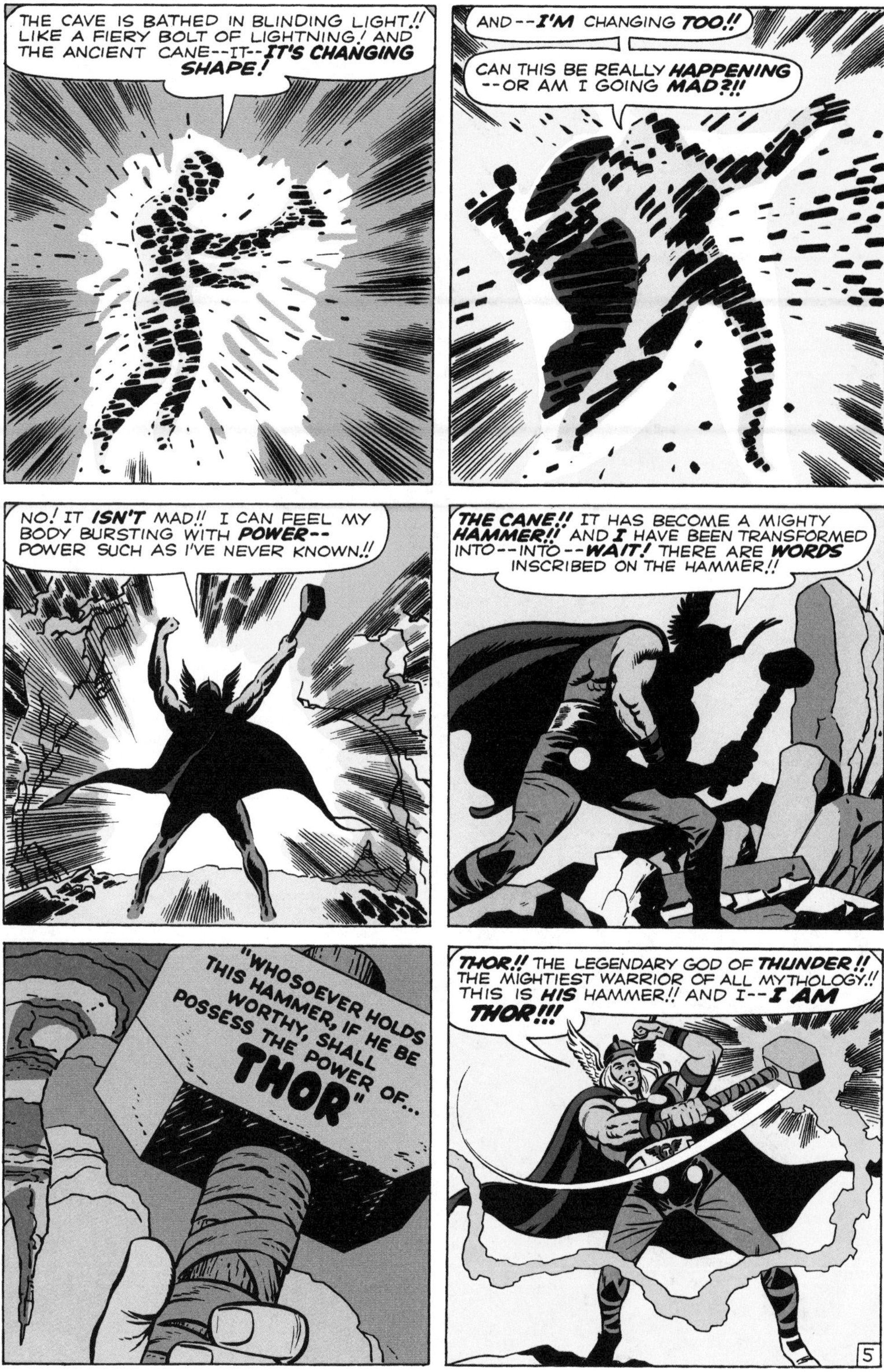
THE CAVE IS BATHED IN BLINDING LIGHT!! LIKE A FIERY BOLT OF LIGHTNING! AND THE ANCIENT CANE--IT--IT'S CHANGING SHAPE!
AND--I'M CHANGING TOO!!
CAN THIS BE REALLY HAPPENING --OR AM I GOING MAD?!!
NO! IT ISN'T MAD!! I CAN FEEL MY BODY BURSTING WITH POWER-- POWER SUCH AS I'VE NEVER KNOWN!!
THE CANE!! IT HAS BECOME A MIGHTY HAMMER!! AND I HAVE BEEN TRANSFORMED INTO--INTO--WAIT! THERE ARE WORDS INSCRIBED ON THE HAMMER!!
"WHOSOEVER HOLDS THIS HAMMER, IF HE BE WORTHY, SHALL POSSESS THE POWER OF... THOR"
THOR!! THE LEGENDARY GOD OF THUNDER!! THE MIGHTIEST WARRIOR OF ALL MYTHOLOGY!! THIS IS HIS HAMMER!! AND I--I AM THOR!!!
5

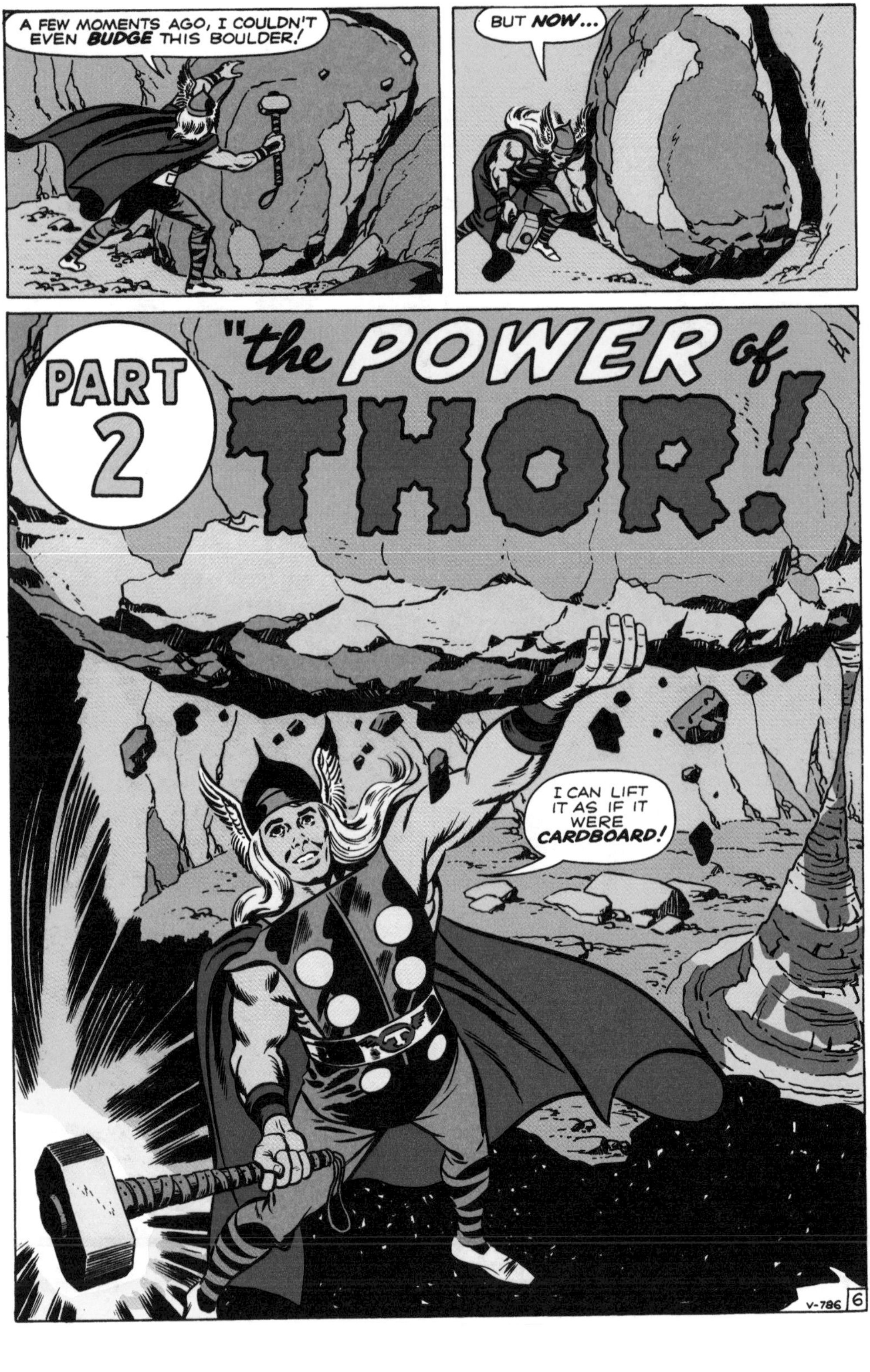
A FEW MOMENTS AGO, I COULDN'T EVEN BUDGE THIS BOULDER!
BUT NOW...
PART 2
"the POWER of THOR!
I CAN LIFT IT AS IF IT WERE CARDBOARD!
V-786
6

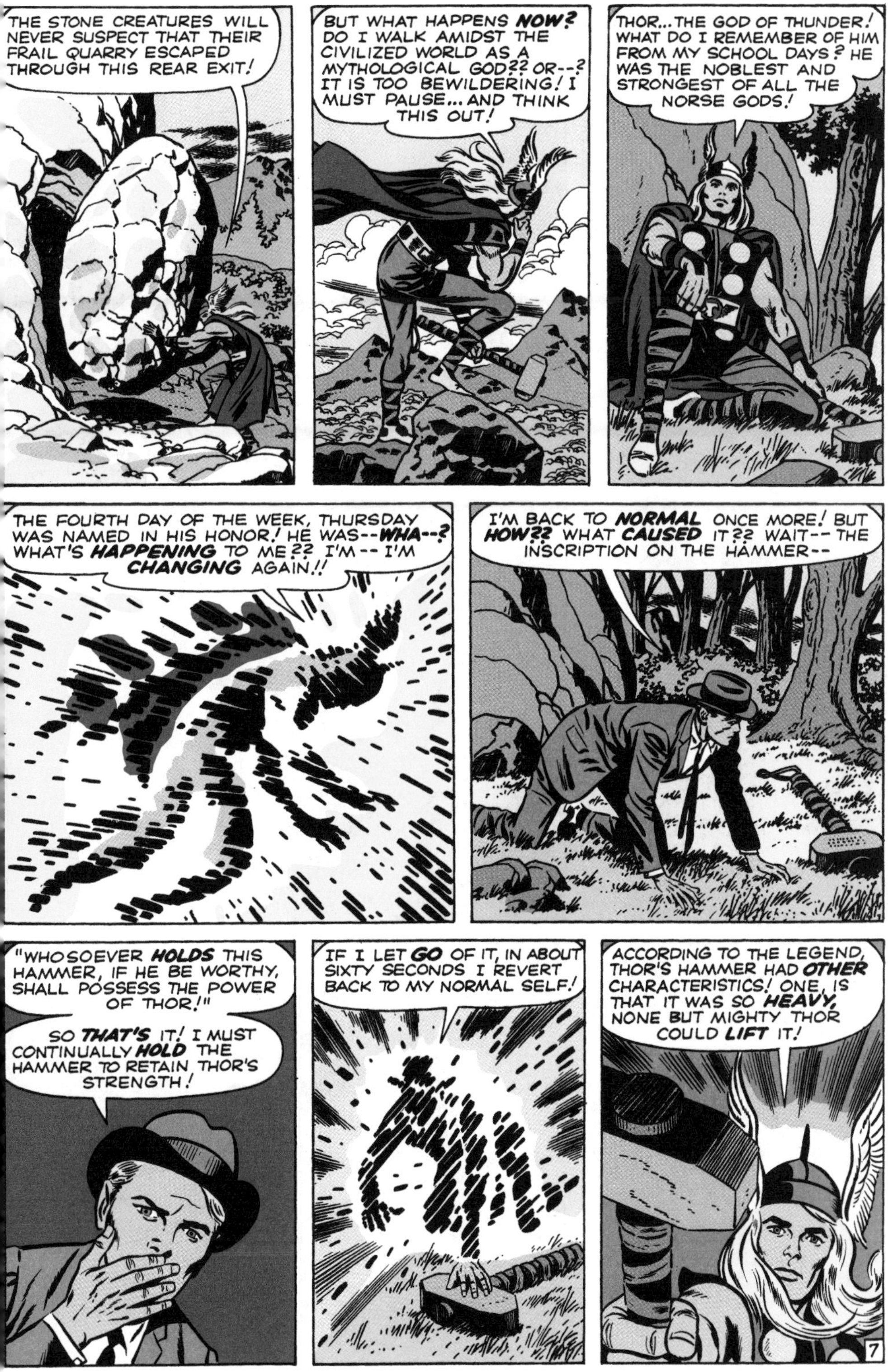
THE STONE CREATURES WILL NEVER SUSPECT THAT THEIR FRAIL QUARRY ESCAPED THROUGH THIS REAR EXIT!
BUT WHAT HAPPENS NOW? DO I WALK AMIDST THE CIVILIZED WORLD AS A MYTHOLOGICAL GOD?? OR--? IT IS TOO BEWILDERING! I MUST PAUSE... AND THINK THIS OUT!
THOR... THE GOD OF THUNDER! WHAT DO I REMEMBER OF HIM FROM MY SCHOOL DAYS? HE WAS THE NOBLEST AND STRONGEST OF ALL THE NORSE GODS!
THE FOURTH DAY OF THE WEEK, THURSDAY WAS NAMED IN HIS HONOR! HE WAS--WHA--? WHAT'S HAPPENING TO ME?? I'M-- I'M CHANGING AGAIN!!
I'M BACK TO NORMAL ONCE MORE! BUT HOW?? WHAT CAUSED IT?? WAIT-- THE INSCRIPTION ON THE HAMMER--
"WHOSOEVER HOLDS THIS HAMMER, IF HE BE WORTHY, SHALL POSSESS THE POWER OF THOR!"
SO THAT'S IT! I MUST CONTINUALLY HOLD THE HAMMER TO RETAIN THOR'S STRENGTH!
IF I LET GO OF IT, IN ABOUT SIXTY SECONDS I REVERT BACK TO MY NORMAL SELF!
ACCORDING TO THE LEGEND, THOR'S HAMMER HAD OTHER CHARACTERISTICS! ONE, IS THAT IT WAS SO HEAVY, NONE BUT MIGHTY THOR COULD LIFT IT!
7

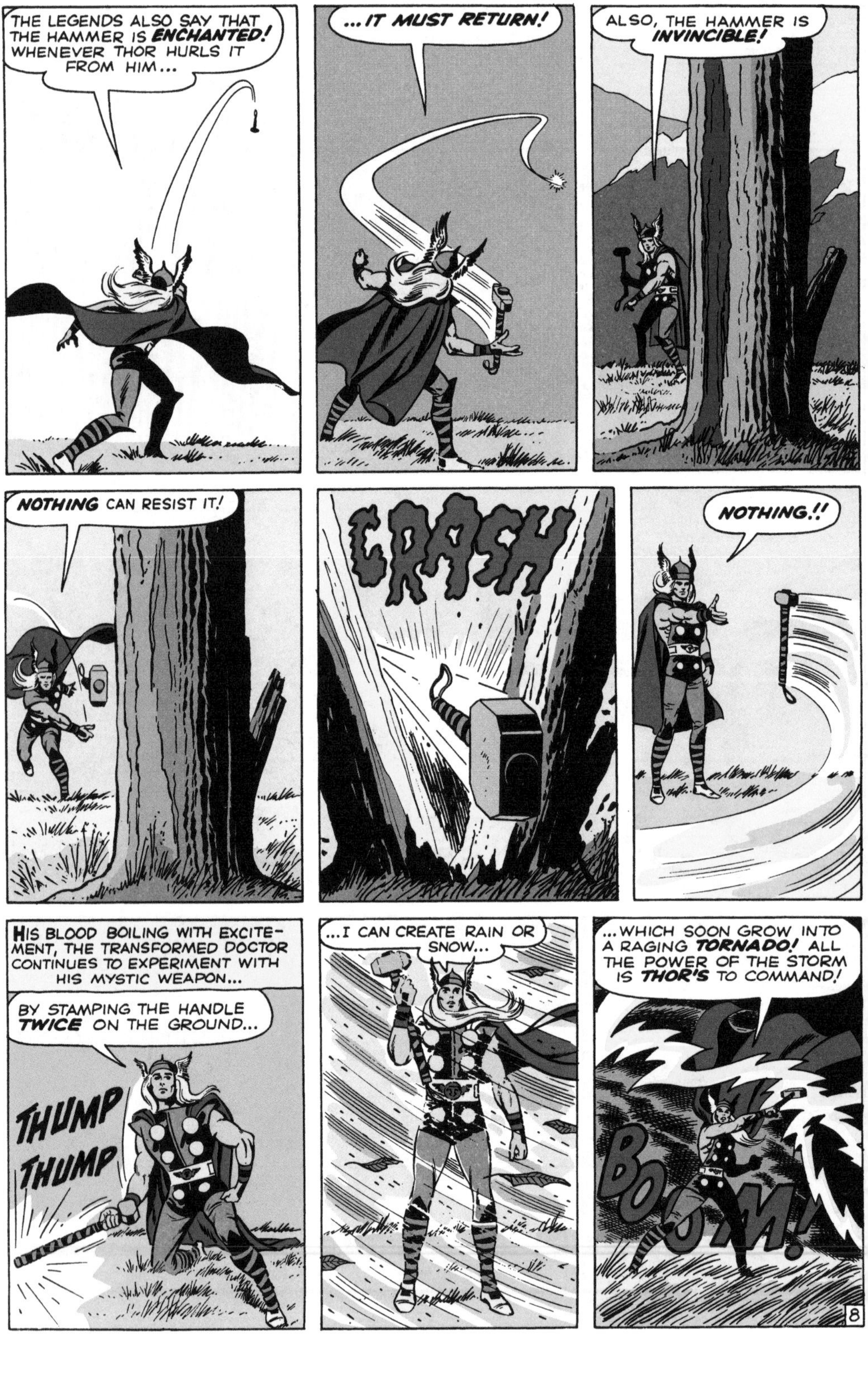

THE LEGENDS ALSO SAY THAT THE HAMMER IS ENCHANTED! WHENEVER THOR HURLS IT FROM HIM...
...IT MUST RETURN!
ALSO, THE HAMMER IS INVINCIBLE!
NOTHING CAN RESIST IT!
CRASH
NOTHING.!!
HIS BLOOD BOILING WITH EXCITEMENT, THE TRANSFORMED DOCTOR CONTINUES TO EXPERIMENT WITH HIS MYSTIC WEAPON...
BY STAMPING THE HANDLE TWICE ON THE GROUND...
THUMP
THUMP
...I CAN CREATE RAIN OR SNOW...
...WHICH SOON GROW INTO A RAGING TORNADO! ALL THE POWER OF THE STORM IS THOR'S TO COMMAND!
BOOM!
8

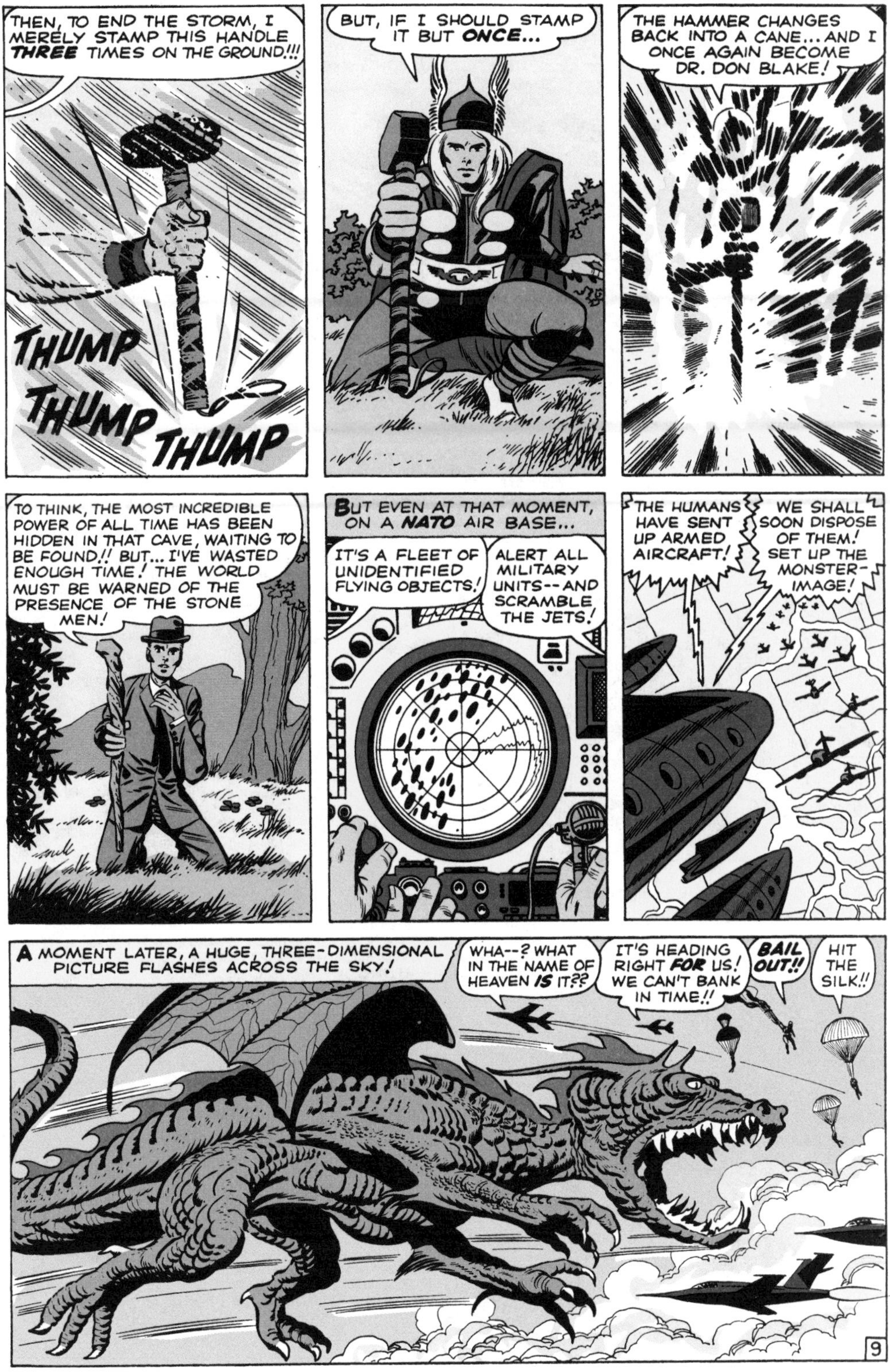

THEN, TO END THE STORM, I MERELY STAMP THIS HANDLE THREE TIMES ON THE GROUND!!!
THUMP THUMP THUMP
BUT, IF I SHOULD STAMP IT BUT ONCE...
THE HAMMER CHANGES BACK INTO A CANE... AND I ONCE AGAIN BECOME DR. DON BLAKE!
TO THINK, THE MOST INCREDIBLE POWER OF ALL TIME HAS BEEN HIDDEN IN THAT CAVE, WAITING TO BE FOUND!! BUT... I'VE WASTED ENOUGH TIME! THE WORLD MUST BE WARNED OF THE PRESENCE OF THE STONE MEN!
BUT EVEN AT THAT MOMENT, ON A NATO AIR BASE...
IT'S A FLEET OF UNIDENTIFIED FLYING OBJECTS!
ALERT ALL MILITARY UNITS--AND SCRAMBLE THE JETS!
THE HUMANS HAVE SENT UP ARMED AIRCRAFT!
WE SHALL SOON DISPOSE OF THEM! SET UP THE MONSTER-IMAGE!
A MOMENT LATER, A HUGE, THREE-DIMENSIONAL PICTURE FLASHES ACROSS THE SKY!
WHA--? WHAT IN THE NAME OF HEAVEN IS IT??
IT'S HEADING RIGHT FOR US! WE CAN'T BANK IN TIME!!
BAIL OUT!!
HIT THE SILK!!
9

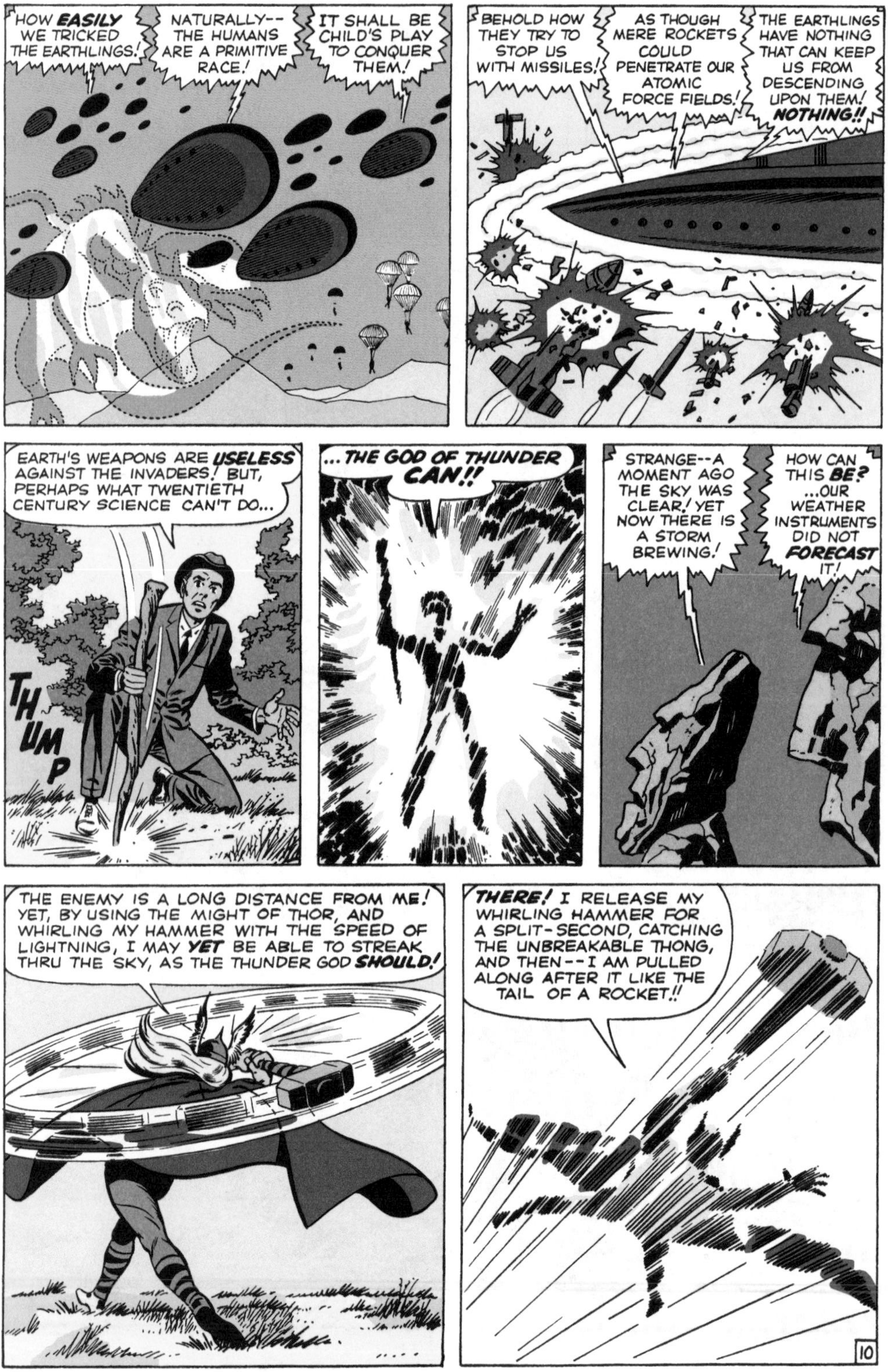
HOW EASILY WE TRICKED THE EARTHLINGS!
NATURALLY-- THE HUMANS ARE A PRIMITIVE RACE!
IT SHALL BE CHILD'S PLAY TO CONQUER THEM!
BEHOLD HOW THEY TRY TO STOP US WITH MISSILES!
AS THOUGH MERE ROCKETS COULD PENETRATE OUR ATOMIC FORCE FIELDS!
THE EARTHLINGS HAVE NOTHING THAT CAN KEEP US FROM DESCENDING UPON THEM! NOTHING!!
EARTH'S WEAPONS ARE USELESS AGAINST THE INVADERS! BUT, PERHAPS WHAT TWENTIETH CENTURY SCIENCE CAN'T DO...
THUMP
...THE GOD OF THUNDER CAN!!
STRANGE--A MOMENT AGO THE SKY WAS CLEAR! YET NOW THERE IS A STORM BREWING!
HOW CAN THIS BE? ...OUR WEATHER INSTRUMENTS DID NOT FORECAST IT!
THE ENEMY IS A LONG DISTANCE FROM ME! YET, BY USING THE MIGHT OF THOR, AND WHIRLING MY HAMMER WITH THE SPEED OF LIGHTNING, I MAY YET BE ABLE TO STREAK THRU THE SKY, AS THE THUNDER GOD SHOULD!
THERE! I RELEASE MY WHIRLING HAMMER FOR A SPLIT-SECOND, CATCHING THE UNBREAKABLE THONG, AND THEN--I AM PULLED ALONG AFTER IT LIKE THE TAIL OF A ROCKET!!
10

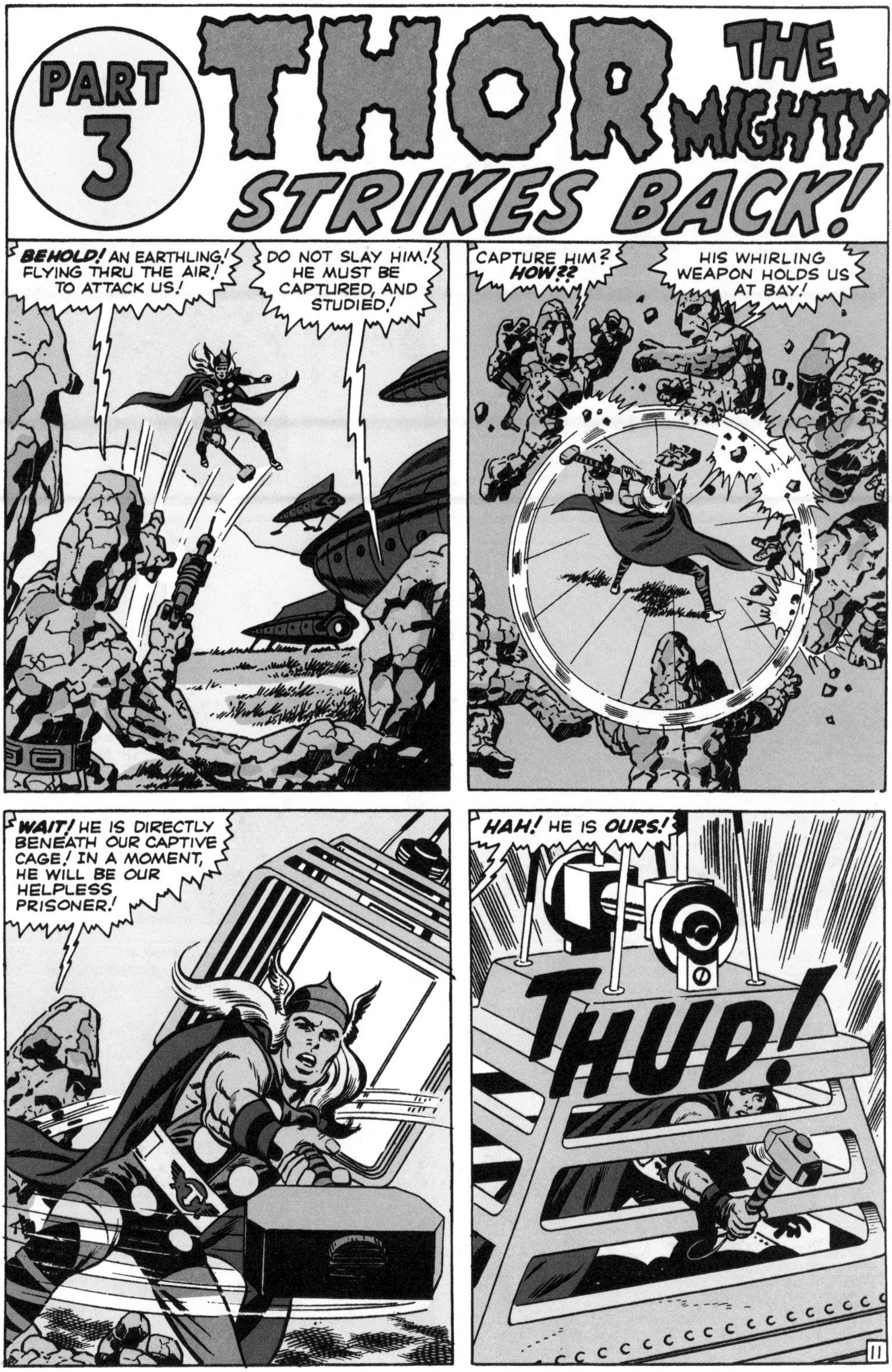
PART 3
THOR THE MIGHTY STRIKES BACK!
BEHOLD! AN EARTHLING! FLYING THRU THE AIR! TO ATTACK US!
DO NOT SLAY HIM! HE MUST BE CAPTURED, AND STUDIED!
CAPTURE HIM? HOW??
HIS WHIRLING WEAPON HOLDS US AT BAY!
WAIT! HE IS DIRECTLY BENEATH OUR CAPTIVE CAGE! IN A MOMENT, HE WILL BE OUR HELPLESS PRISONER!
HAH! HE IS OURS!
THUD!
11

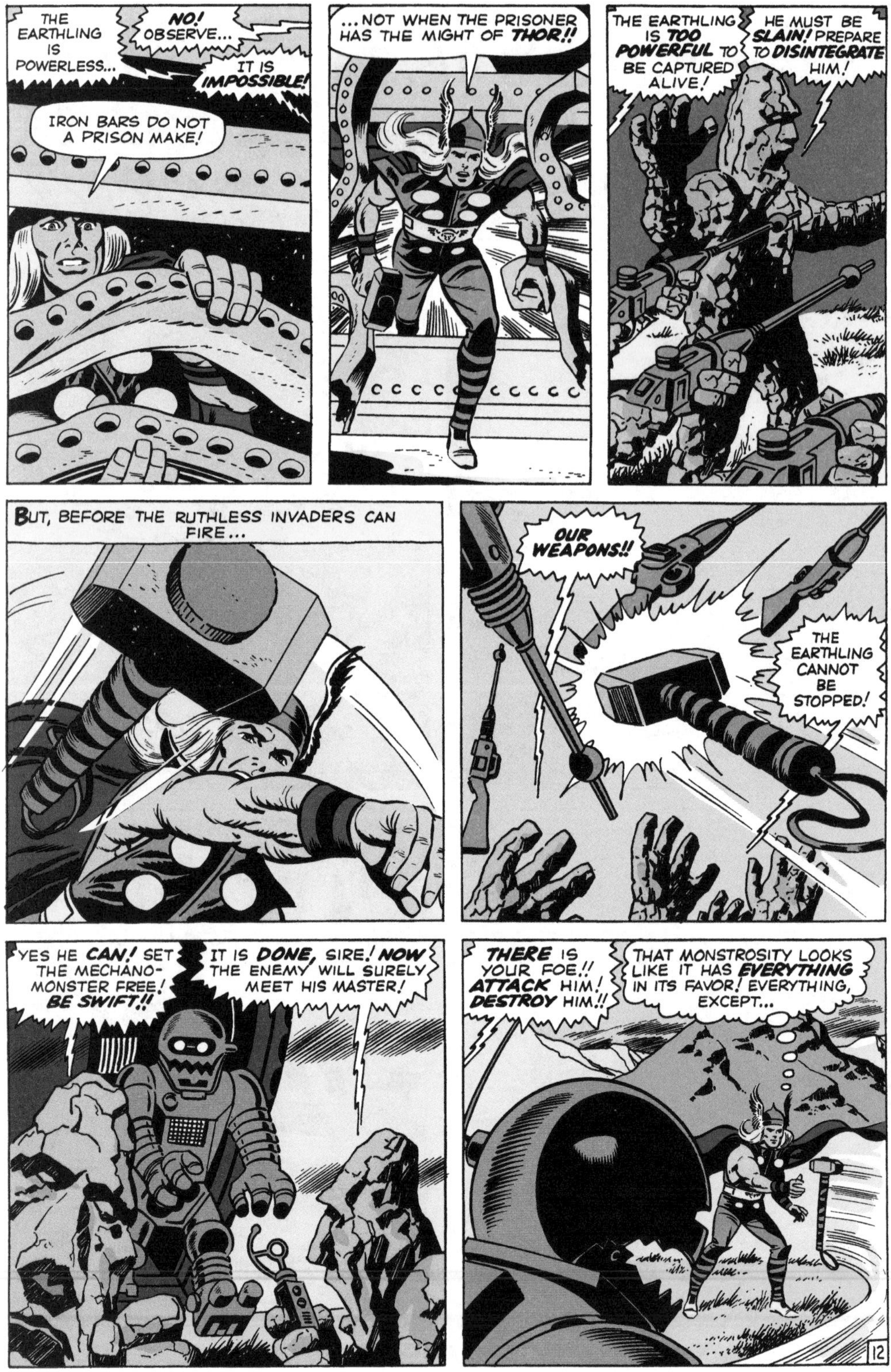
THE EARTHLING IS POWERLESS...
NO! OBSERVE...
IT IS IMPOSSIBLE!
IRON BARS DO NOT A PRISON MAKE!
...NOT WHEN THE PRISONER HAS THE MIGHT OF THOR!!
THE EARTHLING IS TOO POWERFUL TO BE CAPTURED ALIVE!
HE MUST BE SLAIN! PREPARE TO DISINTEGRATE HIM!
BUT, BEFORE THE RUTHLESS INVADERS CAN FIRE...
OUR WEAPONS!!
THE EARTHLING CANNOT BE STOPPED!
YES HE CAN! SET THE MECHANO-MONSTER FREE! BE SWIFT!!
IT IS DONE, SIRE! NOW THE ENEMY WILL SURELY MEET HIS MASTER!
THERE IS YOUR FOE!! ATTACK HIM! DESTROY HIM!!
THAT MONSTROSITY LOOKS LIKE IT HAS EVERYTHING IN ITS FAVOR! EVERYTHING, EXCEPT...
12

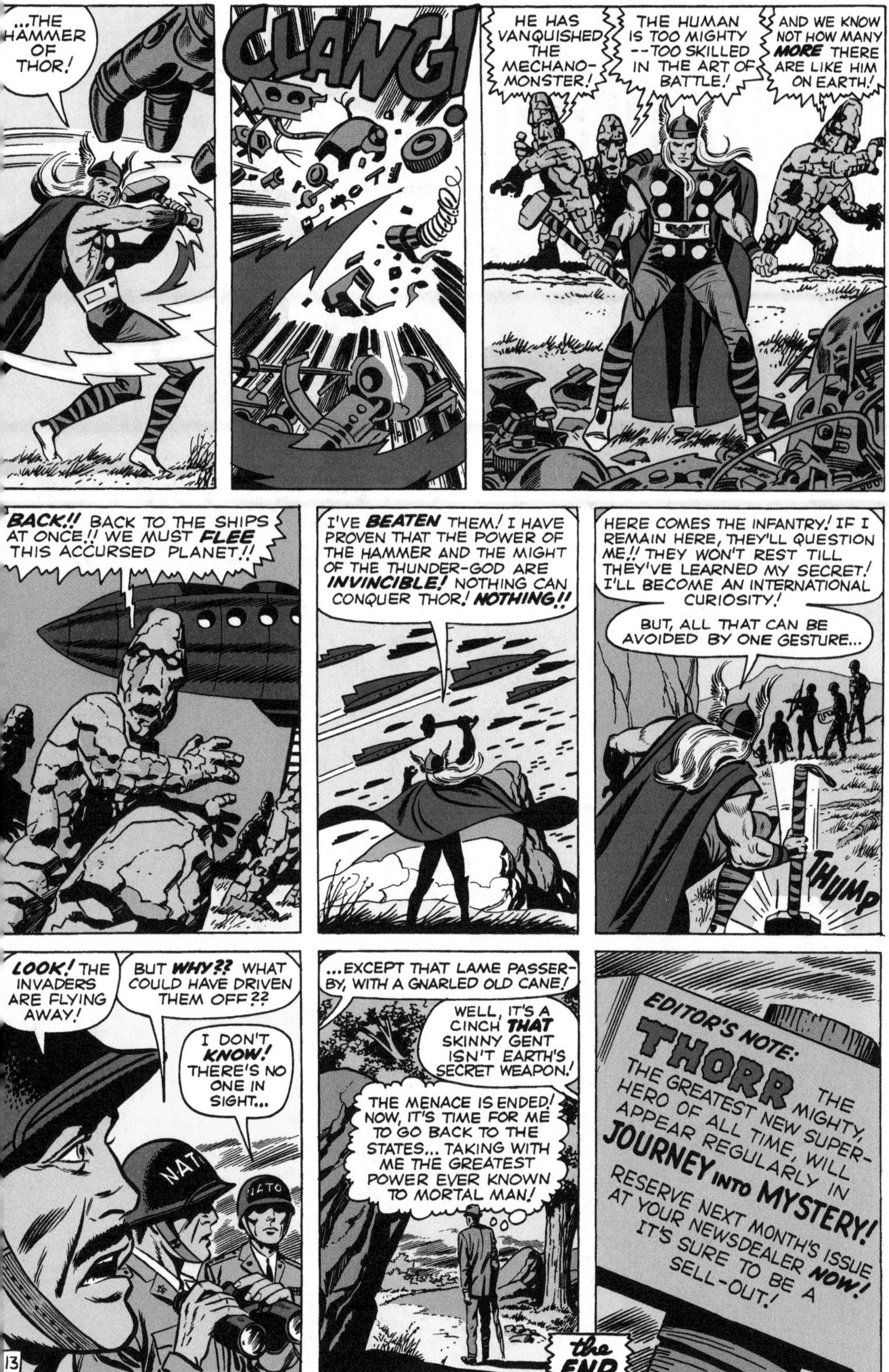

...THE HAMMER OF THOR!
CLANG!
HE HAS VANQUISHED THE MECHANO-MONSTER!
THE HUMAN IS TOO MIGHTY --TOO SKILLED IN THE ART OF BATTLE!
AND WE KNOW NOT HOW MANY MORE THERE ARE LIKE HIM ON EARTH!
BACK!! BACK TO THE SHIPS AT ONCE!! WE MUST FLEE THIS ACCURSED PLANET!!
I'VE BEATEN THEM! I HAVE PROVEN THAT THE POWER OF THE HAMMER AND THE MIGHT OF THE THUNDER-GOD ARE INVINCIBLE! NOTHING CAN CONQUER THOR! NOTHING!!
HERE COMES THE INFANTRY! IF I REMAIN HERE, THEY'LL QUESTION ME!! THEY WON'T REST TILL THEY'VE LEARNED MY SECRET! I'LL BECOME AN INTERNATIONAL CURIOSITY!
BUT, ALL THAT CAN BE AVOIDED BY ONE GESTURE...
THUMP
LOOK! THE INVADERS ARE FLYING AWAY!
BUT WHY?? WHAT COULD HAVE DRIVEN THEM OFF??
I DON'T KNOW! THERE'S NO ONE IN SIGHT...
NAT
NATO
...EXCEPT THAT LAME PASSER-BY, WITH A GNARLED OLD CANE!
WELL, IT'S A CINCH THAT SKINNY GENT ISN'T EARTH'S SECRET WEAPON!
THE MENACE IS ENDED! NOW, IT'S TIME FOR ME TO GO BACK TO THE STATES... TAKING WITH ME THE GREATEST POWER EVER KNOWN TO MORTAL MAN!
EDITOR'S NOTE:
THORR THE MIGHTY, THE GREATEST NEW SUPER-HERO OF ALL TIME, WILL APPEAR REGULARLY IN JOURNEY INTO MYSTERY!
RESERVE NEXT MONTH'S ISSUE AT YOUR NEWSDEALER NOW! IT'S SURE TO BE A SELL-OUT!
the END

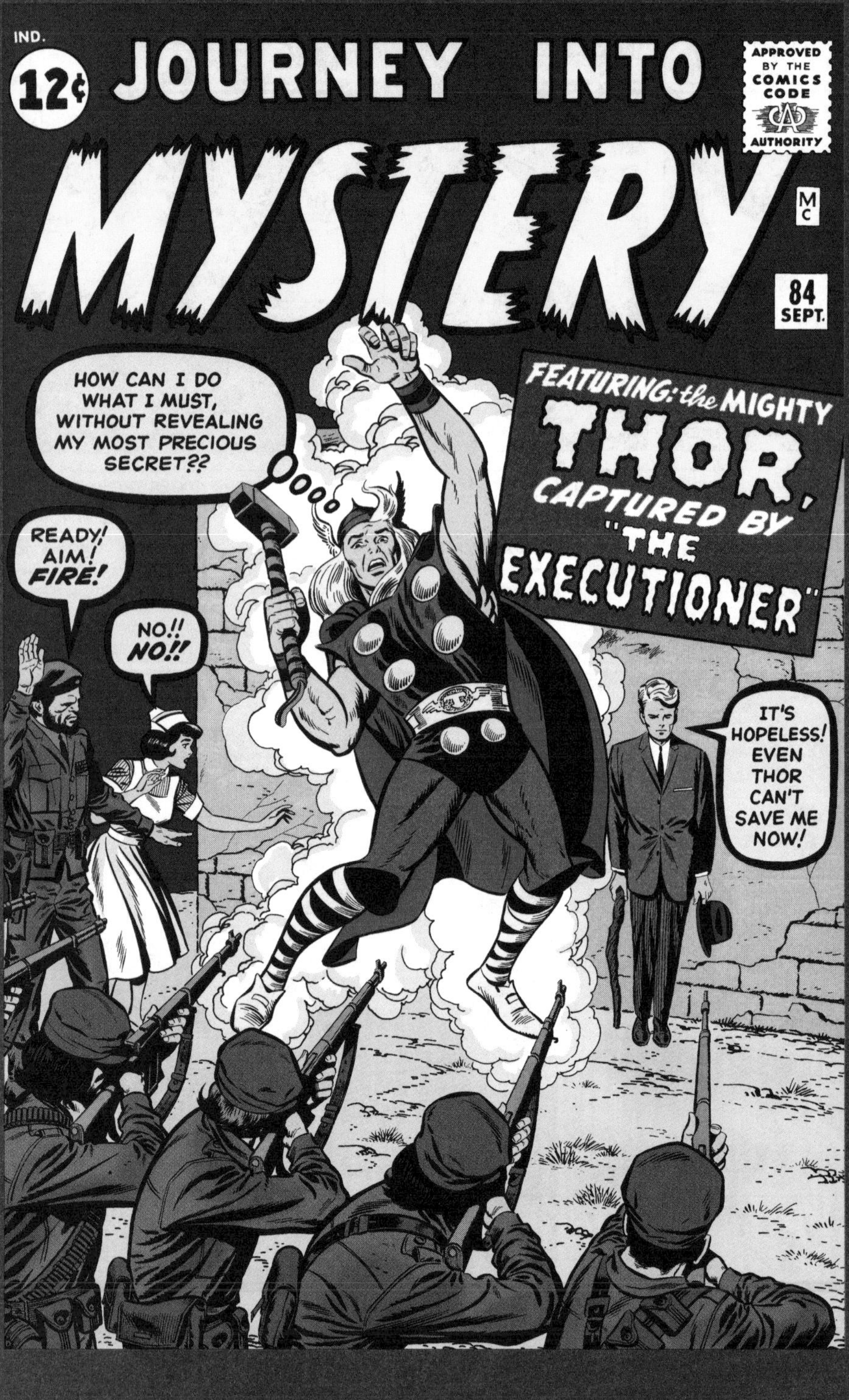

IND.
12¢
JOURNEY INTO
MYSTERY
MC
APPROVED BY THE COMICS CODE AUTHORITY
84
SEPT.
FEATURING: the MIGHTY THOR, CAPTURED BY "THE EXECUTIONER"
HOW CAN I DO WHAT I MUST, WITHOUT REVEALING MY MOST PRECIOUS SECRET??
READY! AIM! FIRE!
NO!! NO!!
IT'S HOPELESS! EVEN THOR CAN'T SAVE ME NOW!

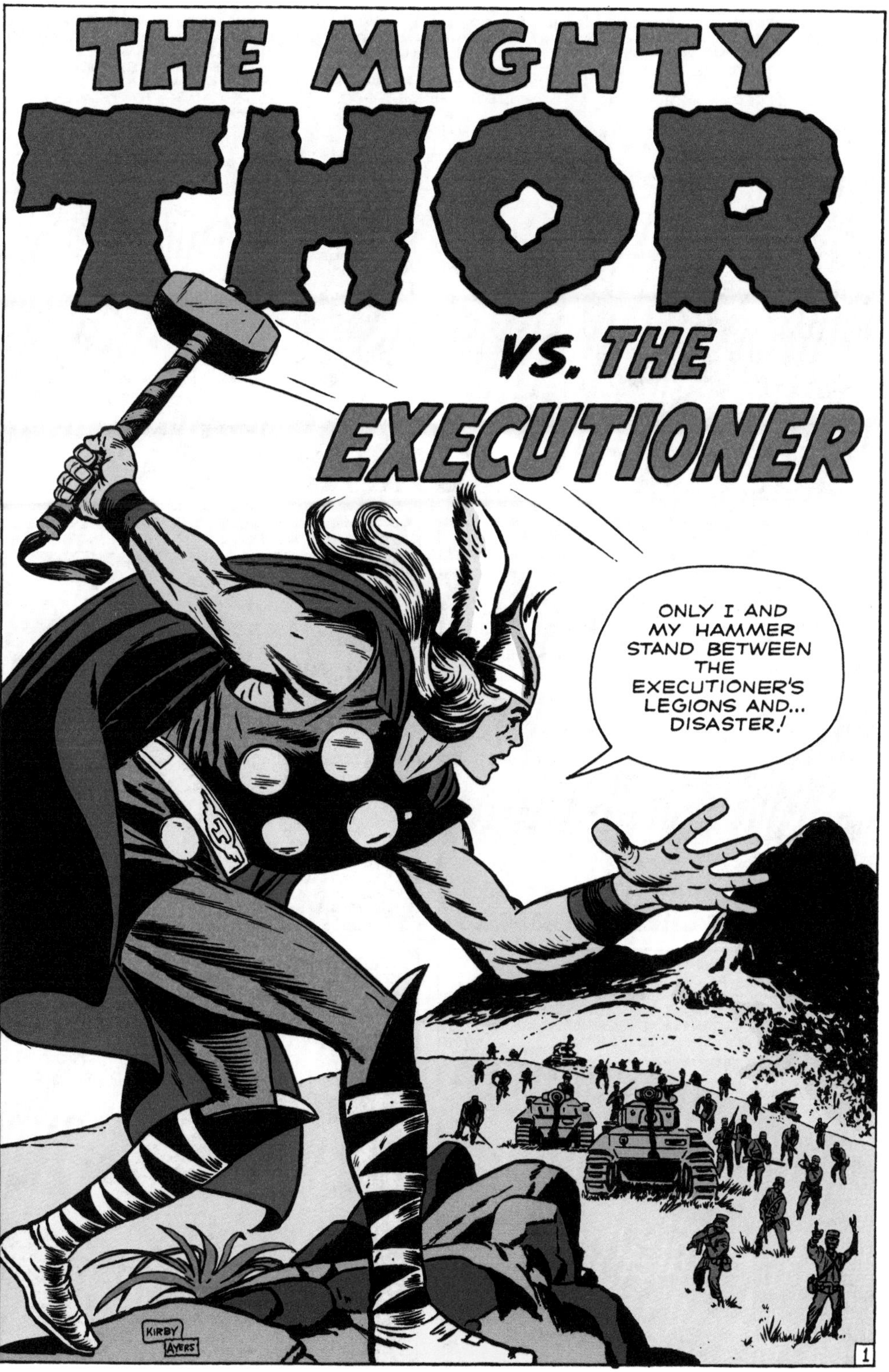
THE MIGHTY THOR VS. THE EXECUTIONER
ONLY I AND MY HAMMER STAND BETWEEN THE EXECUTIONER'S LEGIONS AND... DISASTER!
KIRBY AYERS
1

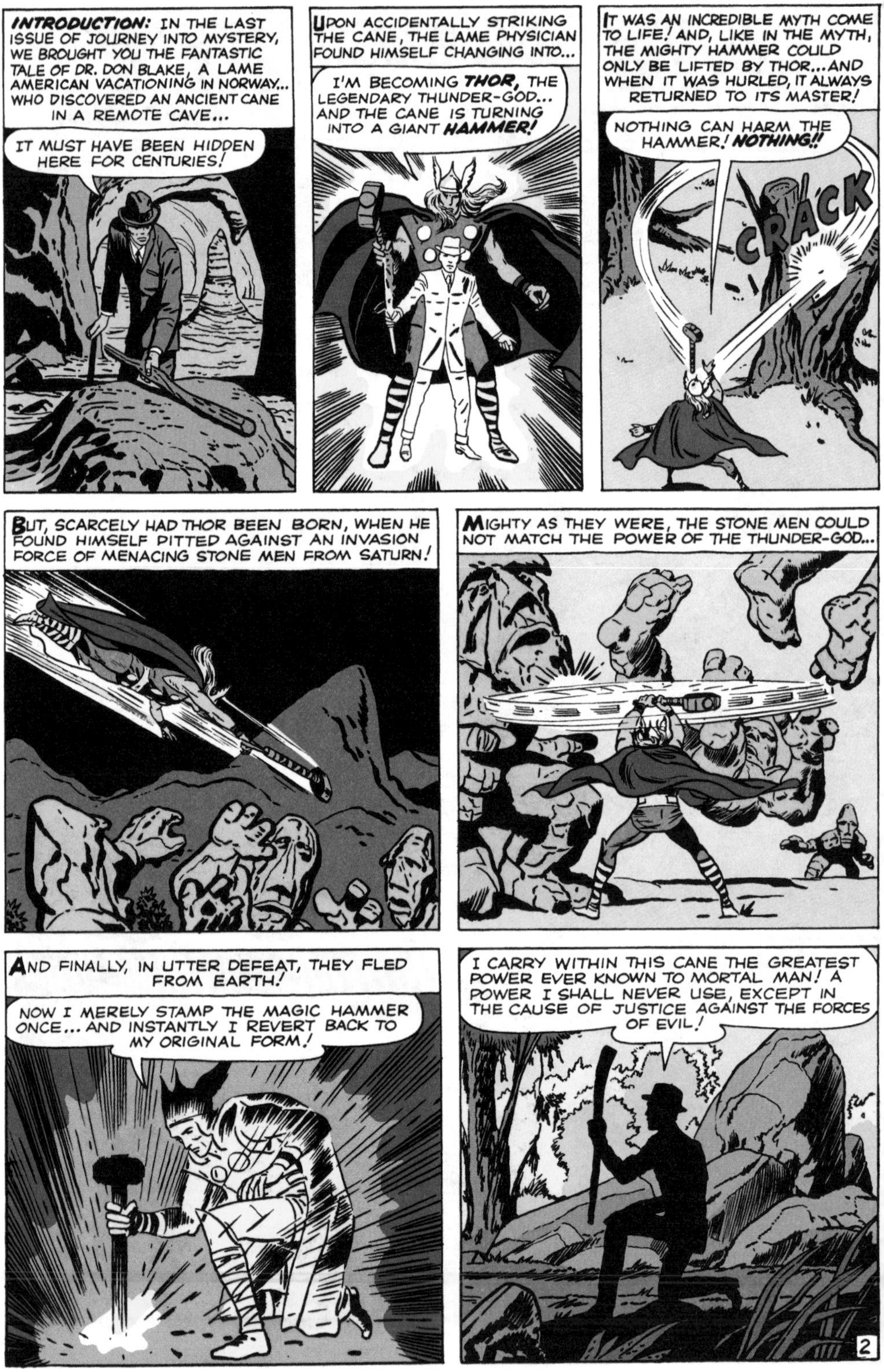
INTRODUCTION: IN THE LAST ISSUE OF JOURNEY INTO MYSTERY, WE BROUGHT YOU THE FANTASTIC TALE OF DR. DON BLAKE, A LAME AMERICAN VACATIONING IN NORWAY... WHO DISCOVERED AN ANCIENT CANE IN A REMOTE CAVE...
IT MUST HAVE BEEN HIDDEN HERE FOR CENTURIES!
UPON ACCIDENTALLY STRIKING THE CANE, THE LAME PHYSICIAN FOUND HIMSELF CHANGING INTO...
I'M BECOMING THOR, THE LEGENDARY THUNDER-GOD... AND THE CANE IS TURNING INTO A GIANT HAMMER!
IT WAS AN INCREDIBLE MYTH COME TO LIFE! AND, LIKE IN THE MYTH, THE MIGHTY HAMMER COULD ONLY BE LIFTED BY THOR... AND WHEN IT WAS HURLED, IT ALWAYS RETURNED TO ITS MASTER!
NOTHING CAN HARM THE HAMMER! NOTHING!!
CRACK
BUT, SCARCELY HAD THOR BEEN BORN, WHEN HE FOUND HIMSELF PITTED AGAINST AN INVASION FORCE OF MENACING STONE MEN FROM SATURN!
MIGHTY AS THEY WERE, THE STONE MEN COULD NOT MATCH THE POWER OF THE THUNDER-GOD...
AND FINALLY, IN UTTER DEFEAT, THEY FLED FROM EARTH!
NOW I MERELY STAMP THE MAGIC HAMMER ONCE... AND INSTANTLY I REVERT BACK TO MY ORIGINAL FORM!
I CARRY WITHIN THIS CANE THE GREATEST POWER EVER KNOWN TO MORTAL MAN! A POWER I SHALL NEVER USE, EXCEPT IN THE CAUSE OF JUSTICE AGAINST THE FORCES OF EVIL!
2

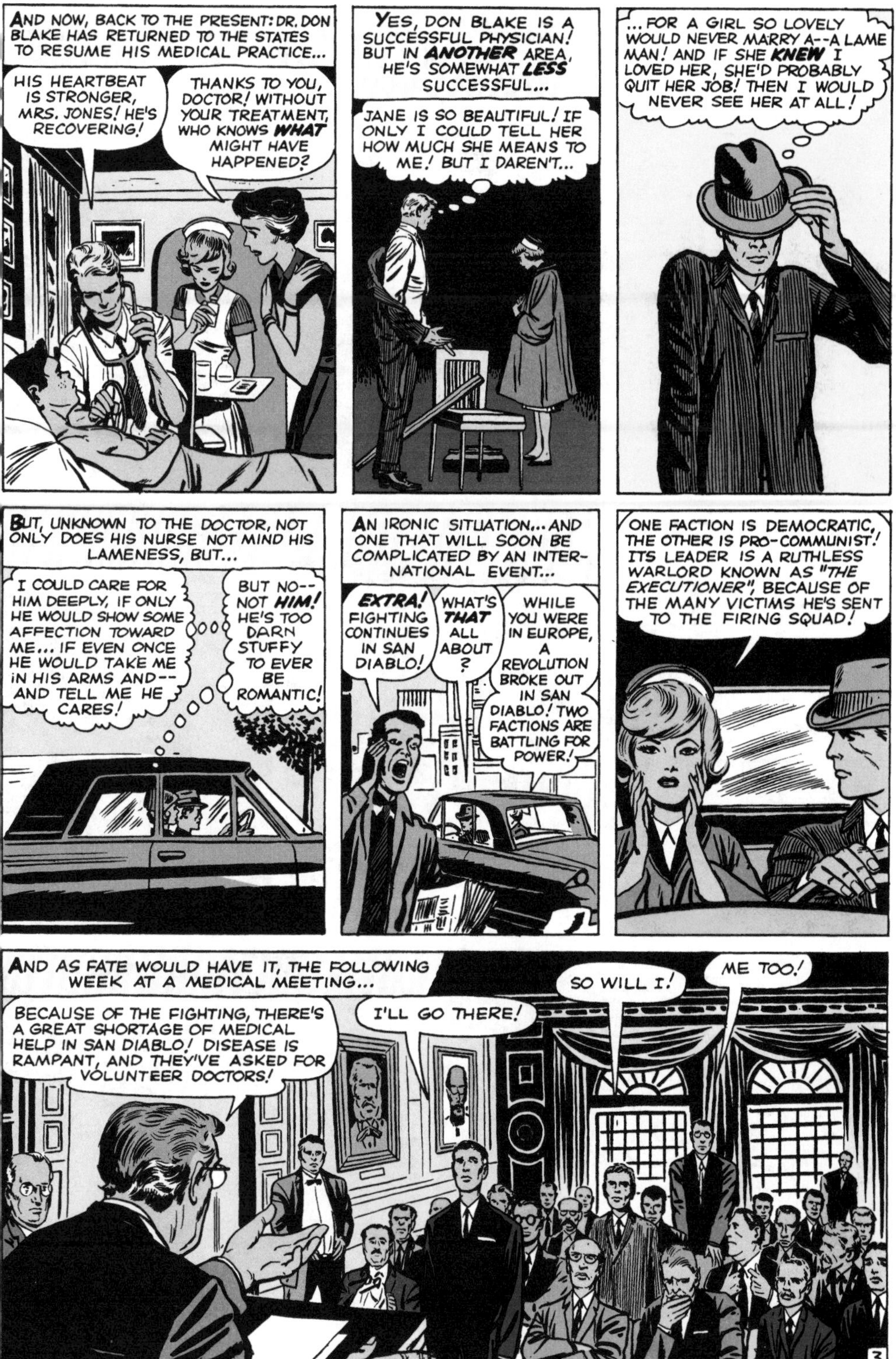
AND NOW, BACK TO THE PRESENT: DR. DON BLAKE HAS RETURNED TO THE STATES TO RESUME HIS MEDICAL PRACTICE...
HIS HEARTBEAT IS STRONGER, MRS. JONES! HE'S RECOVERING!
THANKS TO YOU, DOCTOR! WITHOUT YOUR TREATMENT, WHO KNOWS WHAT MIGHT HAVE HAPPENED?
YES, DON BLAKE IS A SUCCESSFUL PHYSICIAN! BUT IN ANOTHER AREA, HE'S SOMEWHAT LESS SUCCESSFUL...
JANE IS SO BEAUTIFUL! IF ONLY I COULD TELL HER HOW MUCH SHE MEANS TO ME! BUT I DAREN'T...
...FOR A GIRL SO LOVELY WOULD NEVER MARRY A--A LAME MAN! AND IF SHE KNEW I LOVED HER, SHE'D PROBABLY QUIT HER JOB! THEN I WOULD NEVER SEE HER AT ALL!
BUT, UNKNOWN TO THE DOCTOR, NOT ONLY DOES HIS NURSE NOT MIND HIS LAMENESS, BUT...
I COULD CARE FOR HIM DEEPLY, IF ONLY HE WOULD SHOW SOME AFFECTION TOWARD ME... IF EVEN ONCE HE WOULD TAKE ME IN HIS ARMS AND-- AND TELL ME HE CARES!
BUT NO-- NOT HIM! HE'S TOO DARN STUFFY TO EVER BE ROMANTIC!
AN IRONIC SITUATION... AND ONE THAT WILL SOON BE COMPLICATED BY AN INTERNATIONAL EVENT...
EXTRA! FIGHTING CONTINUES IN SAN DIABLO!
WHAT'S THAT ALL ABOUT?
WHILE YOU WERE IN EUROPE, A REVOLUTION BROKE OUT IN SAN DIABLO! TWO FACTIONS ARE BATTLING FOR POWER!
ONE FACTION IS DEMOCRATIC, THE OTHER IS PRO-COMMUNIST! ITS LEADER IS A RUTHLESS WARLORD KNOWN AS "THE EXECUTIONER", BECAUSE OF THE MANY VICTIMS HE'S SENT TO THE FIRING SQUAD!
AND AS FATE WOULD HAVE IT, THE FOLLOWING WEEK AT A MEDICAL MEETING...
BECAUSE OF THE FIGHTING, THERE'S A GREAT SHORTAGE OF MEDICAL HELP IN SAN DIABLO! DISEASE IS RAMPANT, AND THEY'VE ASKED FOR VOLUNTEER DOCTORS!
I'LL GO THERE!
SO WILL I!
ME TOO!
3

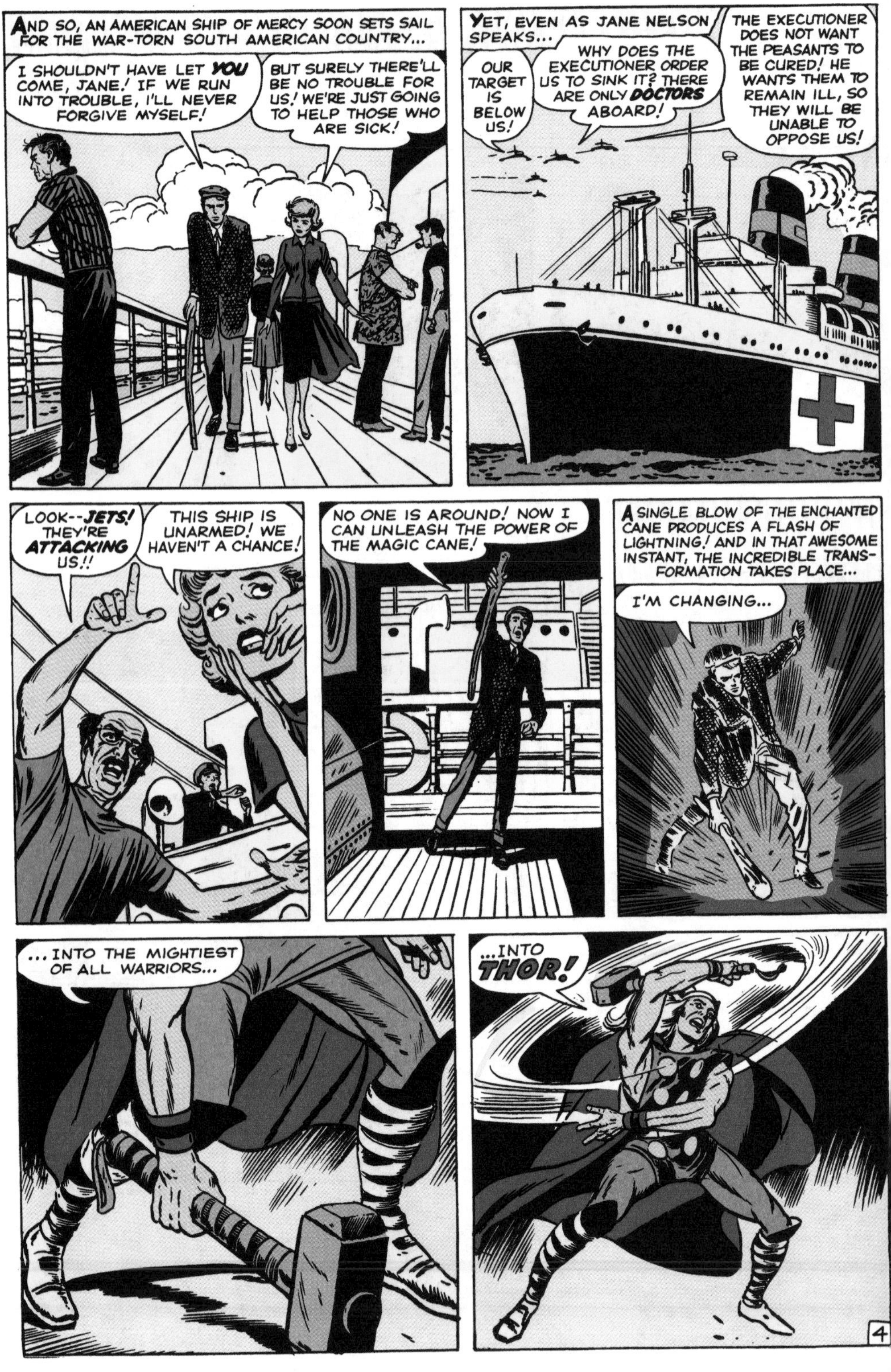
AND SO, AN AMERICAN SHIP OF MERCY SOON SETS SAIL FOR THE WAR-TORN SOUTH AMERICAN COUNTRY...
I SHOULDN'T HAVE LET YOU COME, JANE! IF WE RUN INTO TROUBLE, I'LL NEVER FORGIVE MYSELF!
BUT SURELY THERE'LL BE NO TROUBLE FOR US! WE'RE JUST GOING TO HELP THOSE WHO ARE SICK!
YET, EVEN AS JANE NELSON SPEAKS...
OUR TARGET IS BELOW US!
WHY DOES THE EXECUTIONER ORDER US TO SINK IT? THERE ARE ONLY DOCTORS ABOARD!
THE EXECUTIONER DOES NOT WANT THE PEASANTS TO BE CURED! HE WANTS THEM TO REMAIN ILL, SO THEY WILL BE UNABLE TO OPPOSE US!
LOOK--JETS! THEY'RE ATTACKING US!!
THIS SHIP IS UNARMED! WE HAVEN'T A CHANCE!
NO ONE IS AROUND! NOW I CAN UNLEASH THE POWER OF THE MAGIC CANE!
A SINGLE BLOW OF THE ENCHANTED CANE PRODUCES A FLASH OF LIGHTNING! AND IN THAT AWESOME INSTANT, THE INCREDIBLE TRANSFORMATION TAKES PLACE...
I'M CHANGING...
...INTO THE MIGHTIEST OF ALL WARRIORS...
...INTO THOR!
4

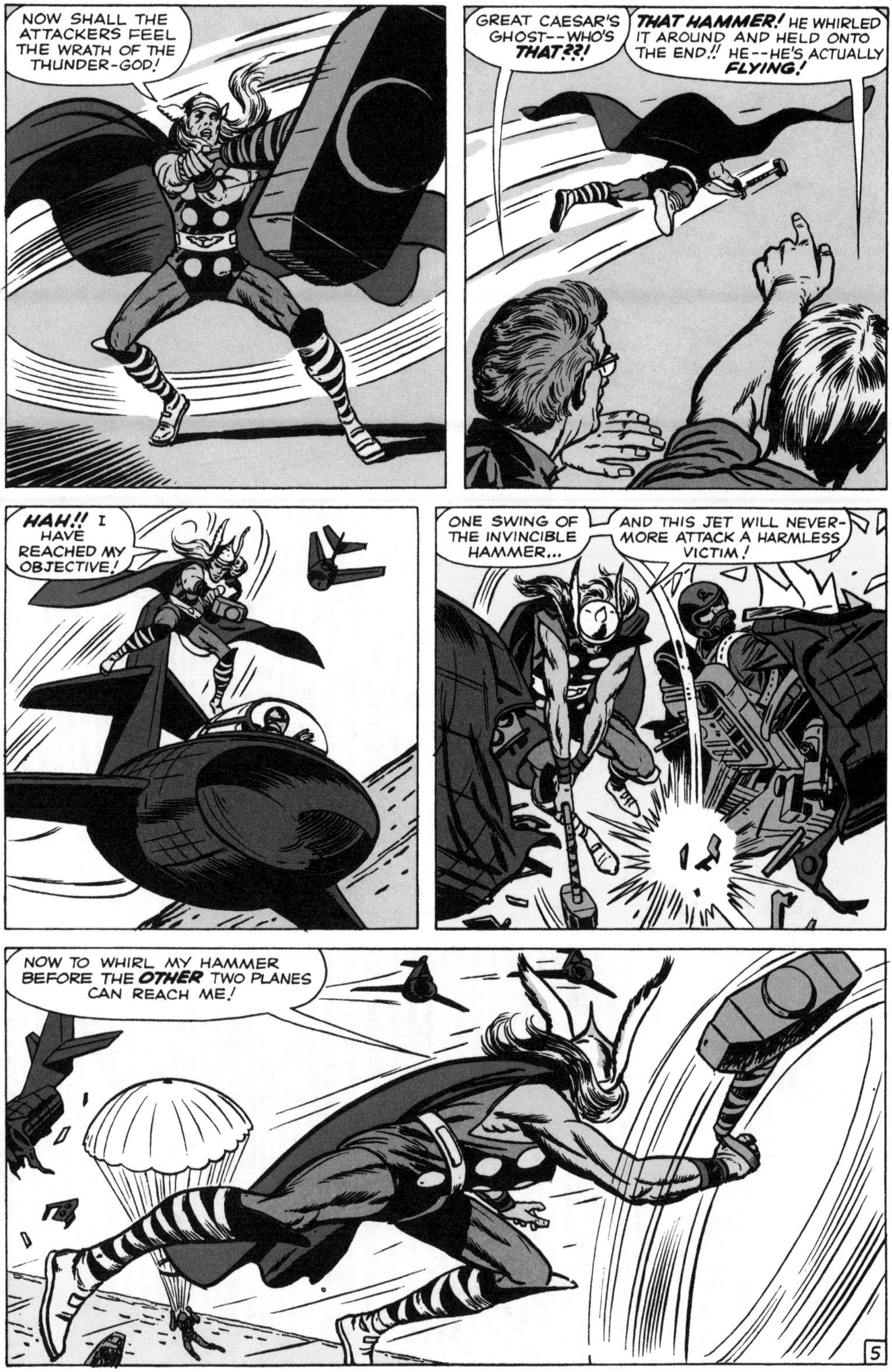
NOW SHALL THE ATTACKERS FEEL THE WRATH OF THE THUNDER-GOD!
GREAT CAESAR'S GHOST--WHO'S THAT??!
THAT HAMMER! HE WHIRLED IT AROUND AND HELD ONTO THE END!! HE--HE'S ACTUALLY FLYING!
HAH!! I HAVE REACHED MY OBJECTIVE!
ONE SWING OF THE INVINCIBLE HAMMER...
AND THIS JET WILL NEVER-MORE ATTACK A HARMLESS VICTIM!
NOW TO WHIRL MY HAMMER BEFORE THE OTHER TWO PLANES CAN REACH ME!
5

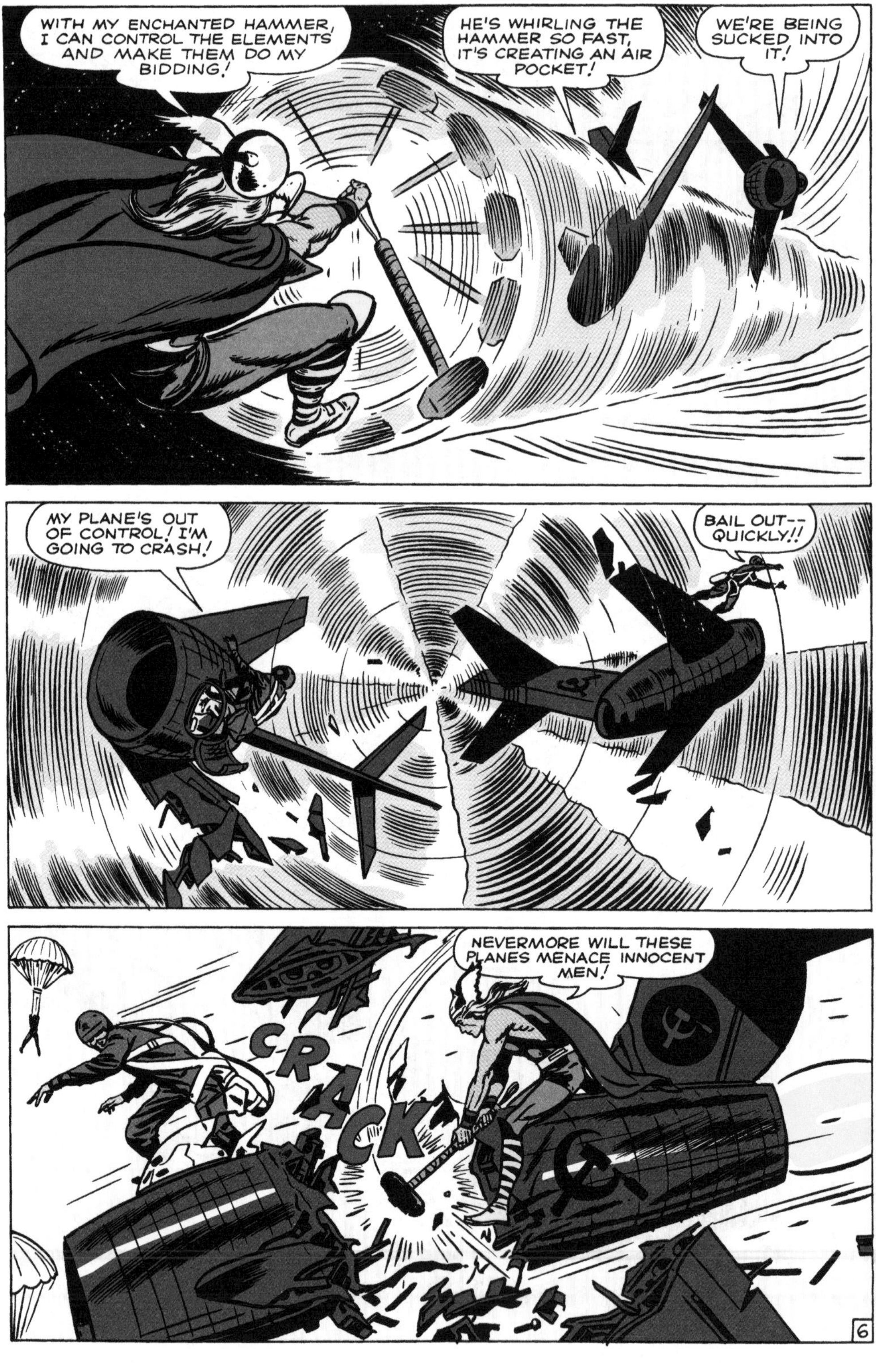

WITH MY ENCHANTED HAMMER, I CAN CONTROL THE ELEMENTS AND MAKE THEM DO MY BIDDING!
HE'S WHIRLING THE HAMMER SO FAST, IT'S CREATING AN AIR POCKET!
WE'RE BEING SUCKED INTO IT!
MY PLANE'S OUT OF CONTROL! I'M GOING TO CRASH!
BAIL OUT-- QUICKLY!!
NEVERMORE WILL THESE PLANES MENACE INNOCENT MEN!
CRACK

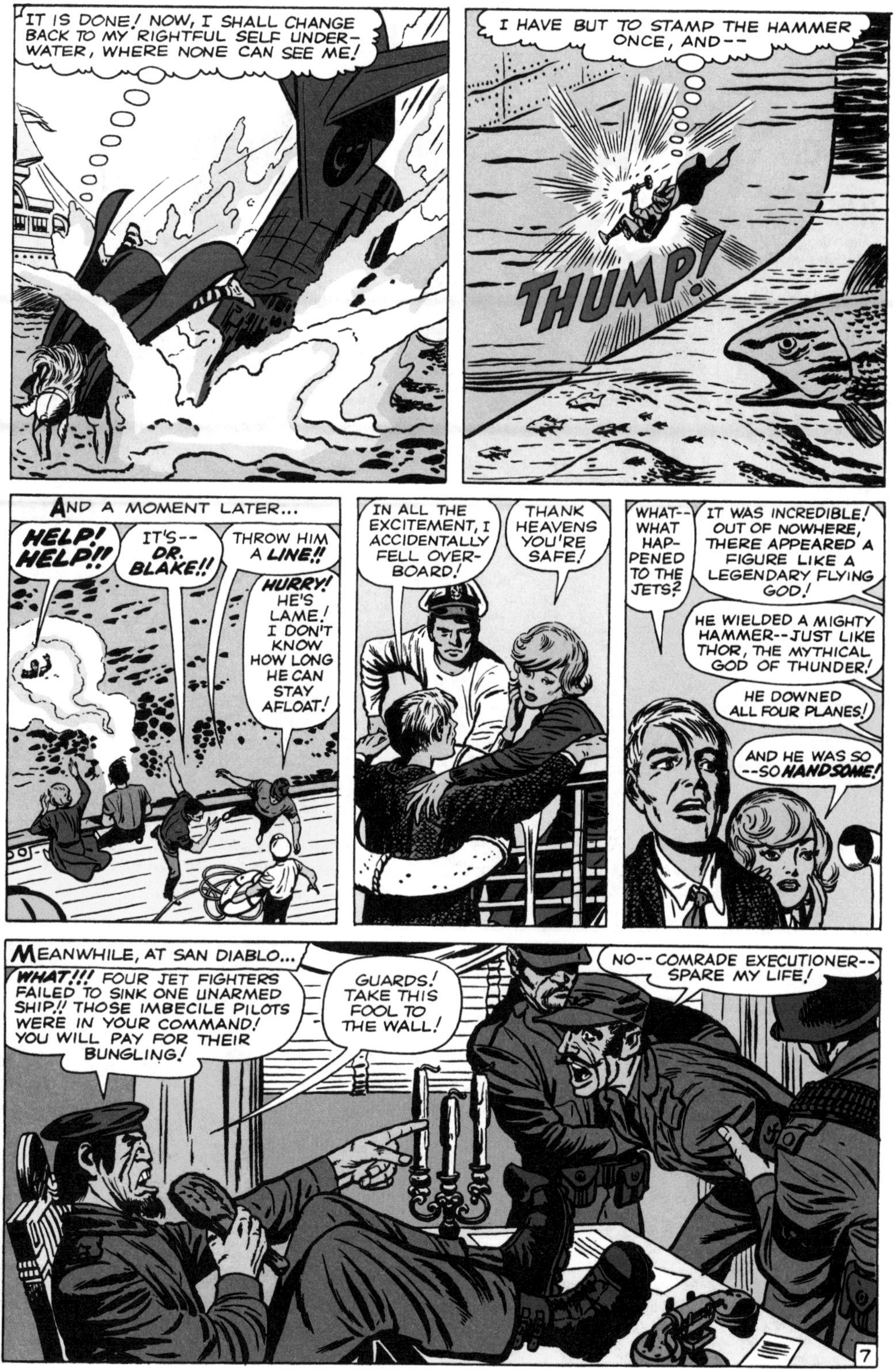
IT IS DONE! NOW, I SHALL CHANGE BACK TO MY RIGHTFUL SELF UNDER-WATER, WHERE NONE CAN SEE ME!
I HAVE BUT TO STAMP THE HAMMER ONCE, AND--
THUMP!
AND A MOMENT LATER...
HELP! HELP!!
IT'S-- DR. BLAKE!!
THROW HIM A LINE!!
HURRY! HE'S LAME! I DON'T KNOW HOW LONG HE CAN STAY AFLOAT!
IN ALL THE EXCITEMENT, I ACCIDENTALLY FELL OVER-BOARD!
THANK HEAVENS YOU'RE SAFE!
WHAT-- WHAT HAP-PENED TO THE JETS?
IT WAS INCREDIBLE! OUT OF NOWHERE, THERE APPEARED A FIGURE LIKE A LEGENDARY FLYING GOD!
HE WIELDED A MIGHTY HAMMER--JUST LIKE THOR, THE MYTHICAL GOD OF THUNDER!
HE DOWNED ALL FOUR PLANES!
AND HE WAS SO --SO HANDSOME!
MEANWHILE, AT SAN DIABLO...
WHAT!!! FOUR JET FIGHTERS FAILED TO SINK ONE UNARMED SHIP!! THOSE IMBECILE PILOTS WERE IN YOUR COMMAND! YOU WILL PAY FOR THEIR BUNGLING!
GUARDS! TAKE THIS FOOL TO THE WALL!
NO-- COMRADE EXECUTIONER-- SPARE MY LIFE!
7

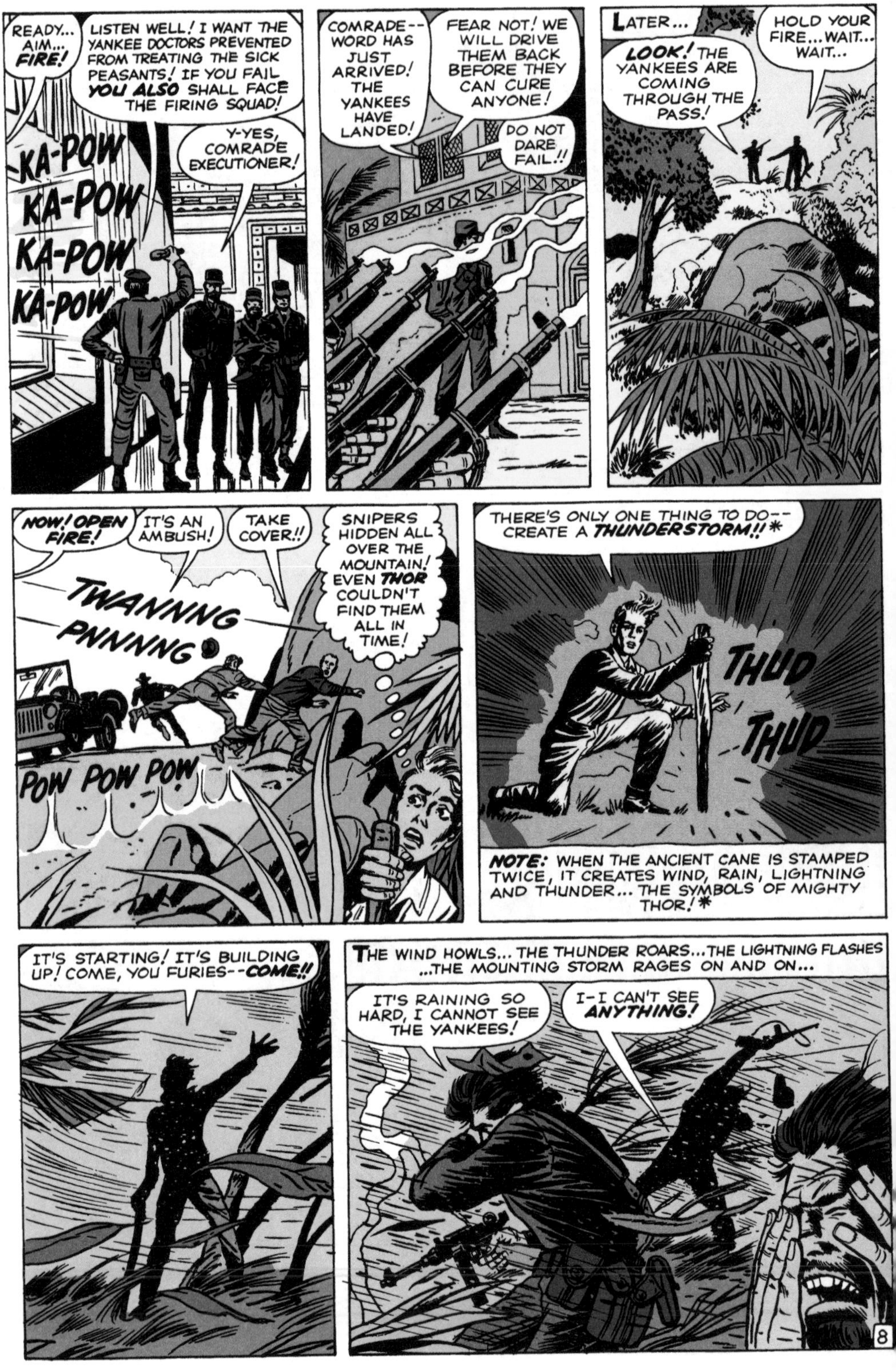

READY... AIM... FIRE!
LISTEN WELL! I WANT THE YANKEE DOCTORS PREVENTED FROM TREATING THE SICK PEASANTS! IF YOU FAIL YOU ALSO SHALL FACE THE FIRING SQUAD!
Y-YES, COMRADE EXECUTIONER!
KA-POW KA-POW KA-POW KA-POW
COMRADE-- WORD HAS JUST ARRIVED! THE YANKEES HAVE LANDED!
FEAR NOT! WE WILL DRIVE THEM BACK BEFORE THEY CAN CURE ANYONE!
DO NOT DARE FAIL!!
LATER...
LOOK! THE YANKEES ARE COMING THROUGH THE PASS!
HOLD YOUR FIRE...WAIT... WAIT...
NOW! OPEN FIRE!
IT'S AN AMBUSH!
TAKE COVER!!
SNIPERS HIDDEN ALL OVER THE MOUNTAIN! EVEN THOR COULDN'T FIND THEM ALL IN TIME!
TWANNNG
PNNNNG
POW POW POW
THERE'S ONLY ONE THING TO DO-- CREATE A THUNDERSTORM!!*
THUD
THUD
NOTE: WHEN THE ANCIENT CANE IS STAMPED TWICE, IT CREATES WIND, RAIN, LIGHTNING AND THUNDER... THE SYMBOLS OF MIGHTY THOR!*
IT'S STARTING! IT'S BUILDING UP! COME, YOU FURIES--COME!!
THE WIND HOWLS... THE THUNDER ROARS...THE LIGHTNING FLASHES ...THE MOUNTING STORM RAGES ON AND ON...
IT'S RAINING SO HARD, I CANNOT SEE THE YANKEES!
I-I CAN'T SEE ANYTHING!
8

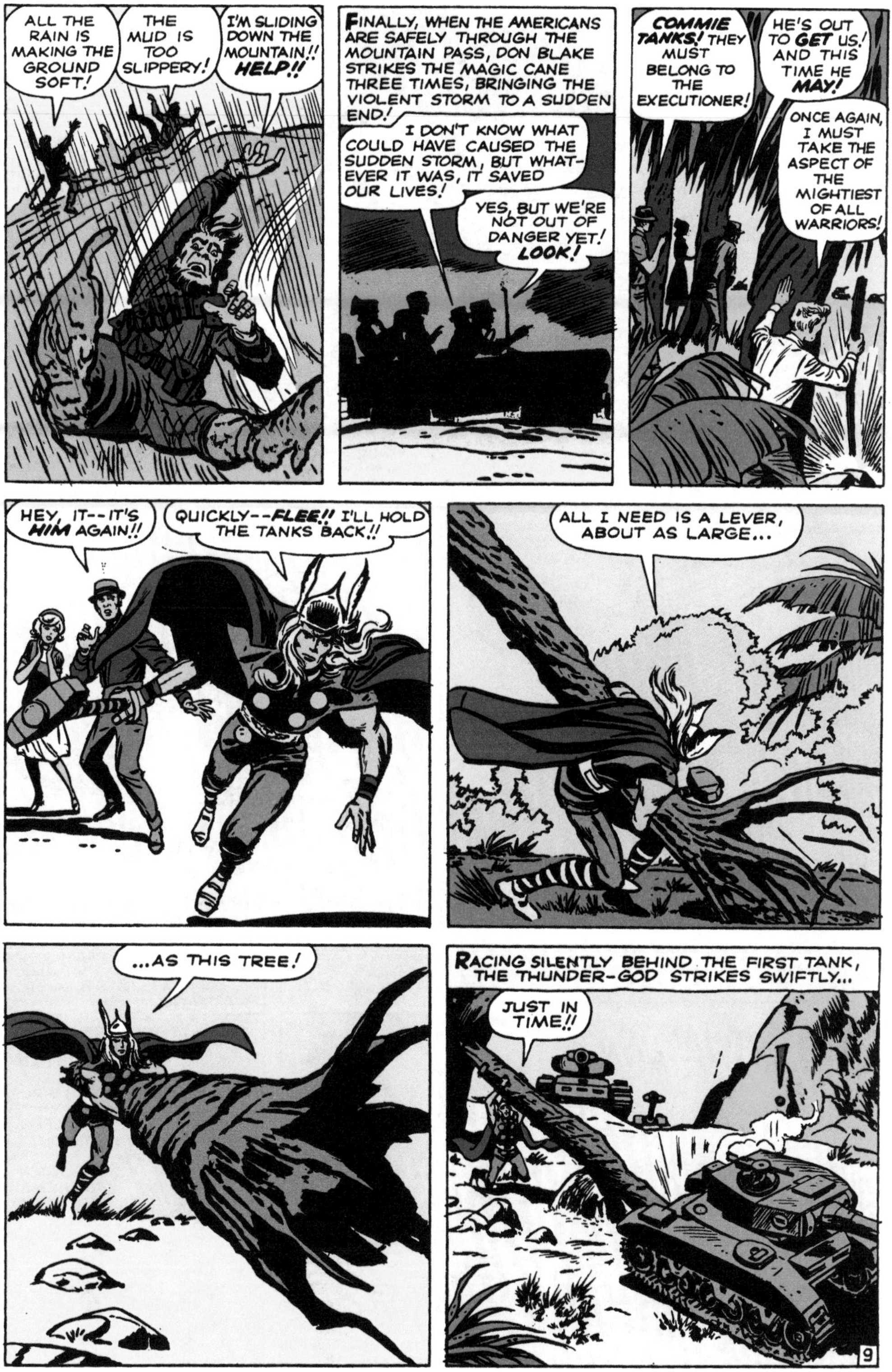
ALL THE RAIN IS MAKING THE GROUND SOFT!
THE MUD IS TOO SLIPPERY!
I'M SLIDING DOWN THE MOUNTAIN!! HELP!!
FINALLY, WHEN THE AMERICANS ARE SAFELY THROUGH THE MOUNTAIN PASS, DON BLAKE STRIKES THE MAGIC CANE THREE TIMES, BRINGING THE VIOLENT STORM TO A SUDDEN END!
I DON'T KNOW WHAT COULD HAVE CAUSED THE SUDDEN STORM, BUT WHATEVER IT WAS, IT SAVED OUR LIVES!
YES, BUT WE'RE NOT OUT OF DANGER YET! LOOK!
COMMIE TANKS! THEY MUST BELONG TO THE EXECUTIONER!
HE'S OUT TO GET US! AND THIS TIME HE MAY!
ONCE AGAIN, I MUST TAKE THE ASPECT OF THE MIGHTIEST OF ALL WARRIORS!
HEY, IT--IT'S HIM AGAIN!!
QUICKLY--FLEE!! I'LL HOLD THE TANKS BACK!!
ALL I NEED IS A LEVER, ABOUT AS LARGE...
...AS THIS TREE!
RACING SILENTLY BEHIND THE FIRST TANK, THE THUNDER-GOD STRIKES SWIFTLY...
JUST IN TIME!!
9

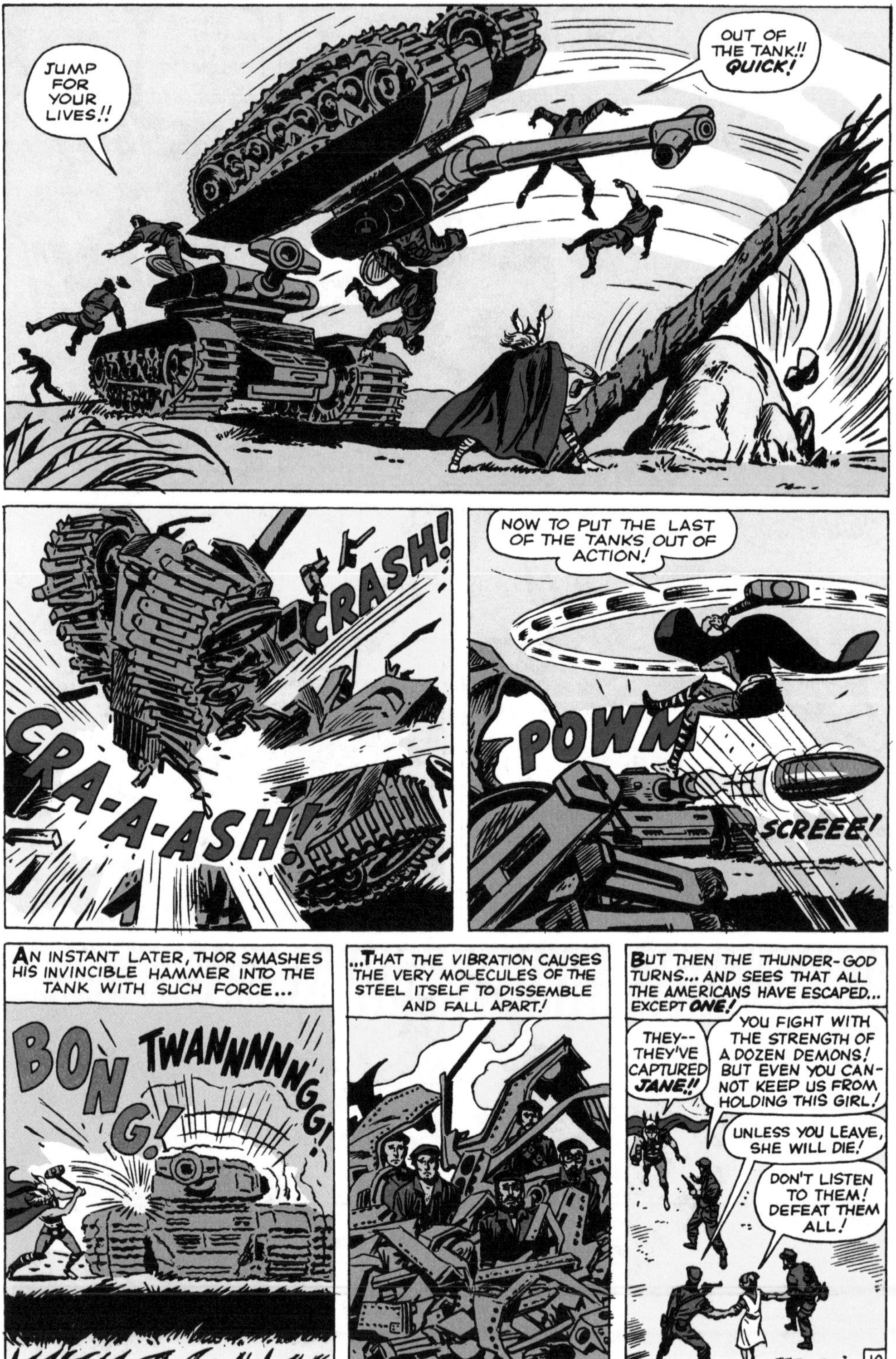
JUMP FOR YOUR LIVES!!
OUT OF THE TANK!! QUICK!
CRASH!
CRA-A-ASH!
NOW TO PUT THE LAST OF THE TANKS OUT OF ACTION!
POWM
SCREEE!
AN INSTANT LATER, THOR SMASHES HIS INVINCIBLE HAMMER INTO THE TANK WITH SUCH FORCE...
BONG!
TWANNNNNGG!
...THAT THE VIBRATION CAUSES THE VERY MOLECULES OF THE STEEL ITSELF TO DISSEMBLE AND FALL APART!
BUT THEN THE THUNDER-GOD TURNS... AND SEES THAT ALL THE AMERICANS HAVE ESCAPED... EXCEPT ONE!
THEY-- THEY'VE CAPTURED JANE!!
YOU FIGHT WITH THE STRENGTH OF A DOZEN DEMONS! BUT EVEN YOU CANNOT KEEP US FROM HOLDING THIS GIRL!
UNLESS YOU LEAVE, SHE WILL DIE!
DON'T LISTEN TO THEM! DEFEAT THEM ALL!
10

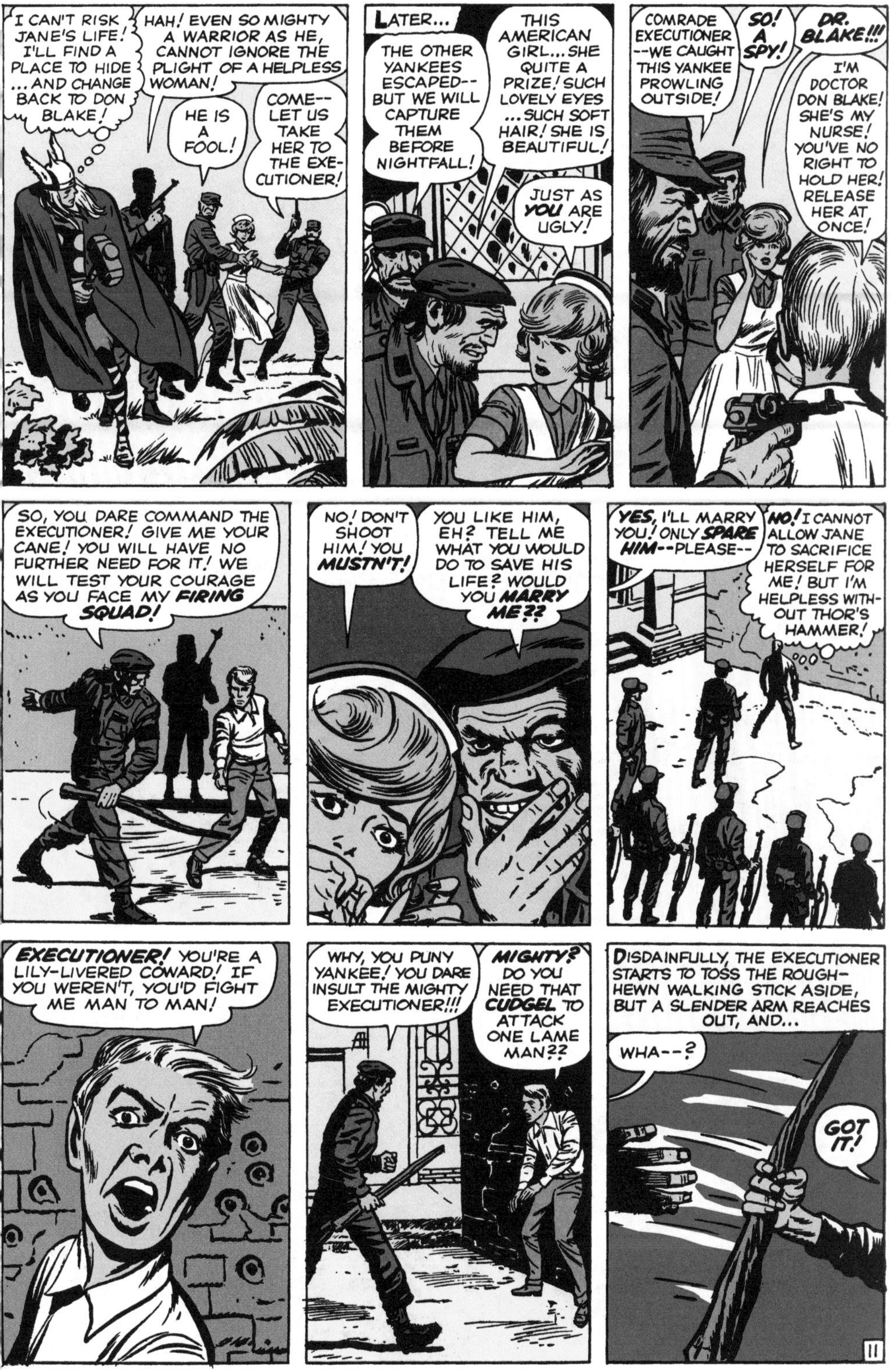
I CAN'T RISK JANE'S LIFE! I'LL FIND A PLACE TO HIDE ... AND CHANGE BACK TO DON BLAKE!
HAH! EVEN SO MIGHTY A WARRIOR AS HE, CANNOT IGNORE THE PLIGHT OF A HELPLESS WOMAN!
HE IS A FOOL!
COME-- LET US TAKE HER TO THE EXECUTIONER!
LATER...
THE OTHER YANKEES ESCAPED-- BUT WE WILL CAPTURE THEM BEFORE NIGHTFALL!
THIS AMERICAN GIRL... SHE QUITE A PRIZE! SUCH LOVELY EYES ...SUCH SOFT HAIR! SHE IS BEAUTIFUL!
JUST AS YOU ARE UGLY!
COMRADE EXECUTIONER --WE CAUGHT THIS YANKEE PROWLING OUTSIDE!
SO! A SPY!
DR. BLAKE!!!
I'M DOCTOR DON BLAKE! SHE'S MY NURSE! YOU'VE NO RIGHT TO HOLD HER! RELEASE HER AT ONCE!
SO, YOU DARE COMMAND THE EXECUTIONER! GIVE ME YOUR CANE! YOU WILL HAVE NO FURTHER NEED FOR IT! WE WILL TEST YOUR COURAGE AS YOU FACE MY FIRING SQUAD!
NO! DON'T SHOOT HIM! YOU MUSTN'T!
YOU LIKE HIM, EH? TELL ME WHAT YOU WOULD DO TO SAVE HIS LIFE? WOULD YOU MARRY ME??
YES, I'LL MARRY YOU! ONLY SPARE HIM--PLEASE--
NO! I CANNOT ALLOW JANE TO SACRIFICE HERSELF FOR ME! BUT I'M HELPLESS WITHOUT THOR'S HAMMER!
EXECUTIONER! YOU'RE A LILY-LIVERED COWARD! IF YOU WEREN'T, YOU'D FIGHT ME MAN TO MAN!
WHY, YOU PUNY YANKEE! YOU DARE INSULT THE MIGHTY EXECUTIONER!!!
MIGHTY? DO YOU NEED THAT CUDGEL TO ATTACK ONE LAME MAN??
DISDAINFULLY, THE EXECUTIONER STARTS TO TOSS THE ROUGH-HEWN WALKING STICK ASIDE, BUT A SLENDER ARM REACHES OUT, AND...
WHA--?
GOT IT!

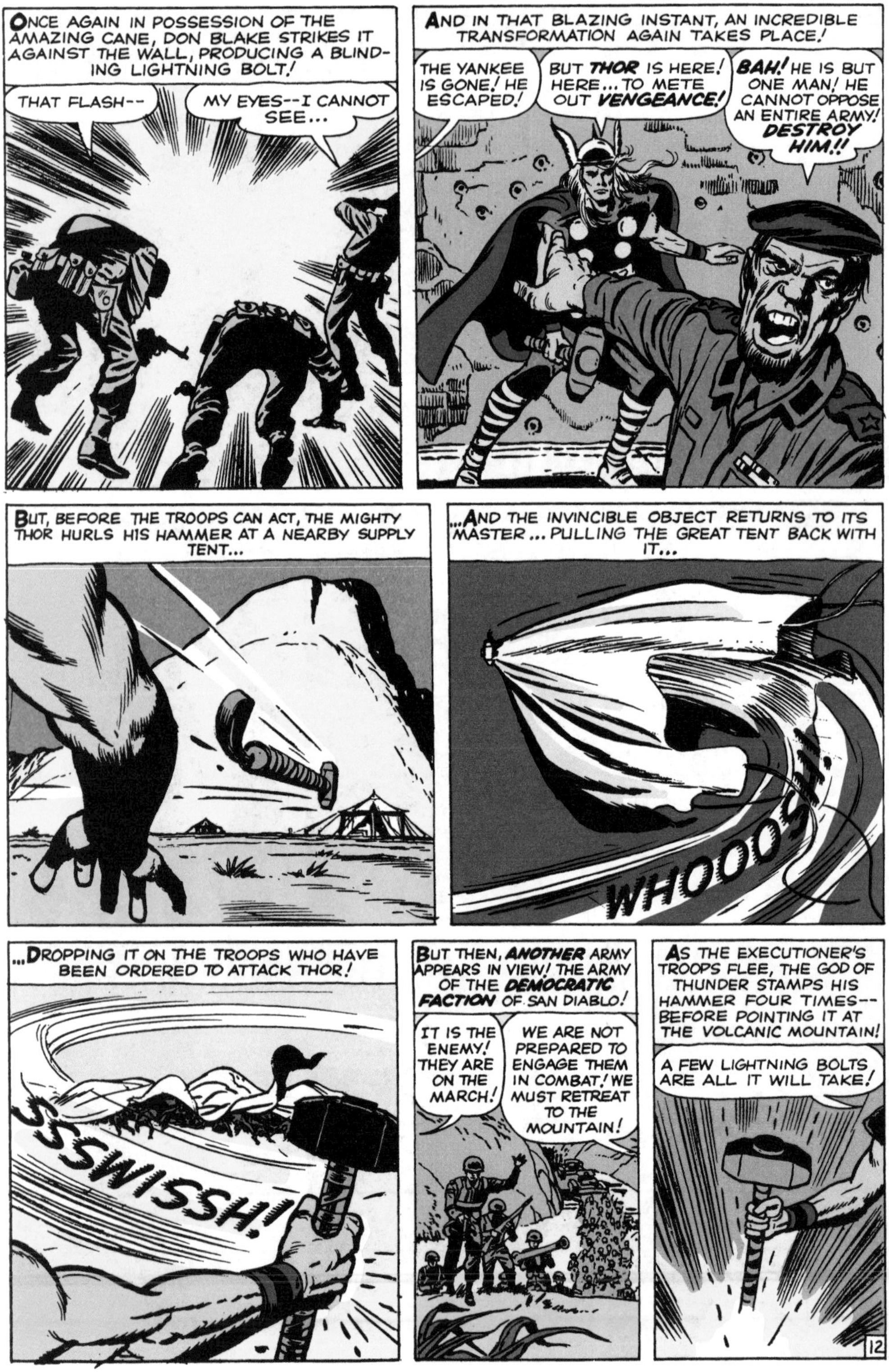
ONCE AGAIN IN POSSESSION OF THE AMAZING CANE, DON BLAKE STRIKES IT AGAINST THE WALL, PRODUCING A BLINDING LIGHTNING BOLT!
THAT FLASH--
MY EYES--I CANNOT SEE...
AND IN THAT BLAZING INSTANT, AN INCREDIBLE TRANSFORMATION AGAIN TAKES PLACE!
THE YANKEE IS GONE! HE ESCAPED!
BUT THOR IS HERE! HERE...TO METE OUT VENGEANCE!
BAH! HE IS BUT ONE MAN! HE CANNOT OPPOSE AN ENTIRE ARMY! DESTROY HIM!!
BUT, BEFORE THE TROOPS CAN ACT, THE MIGHTY THOR HURLS HIS HAMMER AT A NEARBY SUPPLY TENT...
...AND THE INVINCIBLE OBJECT RETURNS TO ITS MASTER... PULLING THE GREAT TENT BACK WITH IT...
WHOOOOSH!
...DROPPING IT ON THE TROOPS WHO HAVE BEEN ORDERED TO ATTACK THOR!
SSSWISSH!
BUT THEN, ANOTHER ARMY APPEARS IN VIEW! THE ARMY OF THE DEMOCRATIC FACTION OF SAN DIABLO!
IT IS THE ENEMY! THEY ARE ON THE MARCH!
WE ARE NOT PREPARED TO ENGAGE THEM IN COMBAT! WE MUST RETREAT TO THE MOUNTAIN!
AS THE EXECUTIONER'S TROOPS FLEE, THE GOD OF THUNDER STAMPS HIS HAMMER FOUR TIMES-- BEFORE POINTING IT AT THE VOLCANIC MOUNTAIN!
A FEW LIGHTNING BOLTS ARE ALL IT WILL TAKE!
12

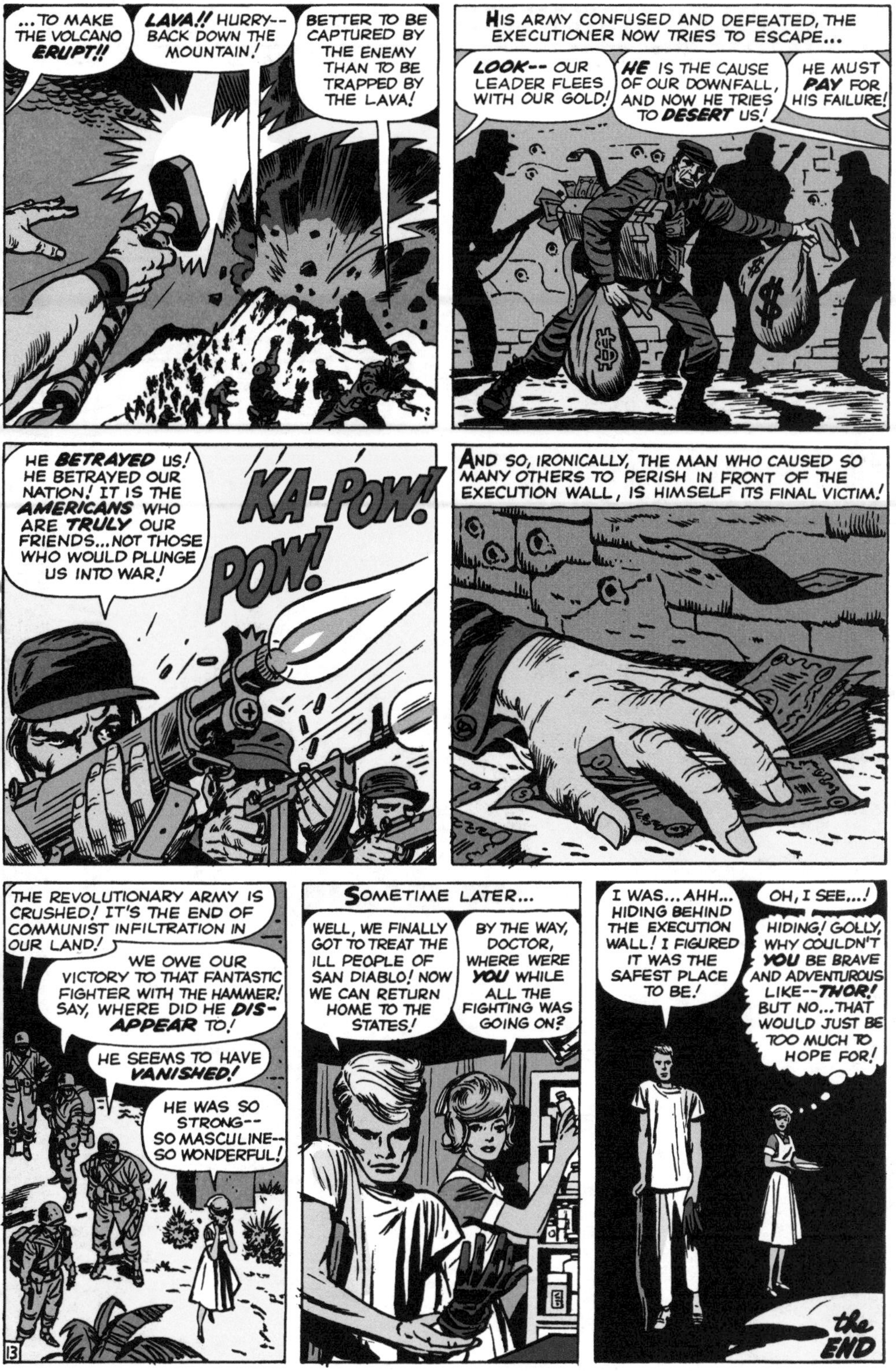
...TO MAKE THE VOLCANO ERUPT!!
LAVA!! HURRY-- BACK DOWN THE MOUNTAIN!
BETTER TO BE CAPTURED BY THE ENEMY THAN TO BE TRAPPED BY THE LAVA!
HIS ARMY CONFUSED AND DEFEATED, THE EXECUTIONER NOW TRIES TO ESCAPE...
LOOK-- OUR LEADER FLEES WITH OUR GOLD!
HE IS THE CAUSE OF OUR DOWNFALL, AND NOW HE TRIES TO DESERT US!
HE MUST PAY FOR HIS FAILURE!
HE BETRAYED US! HE BETRAYED OUR NATION! IT IS THE AMERICANS WHO ARE TRULY OUR FRIENDS...NOT THOSE WHO WOULD PLUNGE US INTO WAR!
KA-POW!
POW!
AND SO, IRONICALLY, THE MAN WHO CAUSED SO MANY OTHERS TO PERISH IN FRONT OF THE EXECUTION WALL, IS HIMSELF ITS FINAL VICTIM!
THE REVOLUTIONARY ARMY IS CRUSHED! IT'S THE END OF COMMUNIST INFILTRATION IN OUR LAND!
WE OWE OUR VICTORY TO THAT FANTASTIC FIGHTER WITH THE HAMMER! SAY, WHERE DID HE DIS-APPEAR TO!
HE SEEMS TO HAVE VANISHED!
HE WAS SO STRONG-- SO MASCULINE-- SO WONDERFUL!
13
SOMETIME LATER...
WELL, WE FINALLY GOT TO TREAT THE ILL PEOPLE OF SAN DIABLO! NOW WE CAN RETURN HOME TO THE STATES!
BY THE WAY, DOCTOR, WHERE WERE YOU WHILE ALL THE FIGHTING WAS GOING ON?
I WAS...AHH... HIDING BEHIND THE EXECUTION WALL! I FIGURED IT WAS THE SAFEST PLACE TO BE!
OH, I SEE...!
HIDING! GOLLY, WHY COULDN'T YOU BE BRAVE AND ADVENTUROUS LIKE--THOR! BUT NO...THAT WOULD JUST BE TOO MUCH TO HOPE FOR!
the END

COLLECTION COVER INKS BY CHRIS SAMNEE

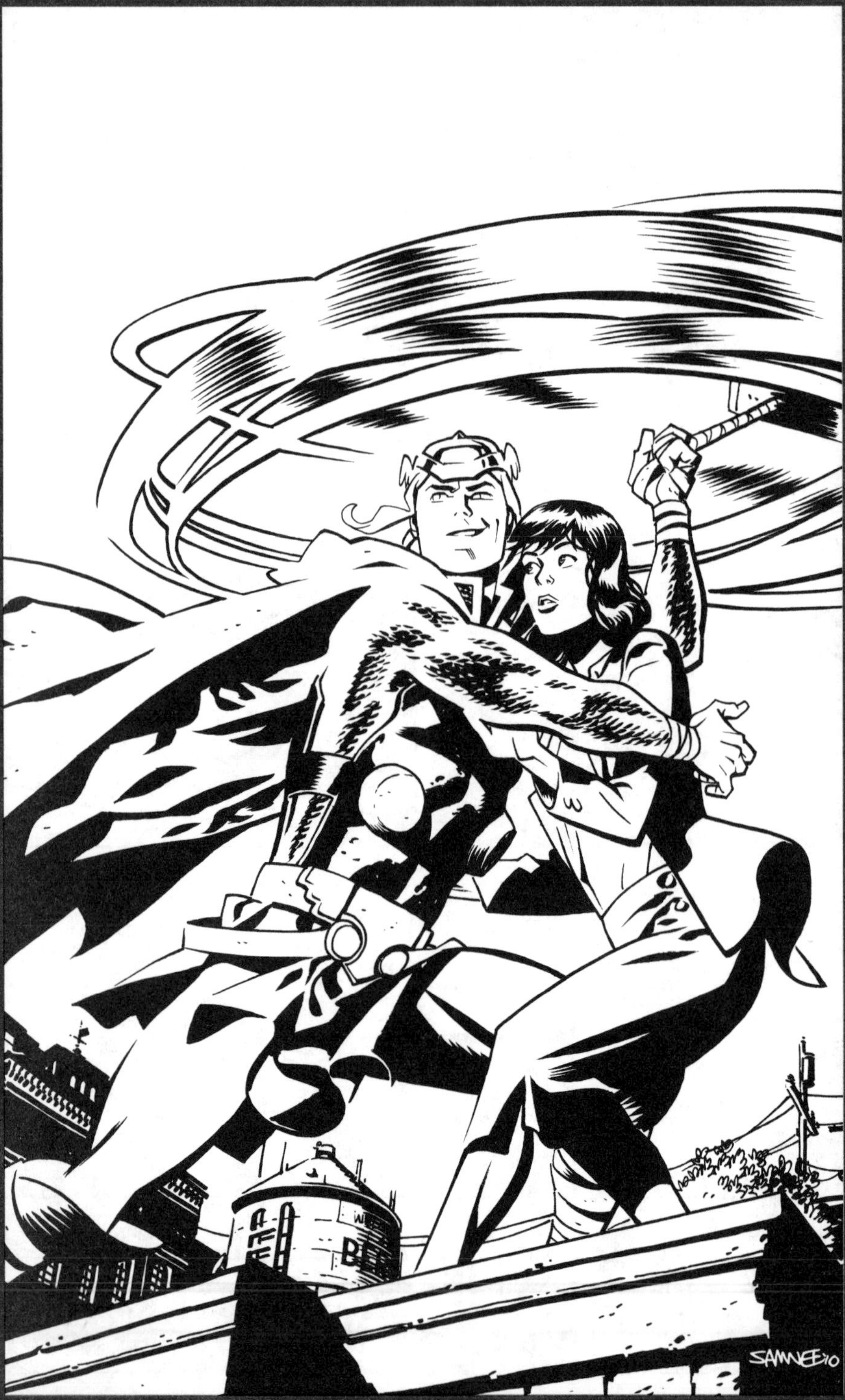
SAMNEE'10

COLLECTION COVER COLORS BY MATTHEW WILSON

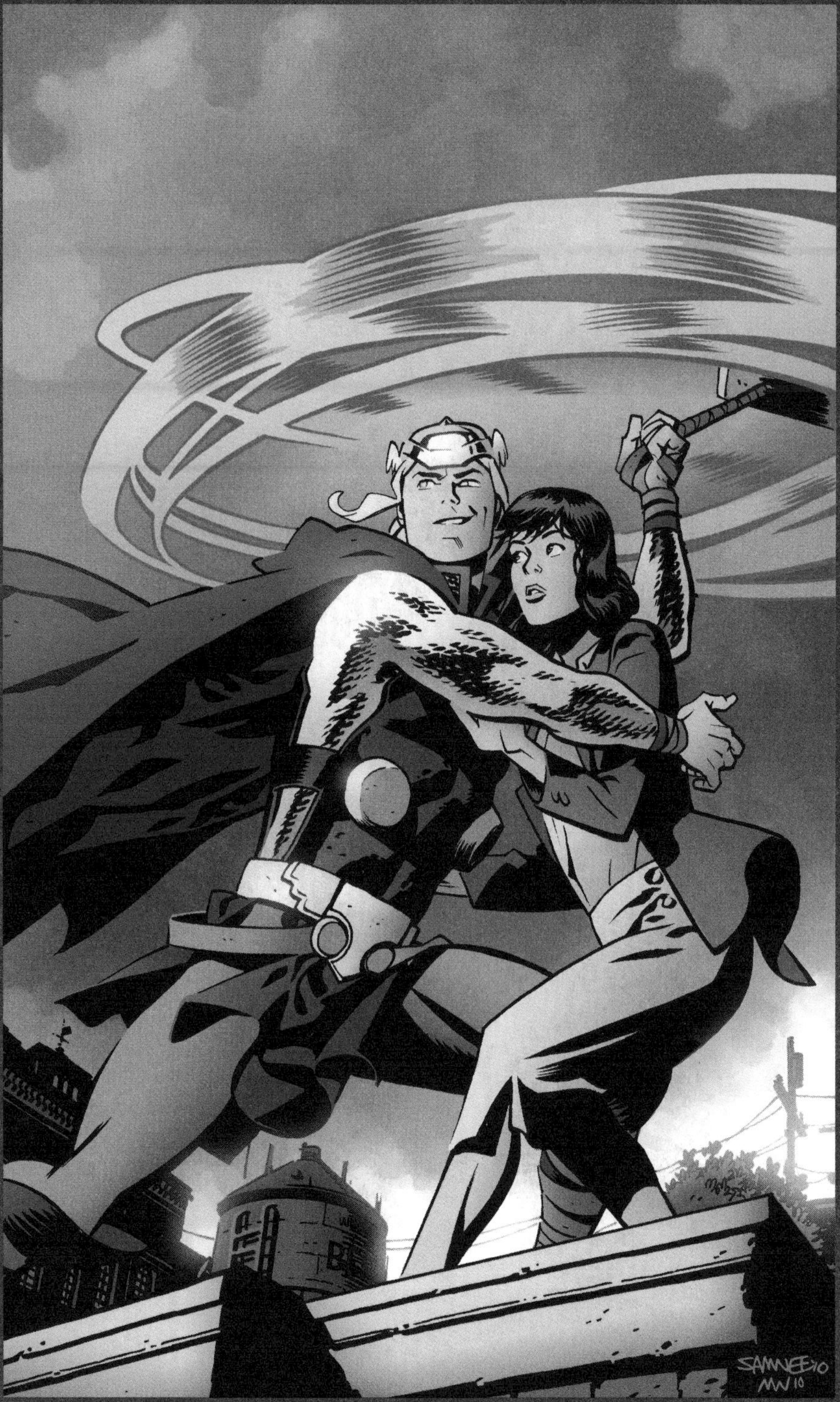

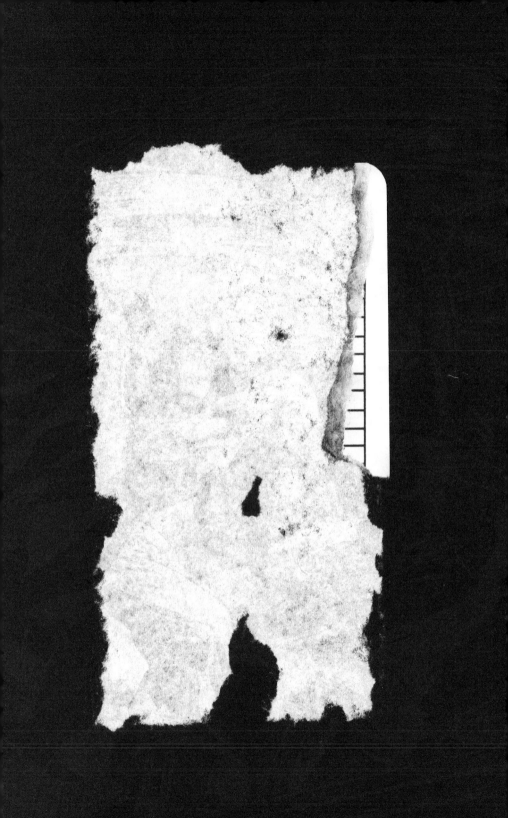